GLOBALIZATION AT RISK

GLOBALIZATION AT RISK

Challenges to Finance and Trade

Gary Clyde Hufbauer and Kati Suominen

Yale UNIVERSITY PRESS

New Haven and London

Yale University Press books may be purchased in quantity for educational, business, or promotional use. For information, please e-mail sales.press@yale.edu (U.S. office) or sales@yaleup.co.uk (U.K. office).

Set in Galliard Old Style type by Westchester Book Services
Printed in the United States of America by Sheridan Books, Ann Arbor, Michigan

Library of Congress Control Number: 2010928702
ISBN 978-0-300-15409-2

A catalogue record for this book is available from the British Library.

This paper meets the requirements of ANSI/NISO Z39.48-1992 (Permanence of Paper).

10 9 8 7 6 5 4 3 2 1

TO THE MEMORY OF PROFESSOR LORD
NICHOLAS KALDOR AND TO THE WHARTON
EXECUTIVE MBA CLASS 33

CONTENTS

PREFACE

Globalization is contentious. It has emerged as one of the leading buzzwords in policy communities around the world and has spurred a massive body of academic, policy, and business literature. Two warring camps are happily at battle—the proglobalizers and the antiglobalizers. In between are the globalization skeptics, for whom open markets are good in principle, but only if and when they are tamed by sturdy policies and regulations.

Among the more popular, recent works in the pro camp are *Why Globalization Works* by *Financial Times* columnist Martin Wolf and *In Defense of Globalization* by Columbia University economist and committed free trader Jagdish Bhagwati. Bhagwati's colleague and former World Bank chief economist Joseph Stiglitz is, if not on the other side of the fence, then *on* the fence with his *Globalization and Its Discontents*, as is Harvard's Dani Rodrik with *Has Globalization Gone Too Far?* Harvard professor Naomi Klein's *No Logo* offers a disparaging take on the putative shortcomings of neoliberalism; in addition, George Soros, who built his wealth in global currency markets, critic of the International Monetary Fund (IMF) Susan George, and America's most renowned dissident, Noam Chomsky, have lobbied their own heavy criticisms against globalization. Thomas Friedman's *The World Is Flat* ranks among the most famous of commentaries, as more a description of the global factory than its outright celebration.

It would appear that the globalization literature has gone too far, so why write another book on the subject? There are three reasons:

First, globalization is a rapidly moving target. The 2008 global crisis precipitated events that were unimaginable just months before: a bewildering roller coaster in stock markets, nationalization of banks in the United States and Europe, destruction of trillions of dollars of wealth within months, and a collapse in oil prices that had been sky-high just a few months earlier. These events have hurried in a fierce yet far from resolved debate about ways the system could be fixed and similar shocks averted—as well as about the future of the free market paradigm and unfettered global flow of goods, services, and money. Our aim is to summarize and inform that debate with levelheaded analysis and policy recommendations.

Second, while there are a great many diagnoses about the rise and advance of globalization and catchall catalogues on the different aspects of globalization from trade to social movements and migration, there are but few practical road maps for improving upon globalization or managing the real risks to globalization. And yet, this issue is crucial, particularly in the face of the "Great Crisis" set in motion in the fall of 2008, fears about a prolonged recession and L-shaped recovery at best, concerns over a Doha Trade Round collapse, uncertainties about the future of global finance, and protectionist political winds around the world that can risk turning into a gale.

Third, while ivory towers and international institutions are producing a steady stream of rigorous analyses on the extent and impacts of globalization, there are but few accessible compilations of the results of serious technical work that would reach and inform the public debate. Although much is changing—for example, there are numerous superb analyses and proposals circulating in the blogosphere, at times from unexpected sources—the more popular published literature tends to be dominated by catchy sound bites and impractical prescriptions that can be outright condescending to the nonexpert reader. We will strive to bridge that gap— translating the best of academic studies into accessible but still substantive prose on critical issues facing the global economy.

Globalization, our dependent variable, is in this monograph operationalized as expansion in cross-border trade and financial flows. There are arguably many different globalizations—social networks, media and entertainment, and so forth—but we believe that a clear and strict definition gives focus to our inquiry and relevance for our policy recommendations. Moreover, we argue that trade and financial flows are perhaps the most powerful forms of globalization in terms of their immediate effects on domestic growth and economic activity in countries around the world. The recent "fail or bail" policies vis-à-vis financial services firms around the world have attested to that.

This book is an assessment of globalization, a stocktaking on some of the reputedly sturdiest challenges to the future of globalization—particularly now, as the world emerges from the mightiest economic crisis in decades— and an action plan to both further and better globalization. We have three main theses:

First, globalization can be and is a force of great good, one that has delivered us heady economic benefits that would have remained unrealized in a less-globablized world. Globalization is also a key force that is delivering the world out of the catastrophic Great Crisis.

However, and second, the fact that policies are at the heart of globalization also means that globalization is not automatic: it requires a set of active domestic and multilateral policies to keep going and to grow better. Conversely, policy barriers can curtail globalization and its benefits, and even grind them to a halt. This is precisely what raises concerns about the future of globalization. The institutions and policies that have furthered globalization have long been under serious pressures, public support for open markets has been undercut by job churn and outsourcing, and the ongoing market turmoil tempts ad hoc policy measures that can have the unintended consequence of derailed economic exchange.

Third, whether and how exactly the risks to globalization can be overcome and its benefits carried over to the twenty-first century depends on smart policies, sustained political support, and tireless work in bureaucracies around the world. It also requires institutional engineering and coordination at the domestic, regional, and multilateral levels. This book is purported to inform and fuel that critical work.

ACKNOWLEDGMENTS

This volume would not have been possible without the support of numerous individuals and institutions. We are grateful to our tenacious research assistants—Santiago Florez Gomez, Andrew Green, Carlos M. Gutierrez Jr., and Jisun Kim.

Anonymous referees critically shaped our approaches in this volume, for which we give thanks. We are also deeply indebted to dozens of colleagues in Washington and beyond who have, over our careers, provided penetrating insights and fresh angles, enriching our work.

We also wish to thank the exceptional team at the Economics Program of the German Marshall Fund in Washington for the outstanding support of Kati Suominen's authorship. Our thanks as well to Antoni Estevadeordal at the Integration and Trade Sector of the Inter-American Development Bank for his support of the project from its inception.

Yale University Press patiently extended our deadlines and proceeded promptly to prepare the volume for publication. We are particularly grateful to our acquisitions editor, Michael O'Malley, for suggesting the volume to us, and to Jack Borrebach, Niamh Cunningham, and Michael Haggett and Fran Lyon for their excellent work on sharpening the manuscript. The remaining errors are ours.

We dedicate this volume to sources of inspiration: to the memory of Professor Lord Nicholas Kaldor, the mentor who launched Gary

Hufbauer on a career in international economics, and to the Wharton Executive MBA Class of May 2009, superb and steadfastly optimistic companions to Kati Suominen during this epic time in the global economy.

GLOBALIZATION AT RISK

1

A Bleak New Era

The years 2008 and 2009 set new and discouraging records for the world economy. The financial crisis spread with epic speed, destroying $50 trillion of wealth and shrinking world output on a scale not seen since the Great Depression. In many nations, unemployment figures were the highest in three decades. The crisis—which we name the "Great Crisis"—mounted the biggest challenge yet seen to globalization. It caused the largest decline in international trade since the Second World War, a severe contraction in cross-border direct investment, and at its worst, wiped out half the value of global financial assets.

In 1917, Vladimir Ilyich Lenin published a famous pamphlet, *Imperialism, the Highest Stage of Capitalism*. Today, one could write *Globalization, the Highest Stage of Free Markets*. History has declared capitalism and economic globalization the winners of the twentieth century. But liberal economic policies that enabled globalization and lifted worldwide income to levels unimaginable during the Second World War are now at risk. Economic hardship provokes many legislators to keep imports out, keep jobs at home, and clamp down on global capital.

The paradigm of free markets has been badly tarnished. Honest toil goes without reward. Dozens of banks are decimated, thousands of entrepreneurs have seen their dreams crushed, and millions of people are falling back into poverty. Celebrated investment managers are jailed for their

Ponzi schemes; corporate chieftains are excoriated in public hearings and held hostage by employees—payback for big bonuses and mediocre management. Electorates are infuriated, trust is lost, and calls for cracking down are loud.

All this happened not because of failures at the periphery of globalization but because of failures at the very center—Wall Street, the capitalist heart of America, and Washington, its sleepy guardian. Globalization was a hapless handmaiden in spreading the crisis.

The good news is that the world was spared from 1930s-style beggar-thy-neighbor protectionism, owing in large part to the frightening lessons of the Depression era and a completely different response in monetary and fiscal policy. In the 1930s, central banks were slow to boost the money supply, and a fiscal policy response was viewed as a problem, not an answer. All that has changed.[1] International commitments made over the past sixty years to liberalize world trade and finance, defended by thousands of vocal proponents of free markets ensconced in industry, academia, the media, and national governments, have preserved the open global economy. The record during the crisis was not perfect—countries engaged in innovative practices to keep jobs at home and foreigners out—but even misguided actions were a far cry from measures taken eight decades ago.

Yet history has shown that countries can shy away from openness when economic life sours. Electorates become weary of bailing out banks and wary of their future; anxiety tempts heavy-handed regulation and a search for alternative economic models. Trade and investment cooperation become fragile: prior eras of integration have shown that economic hard times, populist politics, and isolationist sentiments are comfortable bedfellows.

Globalization has often faced challenges since the Second World War, but its record of delivering results saved the day in the aftermath of past episodes: the breakdown of Bretton Woods in the 1970s, the oil crises of the 1970s and 1980s, the Latin American debt crisis of the 1980s, the Asian financial crisis of the 1990s, and the attacks of September 11, 2001. Yet we cannot be confident that globalization will always be the savior. The vast magnitude and lightning spread of the 2008 crisis, and the undeniable fact that Wall Street was its epicenter, put at risk any progress toward the unfettered flow of money, goods, and services across borders.

Even if protectionist dominoes did not tumble all at once, countries could—and have—cut corners in their trade and financial regimes. Herein lies the grand policy paradox of the hour: while dire straits underline the importance of pro-globalization policies as a vehicle for reviving the world economy, debacles in the United States and elsewhere tempt a turn to nationalism and isolationism.

The Response

The ability of global heavyweights to assemble themselves in unprecedented G20 summits has rightly been hailed as a watershed moment in world economic governance. Collective efforts notwithstanding, the conclaves have laid bare the clash between political forces, which are national, and economic forces, which are global. The United States has sought more stimulus and liquidity; the Europeans and Chinese, more regulation. The British and the Japanese fall somewhere in the middle.

The giants among emerging countries—Brazil, China, and India—want markets to stay open for their exports and advanced nations to throw a lifeline to countries that are drowning thanks to follies elsewhere. Out of these demands, the G20 has called a freeze on protectionism and a conclusion of the Doha Trade Round; the assembled nations also pledged to engage in sturdy macroeconomic coordination policed by the International Monetary Fund (IMF), they elevated the Financial Stability Board (a gathering of financial regulators), and they committed more than $1 trillion of new money to the international financial institutions (the IMF, the World Bank, and regional development banks). The promises have been made; the hard task is delivering. And the crucial question is whether, even if delivered, these responses are enough to arrest the economic rout.

Multilateral bodies and cooperative mechanisms from the IMF to the World Trade Organization (WTO) and the G20 system are stretched at their seams in the face of growing membership and new demands from climate change to credit swaps. In the 1940s, the founders of the Bretton Woods system designed governance for a world economy operating on steamships and postal systems; today's institutional architects cope with an economy moving through the air and the Internet at multiple speeds and volumes. Six decades ago, seats at the table were occupied by a handful of countries that had fought on the same side in a brutal war; today, dozens of nations claim an equal say in the global economy. The global institutions have been revamped from time to time, often to meet looming challenges, but incremental realignments may no longer suffice. As well as the system worked between 1945 and 2005, today it is creaking under severe pressure.

Many observers conclude that the crisis calls for a fresh assessment of the jurisdictional mismatch between national politics and the global economy. But a major recalibration seems virtually unattainable: it would not suit the interests of national governments that now run the show.[2] The most likely way a global polity will be created is gradually and bottom-up, by the work of millions of entrepreneurs, financiers, and Facebook friends who partner up across borders. Yes, we dare argue that the very force of globalization will drive global politics. If a global community—resembling the consolidation of the United States in the nineteenth century and the rise of an integrated Europe in the twentieth century—ever materializes, it will not emerge from the fiat of national leaders summing once a year. Leaders cannot abandon aspects of national sovereignty that their peoples treasure, but they can facilitate the transition to cooperation when the need is clear.

Many also have called for a revision of global governance—the establishment of a Bretton Woods II that would redesign or perhaps even abolish key bodies such as the IMF, the World Bank, or the WTO. But time is not on the side of these advocates: there is a certain path dependence in the veteran institutions, certain entrenched interests that are embedded in them, and certain wisdom garnered over the years. A full-blown revision is not due, nor could it be accomplished. It would not necessarily improve on the existing model. Rather, incremental change will remain the name of the game and perhaps for the right reason—its upside is thoughtfulness and consensus building.

There are no quick or easy fixes.

What Now?

In the wake of the crisis, economic policy making is no longer about fine-tuning the business cycle or boosting growth rates. The whole design of the economic system is now up for grabs. We are in for years of reexamination of the policy framework of trade and financial regimes—

just as we are due for an impassioned debate not seen since the time when Americans took sides behind Milton Friedman and John Kenneth Galbraith about the relationship between private and public sectors and the size and shape of social contracts.

While globalization is an antidote for the poverty that accompanies autarky, it also makes nations more vulnerable to external shocks. And while global trade and finance are engines of wealth and new opportunity, they can transmit devastating losses both for those unprepared to take advantage and for those swept by a storm not of their making. Yet, there are no alternatives that come even close to generating the long-term benefits created by free economic exchange on a global scale.

Adam Smith's invisible hand is perhaps the most durable law of economics. But collective actions by rational market players can result in collective disasters unless somehow coordinated. Nation-states have advanced far in harnessing the creativity and productivity of humanity while regulating the downside incentives for unfair play. However, incentives for individually profitable actions that risk proving collectively harmful actions often accompany innovations in farming, industry, and especially finance. Alternative economic systems do not even come close to capitalism in delivering heady opportunities, individual energy, and breakthrough innovations. The challenge facing every market economy is to anticipate and regulate the bad, while letting the good flourish unfettered.

As the world emerges from the crisis, the indictment should be of foul play by some capitalists, not of capitalism; of imperfect regulation and irrational exuberance on a global scale, not of globalization.

The first purpose of this book is to stress these notions—to temper temptations for harsh judgments and reduce risks to globalization. Unlike the ideological descendants of Lenin, we staunchly defend globalization, not condemn it. In our view, the benefits of globalization since the Second World War are resounding. This motivates our inquiry.

The second purpose of this book is to develop a road map for improving globalization. In every crisis lies an opportunity, and the Great Crisis created several for advancing and improving globalization. Many of the proglobalization policies already in train would have been impossible without the calamity. Like other commentators, we seize the opportunity to offer policy recommendations for a better globalization.

The Hard-Earned Gains

Let's take a step back from the tumult of the past three years. There are many reasons for marvel and celebration. The global economy is unprecedentedly integrated. While global gross domestic product (GDP) has expanded by some four times since 1980, world trade has grown more than sixfold, the stock of foreign direct investment has shot up by twenty times, and portfolio capital flows have surged more than tenfold. Global financial assets are roughly four times the size of GDP of the entire planet. Multinational companies (MNCs) today number some 80,000, more than double the levels of 2000. In 2007, the cross-border mergers and acquisitions rose to total a record $1.8 trillion, 21 percent above the levels attained at the turn of the millennium.

The advance of globalization has made virtually all countries more dependent on the global marketplace. At the dawn of the twenty-first century, the combined sum of external assets and liabilities averaged around 100 percent of GDP in low-income countries, around 150 percent of GDP in middle-income countries, and more than 550 percent of GDP in high-income countries.[3] International investors now hold 14 percent of U.S. equities, up from 4 percent in 1975; 27 percent of American corporate bonds, up from 1 percent; and 52 percent of Treasury securities, up from 20 percent.

The ratio of merchandise trade (imports plus exports) to world GDP grew from 2 percent in 1800, to 22 percent in 1913, reaching 30 percent in 1950, and more than 60 percent today. Over a period of fifty years, between 1950 and 2000, the growth of trade surpassed the growth of output in every world region. Trade as a share of national GDP skyrocketed from 20 percent to 100 percent of GDP in Japan, from 40 to above 80 percent in Canada, from 60 to 80 percent in Western Europe, from 35 to about 60 percent in Latin America, from 50 to 70 percent in sub-Saharan Africa, and from 10 to 20 percent in the United States.[4]

The share of inward foreign direct investment (FDI) stocks of global GDP is now 27 percent; for Europe, the ratio exceeds 40 percent of GDP; for developing countries as a group, 30 percent of GDP; and for the United States, 15 percent. Small countries rely heavily on MNCs to supply capital and create jobs. Today, Luxembourg, Belgium, Hong Kong, and Singapore are more than 60 percent "transnationalized," Trinidad and

Tobago and Estonia are more than 40 percent so, and Chile, Jamaica, the Netherlands, and various Eastern European countries hover above 30 percent.[5]

Globalization has had many drivers, including technology: containerization has boosted global trade, computers have assisted global financial flows, and airplanes have increased global business travel. Another engine of globalization is economic growth: greater prosperity means greater demand for goods, services, and capital from beyond any one country's borders. But a good share of globalization owes its growth to open domestic policies that are conducive to free cross-border flows of trade and capital in the leading economies.

In finance, the 1980s and 1990s saw capital account opening, accompanied by a wave of financial deregulation around the world—relaxing tight rules that governed banking and insurance and approving new investment vehicles.[6] Rules and supervision were simplified and increasingly harmonized across markets. U.S. banking deregulation—launched in 1977 and finalized in 1994—removed geographical expansion restrictions facing banks, both within and across states. France, Germany, and many other Western European nations jumped on board, and Japan began a staged liberalization of its capital markets in 1984. The introduction of the euro in 1999 produced another uptick in financial flows. That the eurozone integrates money and credit markets appeals to investors: the common monetary unit eliminates currency risk among the member countries, freeing investors to substitute foreign for domestic securities. Even though wedded to the pound, London became a hub for euro-denominated financial trade.[7]

Trade has been similarly energized by policy. In the postwar era, some two-thirds of the rise of trade among advanced countries can be attributed to global income growth, a tenth to falling transportation costs, and as much as a quarter due to policy reform—mainly tariff cuts.[8] Similarly in the United States, roughly a quarter of U.S. merchandise trade growth in 1980–2005 was due to policy liberalization; three-quarters can be explained by the general expansion of the world economy and the rest by falling transportation costs.[9]

Enlightened governments have slashed tariff and nontariff barriers down to remarkably low levels through unilateral action and by forging new trade agreements both multilaterally and bilaterally with partners around the world. The United States reduced applied tariffs to trade in goods from 20 percent in the wake of the Great Depression to 3.5 percent today (and often to zero for its free trade partners), Germany from 25 percent to the European Union's (EU's) 5.2 percent, the United Kingdom from 23 percent to 5.2 percent, Japan from 6 percent to 5.1 percent, and China from 20 percent to 10 percent. All these economies also cut back on nontariff barriers—quotas, regulations, and so on. They pulled the world behind them through the 1948 General Agreement on Tariffs and Trade (GATT), an instrument of most favored nation (MFN) liberalization.

In its ideal form, MFN means that every member extends its tariff liberalization to all other GATT members, and no member is the victim of discrimination. During the course of the eight completed GATT negotiations, the number of participating countries grew from an inner circle of 23 founders to 152 members today, opening trade among them, each time lowering tariffs and other barriers further. They paved the way for the 1994 formation of the WTO, which provides a forum for trade negotiations, guides the implementation of trade policies, and houses a sturdy, global settlement mechanism for trade disputes—all with a very lean secretariat staff.[10] While much remains to be done, the achievements of the GATT system are in many ways stunning.

Multinational companies both nurtured and jumped on the new possibilities of open trade regimes, investing heavily in overseas operations and carving expansive regional and global production chains. Investment liberalization has hastened this trend. While investment only recently has been formally addressed in multilateral trade talks, the by now 2,600 bilateral investment treaties among no fewer than 179 countries, coupled with a vast web of double tax treaties, have provided legal bases for cross-border corporate investment. Interestingly, while the average odds of FDI occurring between any one pair of countries are 0.6 percent, a tax treaty raises the chances to 0.7 percent, a big increase on a small number.[11] In the United States, almost a third of the inward FDI stock growth and 18 percent of outward FDI stock growth can be attributed to policy liberalization in the past quarter century.[12]

Along with liberalization to foreign investment, trade opening has enabled multinational firms to flourish: companies prefer to locate in countries where they can bring inputs free of tariff barriers and from where they have access to other markets for exporting part of their output. Trade policy is the alpha and omega of globalization. Conversely, multinational-ization and monetary integration—first and foremost the euro—have pro-pelled trade flows.

Trade and global supply chains require strong financial systems for cross-border financial transactions. Institutions of international finance (IFIs) have facilitated the movement toward open markets. The IMF has monitored and supported the global financial architecture and steadied countries shaken by financial shocks due either to their own misguided policies or to storms arriving from foreign shores. The IMF's counsel, while often criticized as draconian, has tempered rash and ill-informed deci-sions, helping countries around the world to avert future troubles. Many an emerging market could well be a declining market were it not for the IMF's emergency lending and policy advice.

In the emerging markets, the turnabout to liberal policies is recent, em-bedded in a broader framework for conceptualizing the nexus between the state and markets. The 1990s "Washington Consensus," fashioned by leading economists and institutions as a reaction to the macroeconomic crises in the spendthrift and protectionist Latin America in the 1980s, was grounded on macroeconomic stability, fiscal discipline, reduced govern-ment involvement in the economy, and trade and investment liberaliza-tion.

The consensus spread and succeeded, in part due to enforcement by the Bretton Woods institutions and endorsement by the academic commu-nity, and in part due to the haunting remembrance of troubles faced by countries that had earlier experienced political and economic instability, such as Mexico in the mid-1990s. Success reinforced the mantra of open markets and helped propel globalization.

The benefits of the globalized marketplace are staggering. Free flows of trade and capital have produced prosperity that would be completely unat-tainable solely through domestic means, lifting millions out of poverty. Globalization has stimulated growth, which the World Bank finds has a direct, one-to-one relationship with poverty reduction. The Peterson In-stitute calculates that the U.S. economy alone has gained no less than $1 trillion annually due to globalization, and stands to gain another $500 billion per year from future policy liberalization. Another study finds that every American household is $15,000 richer each year due to trade opening.[13] European analysts have figured that if no integration had taken place since 1950 in Europe, the EU's GDP per capita would be 20 percent less today.[14]

Companies are saving massive amounts of money on inventory costs—money that can be invested in productive uses—thanks to the "just-in-time" delivery facilitated by open borders. By the early 2000s, Walmart's massive inventory turned over 7.7 times annually—once every month and a half and up from 4.1 times in 1990. Dell's annual inventory turnover is a legendary 91.6 times—one turnover every four days—up from only 1.7 times in 1990.

FDI yields similar growth benefits. According to the Federal Reserve of Dallas, every dollar of FDI "crowds-in" an additional 50 cents in domestic investment and more than 75 cents in domestic savings in emerging markets. Other studies put the crowding-in ratio to one-to-one. FDI is also linked to greater exports. And opening to FDI in services sectors—especially business communication and financial services—also has a complementary effect, particularly when the "commercial presence" of foreign players increases.[15]

Portfolio opening also boosts growth and incomes. The IMF's Romain Ranciere, UCLA's Aaron Tornell, and University of Osnabrück's Frank Westermann conclude that portfolio financial liberalization boosts per capita income growth by 1 percent annually, even when the odds of volatility are factored in. Further studies show that liberalization of equity flows leads to an average of 15 percent appreciation in the value of a country's firms—as well as to real sales growth, investment, profitability, efficiency, and capacity for leverage.[16] Developing nations have seen a sizable drop in the cost of capital and an increase in worker productivity after liberalizing their stock markets.

Preview of This Book

These pieces of news are not new: the facts about the benefits of globalization are well known. But they do not compete with job losses, wage gaps, instability, and the sense of unlevel playing fields and precarious livelihoods. Analysts displaying neat graphs of upward growth trajectories unfailingly lose the debate to the fury of workers laid off from factories, high-flying professionals suddenly left without a corporate employer, and families whose savings evaporate overnight. A persistent, gnawing sense of precariousness, even absent an epic crisis, has in recent decades proven sufficient to build opposition to openness. And while the benefits of globalization are clear, they are often hard to discern directly, thus failing to galvanize a pro-openness counterforce. To cite just one example, on November 10, 2009, the *Washington Post* ran a lengthy account of furniture workers laid off in Hickory, North Carolina, an isolated town with few alternative work opportunities. The article left little doubt that globalization—in the shape of furniture imports from China—was to blame, not only for lost jobs but also for foreclosed homes.

Unlike the furniture workers in Hickory, in most cases, the economic negatives are not caused by globalization but by technological change, educational gaps, inflexible labor markets, domestic economic mismanagement, and the like. However, the losses are often attributed to cross-border flows. And they sustain lingering protectionist impulses, worries that open markets transmit too many disadvantages along with the many benefits, doubts regarding government capacity to manage the potential downsides, and questions about the trickling down of gains. Such thoughts are powerfully amplified by the economic crisis.

But no problem goes without solutions. That is where our book comes in. The first part sets the stage by assessing the advance, drivers, and the many reputed and real effects of globalization. We have already mentioned the drivers and the gains; let's turn to the controversies.

Chapter 2 examines cross-border finance. Financial globalization has become hugely contested because of its downside—occasional, massive, and at times truly devastating volatility. Events unfolding since the Latin American debt crises of the 1980s from Mexico to Asia to Argentina to Russia to Turkey and the current episode show that money can disappear as fast as it comes in, leaving an economy starved for credit and with a currency depreciated at lightning speed. Some argue that financial integration should be curbed in order to reduce national vulnerability to external shocks; others counter by claiming that financial integration is the engine of global wealth and the handmaiden of entrepreneurship, and that crises are infrequent events.

We would argue that worries about contagion are not unfounded: "sudden stops" and "sudden reversals" have often occurred around the world and are rightly feared. Worse yet, global capital tends to be procyclical, flowing to emerging markets when times are good and getting out when things go awry. Lows are really low, highs are taken for normal, and there is no umbrella for the inevitable rainy day.

But the evidence is clear that crises are not necessarily caused by financial integration—or at least not by integration alone. Economic crises seem to recur roughly once a decade, and they have many sources. In the nineteenth century, crises were largely associated with bank failures; between the 1940s and 1960s, crises combined bank failures and sharp devaluations; and since the 1980s, crises have originated in real estate booms and busts. Harvard's Kenneth Rogoff, and University of Maryland's Carmen Reinhart go beyond most studies that examine the crises of the 1980s and 1990s to show that eighteen financial and banking crises in advanced countries over past centuries all involved high levels of debt—both public and private, and often domestic rather than foreign. It is debt of any sort that matters.

This also means that the lens of open versus closed financial systems is the wrong way to look at crises. If something is to be controlled beyond overall excess leverage, it should be dollar-denominated borrowing by emerging nations. Free equity flows—opening stock markets to foreigners— give bang for the buck and are best if left alone. Whereas bank loans denominated in dollars are rigidly valued (until the threshold of default), equity stakes valued in local currency rise and fall with changing fortunes, absorbing much of the shock on both the downside and the upside.

There is a kernel of truth to the claim that innocent bystanders get hit in the globalized world economy. But research shows—and both sides of the debate about global capital flows agree—that countries with good domestic macroeconomic management, governance, financial sophistication, and open trade regimes are generally better at weathering storms. The key is not to shut out international finance; that would be a grave mistake. Rather, it is to devise strong domestic institutions to wade through the bad and take advantage of the good.

Domestic institutions are equally critical for countries to harness trade for growth. Chapter 3 shows that such domestic "complementary policies"—good governance and economic policies, and training of entrepreneurs and exporters—are key in translating trade into economic success.[17] But while trade opening alone is not a magic bullet for growth, the past several decades validate the arguments of Adam Smith and David Ricardo, who believed that specialization would generate higher national incomes.

And yet, as in finance, the effects of trade raised massive political storms. Trade and its two sister phenomena, outsourcing (of inputs from abroad) and offshoring (of final production overseas), have long been faulted for hurting those unable to withstand foreign competition.

These claims contain more myth than reality. Among the most famous is the "one-way myth": that advanced countries outsource and offshore to poor nations, and that workers in the advanced countries never gain, only lose. In fact, a study by Matthew Slaughter shows that the number of manufacturing jobs *insourced* to the United States in 1987–2002 grew by 82 percent, while the number of U.S. jobs outsourced overseas grew by only 23 percent. The United States is a *net exporter* of business services to India, meaning it produces more services sold to India than India produces for the United States. Pioneering studies by Brad Jensen and Lori Kletzer show (just like Ricardo said!) that U.S. firms outsource fewer skilled jobs and insource more skilled jobs.[18] Insourced jobs are usually higher paying than outsourced jobs. This again is good news for America. Other studies show that companies that outsource see a rise in the incomes of the workers in their original home countries—mostly due to the efficiency gains of outsourcing.

Research does not dispute the redistributive effects of trade—although it is very clear that job churn and wage losses are largely *not* caused by trade, but by technological change within national borders. The Organization for Economic Cooperation and Development (OECD) estimates that trade accounted for just 4 percent of all permanent layoffs in Canada, the United States, and the European Union in 2000. Lori Kletzer similarly calculates that, in the United States, 320,000 jobs were lost annually in 1979–1999 due to trade, or some 4 to 5 percent of all layoffs. More recently, the head of the Trade Adjustment Coalition, Howard Rosen, suggests that of the 16 to 18 million jobs lost annually, approximately 3 to 4 million are considered displaced workers who face serious adjustment costs, and of those workers, about 500,000 are displaced by import competition annually—as illustrated by the furniture workers in Hickory, North Carolina.

Adverse effects from trade are generally targeted and temporary, while positive effects are broad and durable. Research also shows that opportunity favors the prepared worker and the educated mind, as trade places a premium on skills. Barring destructive policy barriers, comparative advantage will remain footloose—which means that skill premiums are a stubborn feature of the global economy.

Even when trade does produce job churn or income inequality, trade barriers are not the remedy. For example, one study suggests that prohibitive trade barriers against Chinese and Indian exports would be very costly for the rich countries: by the end of the current century in 2100, they might cost the developed countries as much as 17 percent of their projected output, and reduce the incomes of *high-skilled* workers by around 25 percent in comparison to a free-trade scenario.[19] Better strategies than trade protection are many and plain to see: more and better education, additional and improved infrastructure, tax incentives for work, and so on.

Chapter 4 turns to the record of multinational production in the world economy. We find that the global company is for real. The biggest MNCs—like Walmart, General Electric (GE), Unilever, or Tata—draw revenues that rival the budgets of major OECD economies. They are not only global and operating in the bulk of countries; they are also inherent globalizers, locomotives of international trade and investment. As such, they are fiercely coveted and energetically courted by most nations, developed or developing.

And yet, multinationalization is argued to have created pernicious incentives. Efforts to court MNCs are claimed to drive countries in a frantic race to the bottom, where each nation offers increasingly attractive tax incentives and other sweeteners that are good for global companies but damaging for the countries themselves. At the end of the race in this story, multinationals rule the world and national sovereignty practically disappears.

Interestingly enough, a giant race to the bottom has not really occurred. This is in part because of the great fallacy in the race-to-the-bottom claim—that the state has a single goal, to chase mobile MNCs, and does not respond to other constituencies, such as voters, lobbies, bureaucracies, and the like. It is true that corporate income tax rates have been slashed over the past three decades by nearly all OECD nations. But Michael Devereux of the Center for Economic and Policy Research (CEPR) shows that revenues from corporate taxes in the OECD region were *higher* (prior to the crisis) than at almost any time since the mid-1960s.[20] This is plausible due to the "Laffer curve" effect of cutting tax rates: lower taxes entice more firms to operate as corporations, reduce the incentives for tax avoidance, and encourage production—all of which increases tax collection in absolute dollars.

Further, races to the bottom have had less influence on MNC location decisions than races to the top—improved local investment climates through better education and training, better judges and a stronger rule of law, leaner bureaucracies, less corruption and violence, and better logistics. That is why Singapore and Hong Kong get so much investment compared to, say, Sri Lanka or Burma. Marxist-inspired views about MNCs eviscerating national policy and public safety nets have been turned on their head.

Some fear that multinationals will crowd out local firms and establish cartels, bring only a small part of a productive process to the host country, and create few opportunities for supply and distribution linkages with local firms.

But this view is largely wrong. Research shows that multinationals usually provide fresh capital, create jobs, transfer technology and research and development, and create backward and forward linkages with local firms. The outcome is to transmit operational, managerial, marketing, and exporting skills to local residents. The entry of MNCs also conveys "demonstration effects," raising the bar among local firms vying to do business with the MNC. Rather than crowding out domestic firms and investment, MNCs "crowd in" domestic investment.

The debate over multinationals is not confined to their host economies: workers in home economies often protest that MNCs ship jobs abroad; legislators argue that MNCs avoid a fair share of the tax bill by salting money in tax-haven countries. But a closer look reveals positive outcomes. In some industries, multinationals have cut jobs less aggressively than comparable domestic firms. In the United States, overall employment in manufacturing fell by 18 percent between 2000 and 2005, but U.S.-based multinationals cut jobs only by 12.5 percent. Depending on the study, U.S. multinationals are found to pay workers 6 to 24 percent more on average than domestic companies in the United States, and European MNCs pay 10 to 20 percent more than purely domestic European firms. MNCs exhibit higher value added per worker, employ more capital per worker, and hire more skilled workers than purely domestic firms, even those that are also exporters but with no production abroad. Moreover, when both U.S. and foreign taxes are taken into account, U.S.-based MNCs pay as high a share of profits in taxes as companies without international operations.[21]

Better Globalization

The second part of our book turns to the future. In particular, we tackle a number of risks to globalization that, if not addressed, can easily fester into troublesome frictions in international finance and trade. We focus on four policy agendas of the hour: revamping the global financial system, restarting global trade cooperation, reducing worker anxiety, and preempting the potential threats that national security and environmental concerns pose to global trade and investment.

A book about globalization in today's world would be incomplete without a serious look at the damage caused by the Great Crisis. Chapter 5 sets the stage by surveying the wreckage in global finance, trade, growth, and employment. The news was uniformly bad. Net private capital flows to emerging markets plunged from $929 billion in 2007 to $667 billion in 2008 and $435 billion in 2009.[22] Emerging European nations faced the biggest drop: the volume of $20 billion for 2009 was less than a tenth of the level of $267 billion in 2008, and less than almost one-twentieth of the level of $393 billion in 2007. Emerging Asia attracted $236 billion in 2009, after $164 billion in 2008 and $315 billion in 2007. Latin America netted $131 billion in 2008 and $135 billion in 2009, after $184 billion in 2007. The good news is that the 2009 tally was far better than expected at the start of the year in Asia and Latin America, in particular. Governments and firms in the G10 rich economies were poised to triple their financing requirements to more than $3 trillion in 2009, leaving the Brazils and Indonesias of the world to scramble for private finance.

Global commerce stagnated and started collapsing in late 2008, and shrank by 12 percent in 2009. This was the first decline since 1982, when developing countries were buried in debt and the United States wrestled with double-digit inflation, the largest drop since the Second World War.[23] Global FDI flows also fell, from $1.98 trillion in 2007 to $1.7 trillion in 2008 and further to $1.04 trillion in 2009.[24] The richest economies took the worst hit, with FDI flows falling by 41 percent in 2009, after the already bad 2008.[25] Particularly affected were the United States, the United Kingdom, Spain, France, and Sweden.

What can be done? Chapter 6 centers on the most critical issue, the worst collapse of the global financial system in recent history. Inappropriate regulation, cheap money, and extreme leverage combined to create a perfect storm on Wall Street. The international financial system went overnight from overdrive to a bewildering stock market plunge, followed by quasi-nationalization of banks in the United States and Europe and investor flight from emerging markets.

This chain of events will reverberate throughout the global economy for years. The crisis and contagion will push back against financial liberalization, intended or not. Temptation for tighter capital controls increases after a plunge—as shown by Chile in the 1980s, Malaysia in the 1990s, and Brazil in the 2000s. The urge to regulate is now global. But excessive regulatory zeal can have counterproductive consequences. It is one thing to trim the massive growth of over-the-counter, unregulated derivatives; it is quite another to discourage long-term portfolio investment in equity markets.

While there were many causes for the crisis—mainly in the United States, but also elsewhere—U.S. policy measures are essential for getting the world economy back on track. These should center first and foremost on cleaning up toxic assets and shedding light on balance sheets, ensuring better ratings and valuations, channeling derivatives into regulated markets with margin requirements, demanding serious risk management on Wall Street, and insisting on measures to arrest the most pernicious of bubbles.

If wisely deployed, such measures need not come at the expense of growth. There is a fine line between abetting exuberance and creating undue caution. Finding that line is the task of central bankers and financial regulators, which is why they are given tremendous power, if not big paychecks.

There are two issues to manage going forward. The first is to avoid curbing financial innovation. To be sure, recent innovations—such as collateralized debt obligations (CDOs) and constant proportion debt obligations (CPDOs)—brought enormous grief.[26] But more often than not, financial innovations that were accepted in the marketplace have proven useful over time. They link savers with investors, hedge against commodity and currency fluctuations, and foster cross-border trade and investment. Since the minds of financial innovators will forever outpace the imagination of regulators, rigid approval processes will anyway prove ineffective and possibly counterproductive.

The second issue to handle with care is the scope of penalties. Regulators must tread the line between tough rules that do the job and legal obligations that can trigger a new wave of civil penalties. Class action lawsuits in the securities market, often founded on minor violations, have already become big business. Public policy may not be served by expanding the business of the trial bar further.

Global responses thus far have been lukewarm. At the international level, the crisis exposed the fact that financial regulations are still national, while financial firms are global. Countries that host banks from abroad or whose own banks expand on a global scale are in for regulatory battles with other nations when crises hit. At the domestic level, banks, insurance firms, and pension funds that rely on credit-rating agencies to properly evaluate risk, assuming the agencies will only award a triple-A rating to truly low-risk securities, find themselves hung out to dry. Rule making should center on closing obvious gaps in the regulatory net. But will the rule makers foresee the next big scam and can clashes among nations over rules be avoided? These issues are but a reflection of the broader clash between national prerogatives and global governance that erupted in the G20 and will take years to resolve.

Overall, the G20 is a good vehicle for bridging the domestic and the global: at the leadership level, it focuses minds and bureaucratic processes, yet without a heavy organization that advocates a preset agenda. The G20 lends itself to looser coordination, a plus in the arena of international financial governance, where issues can change quickly and require frequent revisiting. The ad hoc Plaza and Louvre exchange rate agreements of the 1980s were one-shot events, but arguably steadied the world economy sufficiently for it to prosper over the following two decades. By contrast, the laborious Basel I and II texts created common standards, but were largely ignored by giant players in the financial marketplace.

While coordination without bureaucracy can work, the G20 still needs a permanent police force and an insurance agency. For all its shortcomings, the IMF can serve these roles. All but buried in 2007, the Fund was resurrected in 2009. As a vehicle for lending to countries in distress and for providing quality macroeconomic advice and surveillance, with its hundreds of PhDs and accumulated centuries of experience, the IMF is unparalleled. The challenge now is twofold—the G20 must keep the Fund relevant, especially in safeguarding local financial stability, for it to do business, and the Fund must encourage sound domestic policies in rich and poor countries alike.

On the trade front, cooperation is distinct from the loose coordination of global finance—the goal is to lock in policies with no sunset clause. Yet, as chapter 7 shows, multilateral trade cooperation, the key engine of global liberalization, reached an inflection point in 2008. Progress in the Doha Round, launched in 2001, has ground to a halt by discord among the round's power brokers—the United States, the European Union, China, India, and Brazil. Except for trade facilitation, all the so-called "Singapore issues" that were supposed to be part of the Doha agenda—competition policy, government procurement, and investment regulation—were dropped in 2004, due to mounting opposition from developing countries. Talks on the remaining topic, trade facilitation, were watered down to the lowest common denominator. Meanwhile, core agreements on market access in agriculture, manufactures, and services remain blocked.

Global trade talks under the auspices of the GATT have delivered an immense amount of liberalization over past decades and negotiated caps on trade barriers are locked in by international accords. But within these caps, there is plenty of room (or "water") for countries to raise barriers without violating their obligations. Doha is critical for reducing the water level.

But the picture of global trade cooperation is far from romantic. It took a crisis for the G20 leaders to reassemble trade ministers for the November 2009 meeting, and to call for a conclusion of the Doha Round by 2010.

Progress toward the goal is, however, very uncertain. The Doha doldrums not only reflect deep differences between the big players but also mirror structural failures in multilateral negotiations. The apparatus, put in place in the 1940s, is not equipped to handle the pressures of the twenty-first century.

The first new feature is the rising number of WTO members, most of them not heavyweights in global trade; the second is the multiplication of contentious issues; and the third is the rule that "nothing is agreed until everything is agreed" (the single undertaking) coupled with the rule that every member must be on board (the consensus principle). The world trade body is, to paraphrase Tom Friedman, "hot, flat, and crowded." Whereas the prior GATT rounds could be concluded when a consensus was reached among four big players—the United States, the European Union, Japan, and Canada—today, China, India, and Brazil each hold enough sway to make or break the talks, and any group of twenty or more medium-sized countries can do enormous damage.

The fact that we are not witnessing a bonfire of protectionism in these circumstances with a crippled WTO system demonstrates the collective interest of millions of players who benefit from keeping borders open. It also shows the influence of academics, policy makers and observers who relentlessly tout the benefits of open trade regimes. But assurances are not enough; concrete actions must be taken to safeguard us from ourselves. Much of the action in trade goes under the radar. Protectionism is now more opaque, largely consisting of state measures to buttress national champions. According to the Global Trade Alert, during the crisis, new global heavyweights from Russia to India and Indonesia, as well as major trading powers like Germany enacted many measures with effects akin to tariffs such as subsidies to the ailing champions at the expense of principles of nondiscrimination.[27] While small individually, these measures can snowball collectively—in fact, only 5 percent of world trade has gone completely unscathed by protective measures since the G20 November 2008 pledge against protectionism. Concluding the Doha Round would be the best antidote against a new round of protectionist impulses, and would inject fresh confidence into the world of finance and investment.

Bigger reforms lie ahead, once Doha is concluded. Going forward, the WTO's single-undertaking principle and consensus rule will have to be scrapped in favor of plurilateral deals that can be multilateralized when additional WTO members are ready and able to join. These changes will reward members that are ready to take on obligations today, not wait another five or ten years for the footdraggers.

The other front for policy makers is the rapidly proliferating system of bilateral and regional free trade agreements (FTAs). These agreements can serve as building blocks for arrangements that go well beyond the WTO rules in depth and ambition. FTAs can be incubators for approaches that, once tried and proven, can be multilateralized. The North American Free Trade Agreement (NAFTA), for example, pioneered the liberalization of services and the protection of intellectual property, and these innovations were partially adopted in the Uruguay Round. The Information Technology Agreement, signed by the WTO in 1997, was first conceived in the Asia-Pacific Economic Cooperation (APEC) forum, a group that constitutes more than 60 percent of world trade. The model of transposing regional ideas into the multilateral framework might prove to be the answer for controlling greenhouse gas emissions.

Doha Round battles once again show that global trade rules reflect local politics. And the political challenge has been growing in the United States and Europe. Well before the crisis, in a June 2005 CNN/USA Today/ Gallup poll, 48 percent of Americans said trade is a "threat to the economy," as opposed to 44 percent who agreed that trade is an "opportunity for economic growth." This was the first time since 1992 that a plurality of Americans saw foreign trade as a threat. A 2005 Eurobarometer opinion poll showed that 46 percent of EU citizens had negative views of globalization, against 37 percent who voiced positive views. Once the crisis struck, opinion soured further. In a March–April 2008 *New York Times-CBS News* poll, 58 percent of Americans viewed foreign trade as good for the economy, down from 69 percent in 1996, while 32 percent viewed it as bad, up from 17 percent in 1996.[28] At the same time, 68 percent favored trade restrictions to protect domestic industries instead of allowing unrestrained trade, up from 55 percent in 1996.

Chapter 8 descends to the national level to examine answers to the widely feared (if exaggerated) negative effects of trade on jobs and wages, particularly in the United States and Europe. The expanded U.S. Trade Adjustment Assistance (TAA) programs and the older EU Globalization Fund are fine as instruments aimed at allaying the kinds of worries workers entertained in the 1990s and early 2000s. But the economic crisis makes those programs look like feeble nibbles around the edges of a much larger problem, one that requires far broader and sturdier attention. Job losses are real, retirement accounts are decimated, and insecurity stalks millions of families. In the Great Depression, few bankers actually jumped out of Wall Street windows, but the collapse of 2008 has already prompted many suicides. Even in a good economy, job churn is a perennial issue. As much as a quarter of the workforce changes jobs every year; in an economic slump, many never find a new position. Most lost jobs are unrelated to foreign trade and investment, but the global economy takes the lion's share of blame.

While European social safety nets are fluffy and comfortable, in the United States, the precariousness is real and raw. A new policy paradigm— perhaps an upgrade like Capitalism 3.0—is needed.

The new system should marry security with labor mobility. Health and homes should not be the reason people stay put after their jobs have disappeared. Health insurance should be citizen-based and portable from one employer to the next. Wage insurance and lifelong training programs may be in order. When massive job layoffs hit a community, perhaps emergency relief for prudent home mortgages should be available. The longer-term agenda ought to center on the building blocks of U.S. economy: private and public investment in America's crumbling infrastructure and education systems and promoting clean energy with a low carbon footprint.

These challenges raise tough design issues, for instance: engaging private investors without public complaints; avoiding disincentives to work; and keeping in check overly generous and costly security blankets favored in Europe. Bearing the challenges in mind, bold actions are needed to advance globalization and defeat resignation. Bold actions can also sidestep the catch-22 created by the very labels "trade adjustment" and "globalization fund," terms that cement the public perception that trade and globalization threaten our jobs and our way of life.

Chapter 9 centers on new threats looming behind traditional barriers— national security and environmental policies that can disrupt global trade and finance. Climate policies can lead to rules that are justified to limit greenhouse gas (GHG) emissions, yet impose unnecessary barriers to trade;

national security can be cited as the reason for blocking foreign invest-ment, hoarding energy supplies, and strictly regulating container ships. Overriding reasons demand that we arrest global warming, stop terror-ism, and have ample energy to run our factories and heat our homes. The future challenge is to do these things while preserving and expanding the global economy.

It is hard to wiggle out of the trade effects of climate change legislation. As long as countries apply differing standards and various methods of enforcement, costly action at home will cry out for barriers at the border. Yet such barriers can literally be taxing. World Bank simulations suggest that the potential impact of EU trade measures could reduce U.S. exports to Europe by 7 percent; the most energy-intensive industries, such as steel and cement, could suffer losses of up to 30 percent.[29] Of course, if the United States and other major trading nations implement their own GHG trade restrictions, the cumulative trade losses could be greater.

The real problem surrounding the clash between climate and trade is simple—and fixable. Clear multilateral rules do not yet exist to guide countries toward controls that are both effective against GHG and trade-friendly, nor do rules clearly define appropriate responses to excessive and trade-distorting standards.

A good solution, advocated by Hufbauer, Charnovitz, and Kim (2009), would be a new Climate Code that enumerates both permitted and pro-scribed trade measures in the name of climate control.[30] To succeed, a code must enlist a critical mass of countries. It could start out as a small plurilateral agreement, whereby a subset of WTO members commit to a set of rules that is binding among them and that can be enforced between themselves in the WTO dispute settlement system. Although such a code would require consensus of all WTO members to be formally added to the WTO Agreement, that consent might be politically acceptable because it would not require that all WTO members agree to the disciplines of the code, nor would it affect the rights and obligations of countries that are not members of the code.

If such a code could limit disputes coming to the WTO between the United States, the European Union, Canada, Japan, and a few other OECD countries, it certainly would have achieved much. If it could head off disputes involving China and India as well, it would be a splendid accomplishment. Shared leadership by the United States, the European Union, and China is the key for climate change and trade talks alike. In fact, it is no stretch to argue that a casualty of climate-related trade battles could be fatigue in fighting climate change. To minimize trade battles, climate legislation that includes trade-restrictive measures should reflect the core disciplines of the existing WTO system. If and when WTO members negotiate a new code on trade rules with respect to GHG emissions, these core disciplines should become the reference point.

Barriers are also enticing on the investment front. In the years leading up to the crisis, major countries cited national security or public safety concerns to block FDI inflows. Money seems particularly suspicious when it arrives from new sources that have not been confidants in the game of global politics; in the United States and Europe, "strangers" include China and the Middle East.

These troubles will not go away when the crisis passes. Unfair incentives are deployed to retain investments and jobs that might otherwise evaporate. French president Nicolas Sarkozy's early 2009 announcement that he would like Peugeot, Citroen, and Renault to shift production from low-wage nations back to France in return for €7 billion in soft loans resonated in the minds of many national leaders. Fortunately, the European Commission blocked Sarkozy's initiative, but plenty of other examples of investment and job protection can be found.[31] Such maneuvers can boomerang. In March 2009, China cited new antitrust rules for rejecting Coca-Cola Company's $2.3 billion bid for China Huiyuan Juice Group Ltd. Two weeks later, Australia cited national security while stopping the purchase of OZ Minerals, a mining company, by state-owned China Minmetals Corporation. There is not necessarily any connection in the circumstances of each case, but the atmosphere surrounding investment policies is soured.

Measures to keep domestic firms in and foreigners out can invite emulation if not retaliation. Caps on ownership and politicized investment reviews accentuate the hazards of investing abroad. The chill to investment can be mitigated by clear rules and a prompt review, such as is done by the United States (except when Congress gets involved on a particular case). David Marchick and Matthew Slaughter have advocated a global "code of conduct" for reviewing foreign investments, and we agree.[32] The code, based on a handful of principles, would apply to investments tinged by national security and strategic asset concerns.

Conclusion

When markets are interconnected and interdependent, virtually all countries depend on each other for prosperity and growth. In this context, crisis and volatility also spread easily from one country to another. No country can escape a global debacle originating in one of the great powers.

Yet no country alone, not even a great power, can fix the problems facing the world economy. In the past, successful financial talks and trade rounds depended on consensus between the United States, the European Union, Japan, and Canada; today, Brazil, Russia, India, and China hold enough power to influence global policy agendas. Never before has it been so essential for advanced countries to court emerging players, and never before has multilateral agreement been so critical to meet the challenges facing globalization.

Dealing with the global challenges has never been easy. Nation-states run the world. Changes to the governance of the global economy will happen bottom-up within the system, not top-down from mandarins in the IMF, the World Bank, or the WTO.

Globalization is at risk from economic and political pressures intensified by the crisis; a prolonged downturn would be particularly hazardous. But we believe that even in a bleak scenario, the system has built-in forces willing and able to fight tooth and nail to safeguard openness. Economic integration is a fabulous force—if not unstoppable, at least one of the best agents the world has known for spreading growth and prosperity.

Those arguing that the crisis will accelerate the demise of the West and the rise of the East are, in our view, premature. The crisis may not even signal an inflection point in the distribution of global power. The paradox is that, while many are calling an end to *Pax Americana*, it is the United States that is asked to deliver the world out of the mess. In part, this call reflects economic reality; in part, it shows the absence of contending leaders. China may be waiting in the wings, but China's economy is still one-third the size of the United States. The European Union, for all its size and heft, cannot yet speak with a single voice on fiscal affairs or exchange rates. American leadership and finance has been and will remain essential for getting the world economy back on track. The good news is that the American market system, now so tarnished, may be the very factor that enables the United States to rebound faster than other economies.

Calling an end to the capitalist era is downright foolhardy. Yes, capitalism will evolve, but we will remain closer to Francis Fukuyama's *End of History* than to a new economic model. Market capitalism has delivered so much over the past half century that it would be both difficult and unwise to turn the page. If the Great Depression could not destroy capitalism, neither can the financial collapse of 2008.

The Great Crisis, like many of the economic debacles before it, was created by the dark side of forces that, in a system of market capitalism, make computers run and planes fly: the drive for innovation, the penchant for exuberance, and the quest to get rich. Entrepreneurs take risks because they get carried away by euphoria, they cannot conceive of worse times ahead, and they want to see the good times last. There were no mad animal spirits; rather, men and women on Wall Street to Main Street rationally responded to the incentives laid out in front of them. Some strayed from the legal path. But the majority worked the system without gaming it. They saw great deals—many too good to be true. But as die-hard optimists, they grabbed for the brass ring. Let's not curb those spirits, but instead channel them in a better direction. This book suggests how.

2

BOOMING FINANCE

Cross-border flows of finance exploded from under $1 trillion in 1980 and $1.5 trillion in 1990 to more than $11 trillion in 2007 (figure 2.1). In total, global financial assets in 2007—foreign and domestic—almost topped $200 trillion, or three and a half times world gross domestic product (GDP). International investors now hold 14 percent of U.S. equities, up from 4 percent in 1975; 27 percent of American corporate bonds, up from 1 percent; and 52 percent of Treasury securities, up from 20 percent.

The dizzying array of global capital activity—foreign purchases of equity and debt securities, mergers and acquisitions, greenfield corporate investment, cross-border bank lending and insurance, and more—expanded some twenty times since 1980, vastly outpacing the growth of world output and merchandise trade, which went up (in nominal terms) by around three and five times, respectively. As a result, international finance has come to claim an ever-larger share of the world economy and, as we explore in chapter 6, emerged as the epicenter of the Great Crisis. By 2004, the combined sum of external assets and liabilities averaged around 100 percent of GDP in low-income countries, 150 percent of GDP in middle-income countries, and more than 550 percent of GDP in high-income countries.[1]

Before the crisis, U.S. financial outflows reached $1.05 trillion or 8 percent of GDP in 2006, while inflows were nearly double at $1.86 trillion.[2] Emerging markets have seen equally dramatic changes. In 2007, private capital flows to emerging markets topped at a record $929 billion, nearly 7

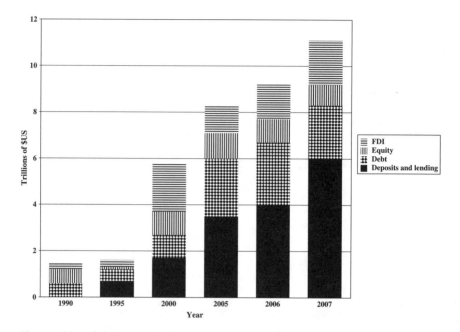

Fig. 2.1 Annual Cross-Border Financial Flows in 1990–2007, by Type.
Source: McKinsey Global Institute.

percent of their combined GDPs.[3] In China, foreign capital inflows reached some $166 billion, or 6 percent of GDP.

New players are shaping global finance. Specialized investors—hedge funds and mutual funds, for example—became major forces in moving portfolio capital to emerging markets in the early 1990s.[4] They were followed by a wave of investors traditionally focused on highly rated debt issued in mature markets: pension funds, insurance companies, and other heavyweight institutional investors. Private equity gathered speed in the 1980s and 1990s, and is now taking off as a cross-border asset class in its own right, due in part to higher returns (at least until 2008) than most public equity and bond markets. Early stage venture capital (VC) is also globalizing: Silicon Valley VC firms place their bets not only on Palo Alto entrepreneurs but also on the Googles of tomorrow that they see blossoming in India and China.

Tables Turning

Big, established players—the United States, the European Union (EU), and Japan—are still the heart of global capital, providing four-fifths of global financial services. They also like each other best. In 2006, flows to emerging markets accounted for only a tenth of global financial inflows and 13 percent of outflows; the rest is among developed markets.[5] The big players are also the engines of global money: the triumvirate of the United States, Britain, and continental Europe alone accounted for 80 percent of the growth of global capital inflows and two-thirds of the growth in outflows between 1996 and 2006.[6] In the precrisis days, the combined EU-U.S. financial market supported nearly 7 million jobs, around $4 trillion in direct investment, and stock and bond transactions of more than $50 trillion.[7]

Despite their still negligible share of the world's whirlpool of money, emerging markets have made rapid forays into global finance. Singapore, Hong Kong, Shanghai, and Seoul have become major financial centers, joining the traditional hubs of New York, London, Frankfurt, and Tokyo. Although the share of global finance held by emerging markets has not changed dramatically in the past decade, there has been a qualitative sea change. Between 1970 and the mid-1980s, the lion's share of capital flows to developing countries was debt, primarily government and secondarily private. Debt typically accounted for about 80 percent of all capital flows; the rest was foreign direct investment (FDI), and there were practically no portfolio equity flows to these countries, mainly due to their own controls.[8]

Unlike the past, when developing countries were big importers of debt finance, now the rich countries are the big importers of debt, on a net basis. Emerging markets deleveraged in the 1990s—their external debts plunged from 82 percent of GDP in 1980–1984 to 50 percent in 1990–1995.[9] The great deleveraging continued, especially after the 1997–1998 Asian financial crisis. Meanwhile, portfolio equity flows as a fraction of total capital flows rose from less than 1 percent in 1980–1984 to almost 19 percent in 1990–1995.

The drop in cross-border debt flows into emerging markets (relative to GDP) partly reflects the fact that major commercial banks have moved into these markets, particularly Latin America and Central and Eastern Europe, often via mergers and acquisitions. As a consequence, lending occurs domestically rather than across borders.[10] Locally funded claims increased fourfold between 1995 and 2002 to $544 billion, or from 14 percent of total claims held by foreign banks on emerging markets in 1995 to 40 percent by the end of 2002. This shift was accompanied by a change from pure lending to other financial services—asset management, equity underwriting, and the like. Bond issuance in local currency in Asia and Latin America rose to rival international issuance.

Unlike the recent past, emerging nations have now built their own reserves and amassed foreign asset holdings—particularly official holdings of foreign exchange. South American countries, which improved their macroeconomic management in the 1990s, built reserve cushions in a commodity boom that lasted through late 2008 and allowed their pension funds to invest abroad. Middle Eastern countries fattened their coffers on the back of spiking oil prices in 2006 and 2007. China, basking in a megaexport boom for more than two decades, raked in nearly $2 trillion in foreign currency reserves and became a financial giant. China now holds a fifth of all U.S. Treasuries held by foreigners, still behind Japan, but well above the share held by Britain.[11] In 2006, China became the world's leading capital exporter, followed by Japan, Russia, Saudi Arabia, and Germany.[12]

Meanwhile, the United States turned itself into the borrower of last resort, sucking in almost two-thirds of global capital imports, followed by Spain, Britain, and France. While the United States has been a capital importer since the 1960s, at the end of 2006, the Treasury reported the largest current account deficit in world history at $857 billion, almost 7 percent of GDP. In order to finance both the current account deficit and its own sizable foreign investments, the United States has to import some $1 trillion of foreign capital annually, or more than $4 billion—the yearly budget of the city of Houston—every working day.[13]

The surge of finance from China and the Middle East to the advanced markets (led by the United States) has in part arrived through sovereign wealth funds (SWFs). These forty or so government-owned investment institutions manage some $3 trillion of global assets. The list is topped by the Abu Dhabi Investment Authority, with some half a trillion dollars,

followed by Norway's Government Pension Fund, the Kuwait Investment Authority, Singapore's Government Investment Corporation, and
the China Investment Corporation (CIC).

Unlike central banks, SWFs do not confine their holdings to Treasury
bills and government-guaranteed debt. Instead, they invest in shares, corporate debt, and sometimes whole companies. In 2007–2008, SWFs invested more than $60 billion in some of the largest financial companies in
the world, mainly in the United States. In 2007, the CIC invested a total
of $8 billion in the investment bank Morgan Stanley and the renowned
U.S. private equity firm Blackstone, and in 2008, China's State Administration of Foreign Exchange (SAFE) made a $2 billion bet on the U.S.
private equity firm TPG. Middle Eastern money also got in the game: the
Abu Dhabi Investment Authority purchased a small stake in Apollo Management in July 2007, and Dubai's Mubadala Development Company
bought 7.5 percent of the Carlyle Group, another giant in private equity, in
September 2007. Before the Great Crisis of 2008, SWFs were projected to
grow to a massive $10–12 trillion by 2015—nearly the size of the entire U.S.
economy.

In sum, global finance has skyrocketed and metamorphosed—into le-
veraging by developed countries, deleveraging by many emerging markets, and increased cross-border securities trading by both. The share of
advanced countries in global cross-border debt liabilities and assets has
grown since the mid-1990s, while their share of global portfolio assets and
liabilities—as well as world trade and reserves—has shrunk (figure 2.2).[14]

From Railways to E-Trade Accounts

Global financial integration is not new. The gilded era of globalization in the late nineteenth century saw massive flows of finance outward from the leading nations of Western Europe to "peripheral" Europe
and the overseas regions of recent European settlement, particularly those
with impressive natural resources—Australia, America, Canada, and Argentina. Net capital outflows were at the time as high as 9 percent of GDP
for Britain and peaked at comparable levels in France, Germany, and the
Netherlands.[15] For the "frontier" recipients, annual inflows entailed current account deficits often exceeding 10 percent of GDP for three decades

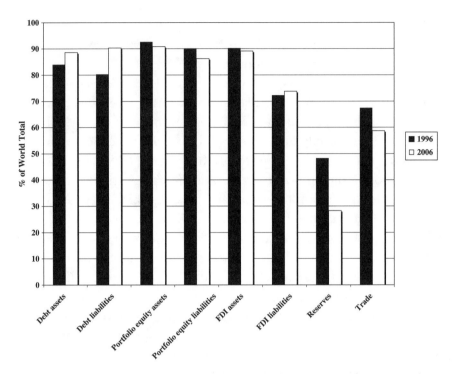

Fig. 2.2 Share of Advanced Countries in Global Trade, Reserves, and Cross-Border Financial Flows in 1996 and 2006 (%). *Source*: Lane and Milesi-Ferretti, "The Drivers of Financial Globalization" (Discussion Paper No. 238, Institute for International Integration Studies, January 2008).

before World War I; even the peripheral Nordic countries had annual inflows accounting for as much as 5 percent of GDP.

But unlike today, when cross-border portfolio and debt flows dominate the picture, much of the booty a hundred years ago went to foreign direct investment in infrastructure projects—port facilities, railway networks, roads, and the like. The goal then was to facilitate the flow of raw materials from the distant lands to European industrial centers. Infrastructure projects went hand in hand with trade liberalization in Europe for raw materials and agricultural goods. The two-way exchange was fruitful: the target countries received investment as well as export revenue—from gold, silver, base metals, agriculture, and eventually petroleum. After the two world wars, direct investment reached into new fields, manufacturing and utilities. However, portfolio flows have in recent times surged to the forefront, regularly surpassing direct investment flows. In the period between 2000 and 2006, cross-border portfolio flows topped FDI by roughly two to one.

Junk Bonds or International Monetary Fund (IMF) Dictates?

What drives the exponential growth in global cross-border capital flows of a portfolio character? Why is there so much money flow from one nation to another, and why now?

Technology has supplied a major jolt. Before, an investor would call his or her well-paid broker a few times a year; today, anyone can log on to E*Trade or Fidelity every day and buy and sell stock virtually anywhere, sending money back and forth across borders. Before, the business of valuing overseas securities was a back-of-the-envelope process compared to today's science of finance. Now, PhD quants from top universities run mathematical models on their computers to value entire countries and asset classes, and to create bewildering new securities.

Computerization was indeed a game changer. It provided for new risk-management techniques, reduced communications costs, and democratized investing, making all of us participants in and captains of the flow of global finance. Futures and options trading, hedging techniques that require complex calculations, and "program trading," which delivers automated transactions in response to preprogrammed price and volume thresholds, are all the fruit of sophisticated computers and software.

Financial innovations gave a further boost to cross-border capital flows. The Eurodollar market fashioned in the City of London in the early 1960s enabled U.S. financial subsidiaries operating abroad to take deposits and make loans in U.S. dollars—free from oversight by the Federal Reserve or other stateside regulators. The 1980s were a heyday for innovators. Legendary financier Michael Milken developed the junk bond market of risky, high-yield bonds in New York as a source of funding for corporate mergers and acquisitions. Securitization was devised to convert nonmarketable instruments, such as credit card debt or auto loans, into publicly traded securities. Mortgage-backed securities known as collateralized mortgage obligations (CMOs) sliced the cash flow from the underlying assets into various categories, or tranches, with different maturities and risks to suit investors with distinct risk appetites.

Created in one country, often the United States, these new financial products found a market among investors elsewhere. They also enabled investors to arbitrage differences in tax and regulatory systems across countries. Offshore special purpose vehicles—set up or controlled by domestic actors to access offshore equity financing—fed the surge of cross-border flows.

But much of the globalization of money would not have happened without policy changes. The initial impetus was capital account liberalization— affecting FDI, portfolio flows, and bank finance alike—in the 1970s and 1980s. This represented a radical departure from the primacy of fixed exchange rates buttressed by capital controls—the gold standard system of the late nineteenth and early twentieth centuries and the Bretton Woods system anchored on the U.S. dollar in the post–Second World War era. The United States tried to combine an open capital market with the dollar pegged to gold in the 1960s and early 1970s, but could not pull off the trick in the face of Vietnam-era spending. After flirting with mild capital controls in the Kennedy and Johnson administrations, the United States abandoned the fixed link between gold and the dollar in 1973.[16] Thus began the era of floating exchange rates and free capital flows.

What compelled the policy choice in the first instance was the problem of current account imbalances. These became so large that they could not be settled in gold without running the vaults dry or taking the painful medicine of gold standard economics. In Europe, financial openness was patchy at the beginning, despite the European Community effort in the 1960s to free intraregional capital flows.[17] In the wake of large U.S. current account deficits and the oil shocks of 1973, some European nations tried to tighten their rules both on capital inflows and outflows.

Weary of the domestic cost of steadying the pound, in October 1979, Britain's new conservative government went ahead and abolished all controls on capital flows. The British current account surplus surged when North Sea oil made the United Kingdom a net oil exporter in 1981, and large-scale capital outflows soon followed. The Netherlands and Germany already had rather open capital markets and rebelled against capital controls in the early 1980s.[18] Further opening ensued: Italy eliminated the special exchange rate regime for capital account transactions in 1982, France let go of controls in 1983, and Belgium dropped its dual exchange system in

1990. The 1987 Single European Act fostered directives to free financial movement throughout the continent. Central and Eastern European countries seeking EU membership opened quickly in the 1990s.

Emerging markets, particularly those in Latin America, which had traveled the rocky road of debt crisis in the early 1980s, adopted the tenets of Washington Consensus in the late 1980s, and followed suit by sharply relaxing capital controls in the 1990s. The emerging markets of East Asia were also forceful advocates of liberalization (figures 2.3 and 2.4).[19] But like in Europe of the 1960s and 1970s, there were also numerous backsliding episodes of new controls in the 1990s and 2000s, from Russia to Brazil to China and India.[20] East Asian countries also rolled back some of their liberalization after the financial crisis of 1997–1998.

Capital account opening was accompanied by a wave of financial deregulation—relaxing tight rules governing banking and insurance, and approving new investment vehicles.[21] Rules and supervision were simplified

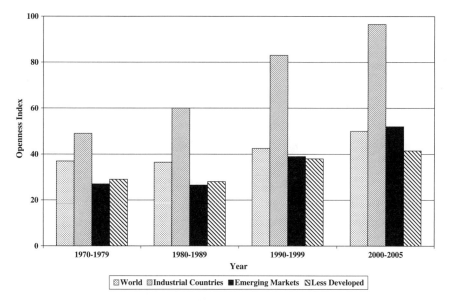

Fig. 2.3 Development of Capital Account Openness in the World and in Industrialized, Less-Developed, and Emerging-Market Countries in 1970–2005 (KAOPEN Index). *Source*: Chinn and Ito, "A New Measure of Financial Openness," *Journal of Comparative Policy Analysis* 10(3) (September 2008): 307–320.

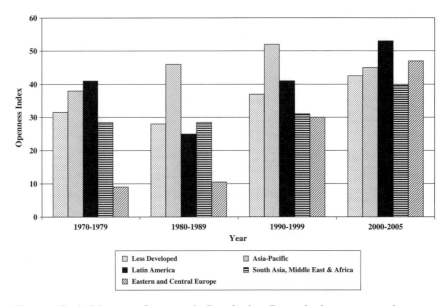

Fig. 2.4 Capital Account Openness in Developing Countries in 1970–2005, by Region (KAOPEN Index). *Source*: A New Measure of Financial Openness," *Journal of Comparative Policy Analysis* 10(3) (September 2008): 307–320.

and increasingly harmonized across markets. The United States and Britain were front-runners. U.S. banking deregulation, launched in 1977 and finalized in 1994, removed geographical expansion restrictions facing banks, both within and across states. France, Germany, and many other Western European nations jumped on board. The continent's markets for financial services would, however, remain segmented for another decade until 1999, when the European Commission unveiled the Financial Services Action Plan, a missive of forty-two measures designed to harmonize the member state rules on securities, banking, insurance, mortgages, pensions and all other forms of financial transactions. Most elements of the plan were adopted by 2004.

For its part, Japan began a staged liberalization of its capital markets in 1984, at the prodding of the United States. American officials anguished over the strength of the dollar relative to the yen and the growing U.S. trade deficit with Japan, and believed that financial liberalization might help reverse these trends. The changes were a dive into the unknown for

Tokyo. In the late 1970s, the Japanese financial system was still strictly regulated. The size of bank loans, interest rates, borrowers, branches, fees, and other business lines were all regulated, and banks were not allowed to compete with each other. Following the reforms, and partly due to them, Japan rose to become a leading financial power and the world's largest international creditor.[22] In 1987, Japan was home to seven of the world's ten largest commercial banks, a coup over the United States. With the opening of capital markets, deregulation expanded Japanese home economy borrowing, helping to build new companies and arguably moderating the business cycle at home and abroad.[23]

The introduction of the euro in 1999 produced another uptick in financial flows. The single currency led to a surge in intra–euro area holdings, to reach nearly a fifth of the world's cross-border holdings.[24] The fact that the eurozone integrates money and credit markets appeals to investors: the common monetary unit eliminates currency risk among the member countries, freeing investors to substitute foreign for domestic securities. Even though wedded to the pound, London became a hub for euro-denominated financial trade.[25]

Trade liberalization, a transformative force in the postwar era, in many ways was key for financial globalization. Merchandise transactions and global supply chains inherently stimulate financial flows: they require trade credits, export insurance, and means of payment across borders. And trade linkages fuel information flows, establishing pathways and appetites for foreign assets.

International talk shops prodded and shaped domestic financial reforms. Multilateral bodies such as the G7 and G8 and subsequently the G20, the Organization for Economic Cooperation and Development (OECD), and the Financial Stability Forum—all serving as meeting grounds and watering holes for senior representatives of national central banks, supervisory authorities, and treasuries—helped open markets, coordinate policies, and converge regulatory systems. The United States held bilateral dialogues with Japan, China, the European Union, and many other economies; the European Union did the same with Japan, China, India, and Russia. The U.S.-EU forum has propelled changes in accounting standards: acceptance in late 2007 by the United States of the International Reporting Standards, and more recently, a pledge by the

European Union and U.S. Securities and Exchange Commission (SEC) to endorse the mutual recognition of their laws governing securities markets. The IMF monitored the global financial regulatory architecture and steadied countries that were shaken by financial shocks. The IMF's counsel, while often criticized as draconian,[26] has tempered decision making and preempted future troubles. Many an emerging market would be deeply troubled were it not for the IMF's emergency lending and policy advice.

Uneven Membership

Within a few decades, sealed domestic markets, fixed exchange rates, and a mosaic of idiosyncratic national regulations were transformed into free-flowing global finance, floating exchange rates, and increasingly convergent regulations. Although national rules still have the last say (except within the European Union), the world of finance is flatter and more fluid than at any time in the twentieth century. The exponential surge in flows of money and trade attests that this setup has fueled business across borders.

Not all countries have been equally swept by the cross-border financial frenzy, however. Even the most integrated emerging markets are still less wired to global money than Europe, Japan, and the United States. Indexes of openness devised by the IMF show that sub-Saharan states, former Soviet Republics, Turkey, and several Latin American nations trail well behind the OECD nations in financial integration.

Granted, some of this is simply due to being latecomers. But capital controls and relatively closed trade regimes are also at play. Domestic financial sophistication—the presence of retail and investment banks, institutional investors, and mutual funds—are essential elements of a modern economy. Domestic players can learn by interacting with foreign firms. Causality also runs the other way: exposure to global markets can educate domestic investors and bring in new instruments and players, sharpening financial savvy. More sophisticated markets whet the appetite of foreign investors.

Domestic financial sophistication and economic development conspire. Former U.S. Federal Reserve governor Frederic Mishkin has famously remarked that finance is "the brain of the economy." In an epic survey, Richard Sylla, economic historian at New York University's business school, argued that financial sophistication has propelled military and economic power, starting from fifteenth-century Italy to seventeenth-century Low Countries, eighteenth-century British government debt and insurance, and nineteenth- and twentieth-century American capital. Japan set out to copy Western financial practices when it decided to industrialize in the late 1860s. Studies focused on more recent years find that an actively traded stock market augurs present and future growth.[27]

The confluence of growth and sophistication makes for a roster of beauty queens and sore losers. Smaller, low-income countries are likely to receive a cold shoulder from investors, while big, diverse, and integrated economies bask in attention.[28] Smaller countries with limited financial systems also are more likely to impose capital controls in an effort to preempt shocks. Data compiled by the World Economic Forum is instructive. Its financial sophistication index recites a summit of likely players—Britain, the United States, Hong Kong, Canada, Sweden, Australia, Ireland, the Netherlands, Germany, Singapore, and Finland. At the bottom of the fifty-two-country list hang Vietnam, China, Ukraine, Russia, Egypt, Indonesia, Nigeria, Venezuela, Argentina, Kazakhastan, and Pakistan. Unsurprisingly, the latter are also less developed—and less open. While there is a lot of variation around the regression line in figure 2.5, the association between financial openness and financial sophistication is unmistakable. Smarts, money, and openness tend to go together.

Financial integration will roll on and well it should, shrinking the gap between countries in their exposure to global capital. But policy will determine the speed of this historic process. In the wake of the financial crisis of 2008, the direction of policy is much disputed, largely because the benefits of financial globalization are all too often punctuated by huge crashes.

Tyrant with a Temper or Benevolent Dictator?

Theoretically, capital account liberalization has clear-cut effects. It allows for more efficient global allocation of capital from capital-rich advanced countries to capital-poor developing economies. This, in turn,

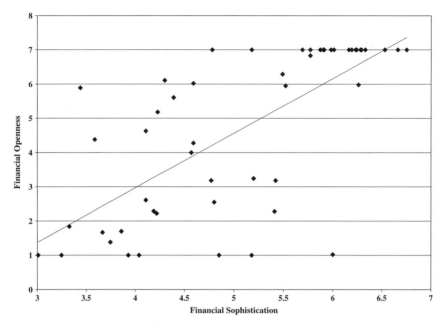

Fig. 2.5 Financial Sophistication and Openness Indexes, Fifty-two Countries, 2007.
Source: Authors, on the basis of World Economic Forum data.

gives a higher rate of return on people's savings in advanced countries and increases growth, spurs employment, and fattens incomes in developing countries.[29] Financial integration also jogs the economy's brain: foreign inflows can facilitate the transfer of technological and managerial know-how and generate competition in domestic financial markets.

But like other cross-border flows, financial globalization has become hugely controversial. The central debate is growth versus volatility. On the one side are those who argue that financial integration makes countries vulnerable to external shocks and undercuts their ability to shape economic policy. This, the argument goes, is particularly true for countries that are not "ready" for the racy world of international finance. The natural policy prescription, most notably advanced by Harvard's Dani Rodrik and the former World Bank chief economist Joseph Stiglitz, recommends capital controls to flatten boom and bust cycles.[30] The argument is that liberalization invites speculative hot money, the sort likely to depart in herds and leave a crisis behind.[31] This school also tends to see FDI as a healthier sort of capital.[32] It is much less volatile—try moving a semiconductor fabrication plant overnight—and it ties down foreign managers and technicians.

In the other corner of the ring are those who see financial integration as the engine of global wealth and the handmaiden of entrepreneurship. How else would that bright young businessperson in Thailand or Kenya raise cash? Controls can discourage foreign investors from bringing money to the country when times are tough for fear that funds will be frozen when political winds change. This, in fact, was exactly what happened in Thailand in 2006, when the country briefly flirted with capital controls to stop foreigners from pushing up the value of the baht: stocks plummeted 15 percent virtually overnight.[33]

Whether a tyrant with a temper or a benevolent dictator, finance is viewed as nothing less than king. So what is the real impact of financial integration?

Contagious Optimism

Critics of global capital are right in that finance is far from steady. Just in the twentieth century, the world has gone through repeated and perhaps more frequent financial crises, where global capital is reallocated at dramatic speeds from one set of markets to another and asset values soar and plummet (table 2.1).

The list of multicountry crises starts with the Latin American debt crisis of the 1980s, which engulfed nearly every country in the region. This was followed by the Mexican debt crisis of 1994, called by IMF managing director Michel Camdessus the "first crisis of the 21st century."[34] Aftershocks were labeled the "tequila effect" when they hit Argentina. Next came the Asian financial crisis of 1997–1998, which rolled across Thailand, Indonesia, Malaysia, and Korea. Then the Russian default of 1998 reverberated across Eastern Europe, Asia, and Latin America. The effects were devastating in national economies, costing from an estimated 7 percent of GDP in Russia to 55 percent of GDP in Indonesia.

Worries about contagion are not unfounded: "sudden stops" and "sudden reversals" are rightly feared. In today's world of computer-driven finance, portfolio inflows can quickly go in reverse when a country is hit with an adverse macroeconomic shock—which in turn amplifies the jitters.

Table 2.1 Major International Financial Crises

1910	Shanghai rubber stock market crisis
1930s	The Great Depression
1973	Oil shocks
1980s	Latin American debt crisis
1987	Black Monday
1989–1991	U.S. Savings & Loan crisis
1990s	Japanese asset bubble collapse
1992–1993	Black Wednesday in Europe
1994–1995	Mexican peso crisis
1997–1998	Asian financial crisis
1998	Russian default
2002	Argentine crisis
2008–2009	The global financial crisis

Source: Authors.

Global capital tends to be procyclical, flowing to emerging markets when times are good and getting out when things go sour, thus providing no cushion for rainy days.

But financial integration *per se* does not cause crises. Economic crises seem to recur roughly once a decade and the downfalls have many sources. In the nineteenth century, crises were largely bank failures; between the 1940s and 1960s, crises combined bank failures and sharp devaluation; and since the 1980s, the origin has been real estate booms and busts.[35] Excessive debt denominated in foreign currency was a common theme in crises that visited emerging markets. When the money starts going out, forced devaluation of the local currency relative to the currency in which debt is denominated—generally the dollar—has been the cocktail that has bankrupted countries from Latin America to Asia.[36] But crises in Japan and the United States cannot be blamed on the rapid departure of hot money from abroad; a collapsing real estate bubble at home was explanation enough.

If excess borrowing is the underlying culprit, foreign lending is not. Former IMF chief economist, Harvard's Kenneth Rogoff, and University of Maryland's Carmen Reinhart go beyond most studies that examine the crises of the 1980s and 1990s to show that eighteen financial and banking crises in advanced countries over past *centuries* all involved high levels of debt—both public and private, and often domestic rather than foreign.[37] According to Rogoff and Reinhart, it is debt of any sort that matters. The aftershocks are most often harsh: in another paper, the authors found that central government debt had increased three years after a financial crisis, on average by 86 percent.[38]

This also means that the lens of open versus closed financial systems is the wrong way to look at crises. Stanford's Peter Henry and Peter Lorentzen suggest that if something is to be controlled in the international realm beyond the general prescription of avoiding excessive debt, it should be dollar-denominated foreign borrowing. Free equity flows—opening stock markets to foreigners—give bang for the buck and are best if left alone.[39]

Openness that abets borrowing in foreign currencies plays a role in precipitating volatility. But the accumulation of foreign money does not lead to financial earthquakes all on its own. Yes, one reason behind contagion is the existence of tight trade and financial links, but another potent cause is the fact that financial institutions lump together markets with common features. If Argentina starts looking suspect, confidence in Brazil begins to erode as well; when China coughs, Thailand gets the flu. While an open capital market can invite speculators to real estate booms in Tokyo, Bangkok, and Miami, this in turn helps breed collective euphoria and those infamous bubbles that have destroyed many a financial titan. But even the world's most renowned crisis scholar, Charles Kindleberger, argued that disappointed investors packed up only at "the revelation of some misfeasance, malfeasance or malversation (the corruption of officials) that occurred during the mania."[40] Open capital markets are not to blame; what should be condemned is bad domestic financial and economic management in a world of open capital markets.

Controlling the Controllers

Capital control advocates—call them the "control group"—got wind in their sails following the Latin American, Asian, and Russian crises. Serious, credible people are members of this group, including the staunch free trader, even libertarian, Jagdish Bhagwati,[41] and the now-Nobel laureate Paul Krugman, who in his 2008 book argued that capital account liberalization was the key reason behind the Asian crisis.[42]

Where the control group may go astray, however, is at the hands of aco-lytes who take the criticisms of global finance to an extreme. Would coun-tries be better off with sturdy capital controls, vintage 1970?

The answer, with some reservations, is no—this would be like arguing to an athlete that the best way to avoid sports injuries is to not engage in sports. While we hold no brief for exotic derivatives that were traded in the trillions at the height of the 2006–2007 housing bubble (see chapter 6), tough capital controls would be akin to the norms of two generations ago that virtually confined university endowments to triple-A bonds and prac-tically ruled out foreign securities for pension funds. The upside of global finance so vastly exceeds the downside that it would be foolish to turn the clock back to 1970.

To be sure, as in many things economic, empirical evidence on the ben-efits of financial opening is mixed. This in no small measure is due to dif-ferent econometric approaches, difficulties in measuring openness, and controlling for the manifold factors other than openness that determine economic growth—natural resources, human and physical capital, pro-ductivity, governance, corruption, and so on. There is also the usual prob-lem of causality: do liberalizing countries grow more because they liberalize, or do they liberalize because they grow? A bird's-eye view of all the ink spilled over these questions is telling: a 2003 survey of studies on the ef-fect of capital account liberalization on growth tallied three papers that found a positive effect, four papers that found no effect, and seven papers that found mixed results.[43] In most studies, however, the effect is not negative, but either zero or positive.

But consider some additional findings. The IMF's Romain Ranciere, UCLA's Aaron Tornell, and University of Osnabrück's Frank Westermann, who factored in the greater propensity for crises created by open markets, concluded that financial liberalization boosts per capita income growth by 1 percent *annually*.[44] A Colombia-Duke-Indiana University team reached a very similar result—that equity market opening has resulted in a 1 percent increase in annual real economic growth.[45] Peter Henry of Stanford showed that the cost of capital has dropped and investment increased when developing countries liberalized their stock markets.[46] Liberalization also leads to a sharp increase in the growth of the country's capital stock, step-ping up the growth rate of output per worker. With Diego Sasson, Henry found that after a typical developing country opens its stock market to inflows of foreign capital, the average annual compensation for each manufacturing worker increases by 25 percent.[47] Another group of authors found that equity market liberalization has reduced consumption volatility, particularly in advanced but also in developing countries.[48] Two further studies found that liberalization leads to a 15 percent appreciation in a firm's equity value—as well as to real sales growth, investment, profitability, efficiency, and leverage.[49]

Besides the good growth effects of freeing finance, there are six reasons why tight controls may not be such a good idea. First, capital controls can easily spill over to the realm of trade. An open trade regime generally requires an open financial regime because exporters and importers need access to international financial markets. By the end of the twentieth century, three-quarters of the countries that had liberalized trade also had liberalized financial flows.[50] The growth in intraregional cross-border trade in Europe was a major reason why capital controls were bulldozed away in the 1980s: exporters and importers could not operate efficiently with the capital control straitjacket on. New controls would likely only stifle trade.

Second, it is hard in practice to distinguish between portfolio and direct investment, both because operating companies (such as GE Capital) can serve as conduits for large flows to unrelated companies and because foreign subsidiaries can buy and sell portfolio instruments. Hence, rigid controls on portfolio finance, if seriously enforced, can curtail the "healthier" sort of capital, FDI, and thus narrow a proven channel for spreading the benefits of advanced technology.[51] Moreover, since FDI goes largely to financial institutions and large firms that trade across borders, bank flows are practically the only source of external finance for most firms that do not trade.[52] So we are back to square one: cutting these firms from external flows could again hurt business investment and limit long-term growth.

Third, capital controls can hamper local entrepreneurs. Compare Thailand, a liberalized economy that has gone through the roller coaster of booms and busts, with India, the nonliberalized economy that has been on something resembling a steady train ride. India's GDP per capita grew by 99 percent between 1980 and 2001, but Thailand's grew by 148 percent—despite the Asian financial crisis that wreaked havoc and left many office buildings in Bangkok half built.[53] In the wake of the Great Crisis, India is now turning in Thailand's direction, not the other way around. MIT's Kristin Forbes summoned a range of microeconomic studies to help understand this. Her collection shows that capital controls can raise the cost of financing, undermine discipline in financial markets and the government, be costly to enforce, and breed corruption.[54]

Fourth, controls certainly do not *drive* growth. One example is the myth of the Chilean Encaje—the tax on short-term capital inflows in force between 1991 and 1998—that is often cited as an example for other countries because it coincided with a Chilean growth boom. Alas, research shows that growth was generated by Chile's smart market-oriented macroeconomic policies and transparent governance; the Encaje, in contrast, increased financial constraints for small public firms, while not really protecting Chile from external shocks.[55]

Fifth, the effectiveness of capital controls for keeping crises at bay is questionable. UCLA professor and former World Bank official Sebastian Edwards finds no clear relationship between capital controls and success at avoiding contagion and crisis.[56] During the economic duress of the 1970s and 1980s, Latin America was unable to contain capital outflows despite pervasive controls. Brazilian controls in the 1990s were largely ineffective.[57] In the meantime, some African countries have enjoyed only minimal inflows despite the absence of restrictions on capital.[58] The link between controls and crises is tenuous because, as shown early by Kindleberger and reaffirmed by Rogoff and Reinhart, foreign capital is not necessarily the dominant cause, let alone the only cause of financial crises.

Sixth, controlling finance is not good politics. Countries with fragile banking systems often prevent households from investing abroad, as this could precipitate a mass exodus of domestic savings at the first sight of bank failure. But seldom are such limits well received by the citizenry, nor should they be. Ailing Argentina did exactly this in 2001, by restricting withdrawals from bank accounts and moving funds abroad; the country erupted in riots that eventually unseated the government. The political catch-22 of slamming domestic savers or allowing capital flight is best resolved by a banking system that savers can bank on.

Honing Institutions

Fortunately, it seems that the control and liberalizing groups are now converging on two issues: (1) the weather is windy and volatile in global financial markets, and (2) financial liberalization has a prerequisite. The general consensus is that good domestic macroeconomic management and governance are keys to weathering volatility and for translating the positives of financial globalization into real domestic development. The benefits of capital account liberalization have been greatest in advanced countries, which not only have the most open capital accounts but also the strongest institutions. Emerging markets that are feeble on governance have not been able to use international financial markets to reduce consumption volatility; rather, crises have been topped off by gaping drops in consumption and incomes alike.

But the new consensus also means that apologetic arguments about poorer countries being at the mercy of global capital are themselves tenuous. Emerging markets need more rather than less financial integration, but they also need to do their homework on managing money. It is clear that with poor regulatory frameworks, the disciplinary role of banks in the lending process will disappear and financial opening will simply produce overinvestment and corruption. Relying on hard capital controls to solve these problems can discourage domestic reform. Capital controls may be a short-term measure, but they are not a long-term solution for the failure to spiff up domestic regulation and revamp macroeconomic management.[59]

Conclusion

Global finance has traveled a staggering trajectory over the past thirty years. Much of the credit goes to technology, financial innovations, and policy changes. The flow of money has at times seemed fickle and irresponsible. But two things are important: financial liberalization is not the only reason for the globalization of finance, and globalization of finance is not the dominant cause of crisis and contagion. Financial globalization is far from perfect, but with the companionship of good domestic governance, global finance has spurred world trade, expanded opportunities for domestic companies in emerging markets, and contributed to fatter pocketbooks worldwide.

Sadly, the political debate on financial globalization seldom draws on rigorous empirical work. Critics have been more vocal than proponents, and that fact has buried many good arguments for the free flow of money. The policy prescriptions, it turns out, are more subtle than either pole would like. First, fix domestic institutions to benefit from the advantages and withstand the disadvantages of global finance; second, cut back on indebtedness of all sorts and maintain equity and FDI flows.

3

EXPANDING COMMERCE

Compared to capricious international finance and lumpy foreign direct investment (FDI), trade is refreshingly steady and predictable. But the seemingly mundane world of trade has transformed over time in various ways, changing the global economy with it.

First, world trade grew faster in the second half of the twentieth century than at any time in history. Total world exports reached $15.8 trillion in 2008, and merchandise trade (exports plus imports) grew by more than 10 percent annually between 1960 and 2008, far faster than the 3.5 percent average before the First World War. The main driver of growth has been trade in manufactured goods (figure 3.1).

Second, trade has become far more important in the global economy. The ratio of merchandise trade (imports plus exports) to world gross domestic product (GDP) grew from 2 percent in 1800 to 22 percent in 1913, reaching 30 percent in 1950 and more than 60 percent today. Over a period of fifty years, between 1950 and 2000, the growth of trade surpassed the growth of output in every world region. As a result, trade (again, imports plus exports) as a share of national GDP skyrocketed from 20 percent to 100 percent of GDP in Japan, from 40 to above 80 percent in Canada, from 60 to 80 percent in Western Europe, from 35 to about 60 percent in Latin America, from 50 to 70 percent in sub-Saharan Africa, and from 10 to 20 percent in the United States.[1]

Third, the lineup of key players in world trade has changed. Some developing countries have turned themselves into manufacturing powerhouses

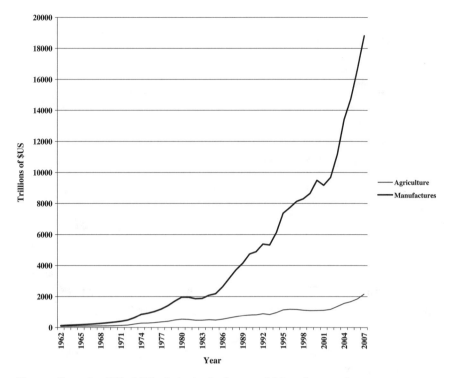

Fig. 3.1 Growth of World Trade in Agriculture and Manufactures in 1960–2008 (trillions of $US). *Source*: UN Comtrade.

by applying the techniques of mass industrialization. Along the way, success has boosted exports from developing to advanced countries more than sixfold, from some 10 percent of global manufactured goods exports in the 1950s to nearly 70 percent by the end of the century.[2]

The change began in the 1980s and early 1990s with the industrialization and export-led growth of the four "Asian tigers"—South Korea, Taiwan, Hong Kong, and Singapore. Since then, North American and European trade growth with developing countries has arrived principally from China and some smaller Asian players (and, for the United States, from trade with Mexico). Year 2004 marked a watershed: for the first time, the United States traded more with developing countries in manufactured goods than with other advanced nations. There is also more trade among developing countries than in prior years. For instance, middle-income coun-

Table 3.1 High-, Middle-, and Low-Income Country Exports in 1965–2007, Select
Years (% of Total by Origin and Destination)

Origin	Destination	1965	1980	1990	2000	2007
High-Income	High-Income	77.1	78.9	85.2	80.3	74.8
	Middle-Income	18.9	18.0	13.4	18.7	23.9
	Low-Income	4.0	3.1	1.4	1.0	1.3
Middle-Income	High-Income	83.4	83.3	84.3	78.7	70.5
	Middle-Income	15.0	15.3	14.1	19.1	26.4
	Low-Income	1.6	1.4	1.6	2.2	3.2
Low-Income	High-Income	78.2	68.7	75.9	69.4	53.3
	Middle-Income	15.4	18.3	13.1	23.0	29.7
	Low-Income	6.4	13.0	11.0	7.5	17.0

Notes:
SITC Rev. 1 for years before 2000/ Standard International Trade
  Classification (SITC) Rev. 2 for years after 2000.
  Country groups are created based on classification used by the World Bank: World Bank's income
groups are divided into four categories according to 2007 GNI per capita. Here, we combined groups of
lower middle income and upper middle income into one group called "Middle-Income."
Source: UN Comtrade.

tries such as Mexico now direct a quarter of their exports to other
middle-income countries, as opposed to only 14 percent in 1990 (table 3.1).

Fourth, unlike prewar specialization along the lines of interindustry
trade (coffee and wheat traded for household furnishings and airplanes),
global commerce is now mostly intraindustry—such as Japan sending finished computers to Malaysia and Malaysia sending semiconductors to
Japan, or Germany selling BMWs in France and France selling Renaults
in Germany. Intraindustry trade now accounts for more than two-thirds
of world manufactures trade. When flowing between advanced economies,
some of this commerce is dubbed horizontal intraindustry trade: goods
are differentiated by features such as different shapes, colors, and sizes,
just for the sheer love of variety by consumers—some want Volvos, others
want Corollas. More recently, there also has been an explosion of vertical
intraindustry trade where the driver is cost differences between components in the supply chain: Nokia of Finland might assemble great mobile
phones, but Irish Intel Ireland might make the best microchip.

The fifth major change in international trade has been the rise of regional and global production chains. Unlike the old integrated style, where production was internalized in a single company and centered in a few locations, today's production is segmented and fragmented—spread over an international network of sites and firms. The global economy has turned itself into a vast assembly plant where pieces are made everywhere, assembled elsewhere, and then consumed around the world. There are but few places where a finished item is made from start to finish—designing and manufacturing the pieces, assembling and packaging them under one single roof, and then consuming them in the same country.

As a result, a growing share of global trade consists of intermediate goods shipped from one nation to another; household items ranging from cars to computers contain parts hailing from multiple countries. Trade in parts and accessories has nearly doubled as a share of global trade over the period 1980 to 2005, rising to some 20 percent of the total and surpassing the shares of capital goods and consumption goods—and, to be sure, also reaping the share of primary and food products (figure 3.2). The explosion of intermediate trade has been particularly striking in Asia, where parts and accessories constitute a quarter of all trade.

Sixth, trade in services—tourism, business process operations, legal and medical services, and the like—has grown faster than trade in goods. With e-mail, the Internet, and other forms of information technology (IT) bursting on the business scene, services that were once plainly nontradable are now made in one country and consumed in another—in other words, "offshored." Why not let Indian technicians handle calls from Microsoft's U.S. clients, when the labor costs are a trifle of American wages and the people speak English and know computers?

The numbers for such "trade in tasks" speak for themselves.[3] World commercial services exports rose more than tenfold in a quarter century, from $365 billion in 1980 to some $3.7 trillion in 2008, or from some 12 percent of goods traded to about 20 percent.[4] As a share of U.S. goods exports, services exports more than doubled between 1980 and 2008, from 17 percent to 40 percent.[5] More than half of annual world FDI flows are sent to service activities abroad.[6] The rise of services has in part been propelled by the rising trade in goods: firms that make manufactured

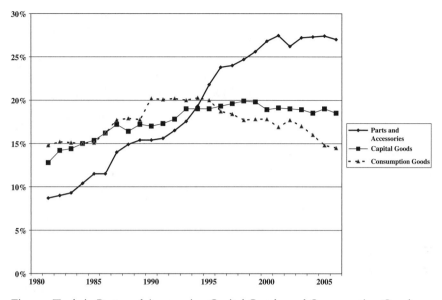

Fig. 3.2 Trade in Parts and Accessories, Capital Goods, and Consumption Goods as a Share of Total Trade in East Asia in 1980–2005. *Source*: UN Comtrade.

goods and grow agricultural commodities need telecom, financial, and transportation services alike to get their merchandise to market.

Despite the rise of "factory globe," we are far from a seamless global marketplace. Integration *between* countries still pales by comparison with integration *within* countries: trade among Canadian provinces bordering the United States is six times that of their trade with the United States, even though the United States and Canada are joined in a free trade pact.[7] More than in finance, a remarkably strong home country bias still persists in global trade. But it is much weaker today than a generation ago. How did we trim that bias?

Steamboats, E-Mail, and Multilateral Trade Rounds

An age-old question is whether the strongest driver for propelling the growth of trade is improved transportation and logistics coupled with far better communications technology, or the reduction of policy barriers. In 1987, Robert Solow won the Nobel Prize in economics for showing (back in the 1950s) that technological progress, not labor or capital accumulation, accounted for the lion's share of economic growth in advanced countries. But it turns out that technological progress is not a magic wand. More is needed to expand output, most important of which is good policy.

This also holds for trade. With the advent of steamships and railroads, many goods could be made in one place and consumed in another. Airplanes and telecommunications further widened the potential geographic space between production and consumption, and the Internet magically enabled trade in detailed tasks. At the same time, enlightened governments have slashed tariffs and nontariff barriers down to remarkably low levels, both through unilateral action and by forging new trade agreements multilaterally and bilaterally with partners around the world. Multinational companies both nurtured and jumped on these new possibilities, creating regional and global production chains.

But while transportation, technology, and policy have combined to spur trade, their relative importance has waxed and waned. Until the First World War, the main engines of commerce were the gold standard (which allowed currency convertibility and almost eliminated exchange rate risk) and a fall in transport costs. According to one estimate, the reduction in trade costs explains as much as 55 percent of the pre–World War I trade boom.[8] At the end of the 1920s, escalating transport costs took a toll on trade.[9] But the real blow came in the 1930s when policy went in reverse— the collapse of the gold standard and soaring tariffs.

In the postwar era, according to one estimate, some two-thirds of the rise of trade among advanced countries can be attributed to global income growth, a quarter to policy reform (mainly tariff cuts), and a tenth to falling transportation costs.[10] Another calculation raises the contribution of falling transport costs to a third of the post–World War II trade boom.[11] More recently, Matt Adler and Gary Hufbauer calculated that roughly a quarter of U.S. merchandise trade growth between 1980 and 2005 was due to policy liberalization.[12] The other three-quarters can be explained by the general expansion of the world economy (72 percent) and falling transportation costs (3 percent).

Now that tariffs and overt nontariff barriers (such as quotas) have been brought to rather low levels, other frictions—red tape, opaque and cumbersome customs procedures, unnecessary delays and sheer unpredictability, creaky logistics, and so forth—are jumping to the fore as targets for countries that want to raise their trade profile. According to the World Bank's *Doing Business Report* data, in Organization for Economic Cooperation and Development (OECD) countries, importing a shipment takes on average less than two weeks, while in developing regions such as South Asia or Southern Africa, it can take up to two months!

Much of the sluggishness in international trade compared to domestic commerce owes to bureaucratic overdrive, such as multiple stamps and signatures required for performing export and import operations. The far-reaching implications of shipping costs are particularly vexing to landlocked countries such as Bolivia or Uzbekistan, which depend on their neighbors for moving goods to ports and beyond, and also to countries distant from the main global markets such as Chile and New Zealand. Consider unfortunate Chad stuck between the Sahara and Nigeria: it takes 102 days to import a shipment, 78 days to export one, and a shipping container costs more than $6,000. Contrast that with Singapore: 4 days for importing, 5 days for exporting, and $439 per container.

Shipping delays have real financial costs. David Hummels, one of the world's renowned transport economists, has established that each extra day a good spends in transit equates to a 0.5 percent tariff on that good. Spend a fortnight at sea; pay a 7 percent effective tariff! Even relatively modest declines in trade facilitation costs can lead to large increases in the trade volumes by encouraging vertical specialization—dividing the production process into geographically separated stages.[13] Speed makes and breaks champions in global trade.

Reducing frictions to trade—everything from port turnaround time to container handling to customs clearance—would generate big gains. According to the World Bank, such "trade facilitation" would boost intra-Asian trade flows by at least $148 billion, or 7.5 percent of the baseline 2004 trade.[14] By contrast, reducing tariffs would generate a gain of "only" $18 billion, and cutting nontariff barriers would boost trade by $35 billion. The Inter-American Development Bank estimates that a 10 percentage point reduction in Latin American trade costs would boost the regional exports to the U.S. market by almost 40 percent.[15] "Barriers" that could be reduced through serious trade facilitation might give a greater trade bang than tariff lowering—in some countries, up to ten times more.

Transport costs, broadly defined, are also increasingly important in a world of just-in-time delivery. For today's global production networks, time is literally money. Indeed, most of the postwar decline in transport costs may not be due to lower shipping charges per ton of freight, but rather a consequence of faster speed. Hummels shows that there is remarkably little evidence of a decline since the mid-1950s in ocean shipping costs for break-bulk, noncommodity freight. However, for some point-to-point routes—such as Shanghai to Long Beach, which takes some twenty-one days to sail—loading and unloading times are much faster. Meanwhile, air shipping costs have dropped dramatically, leading to a rise in ultrafast airborne trade. Helping this is the higher value added in goods of the same weight. Flying microchips is cost-effective because the share of shipping costs is a small portion of the entire cost of a lightweight chip. The same is true for Swiss watches and Parisian apparel. Steel plates, white cotton T-shirts, and the like, meanwhile, can still sail across oceans.

New technologies besides airplanes have been at play. Containerization was hugely important for the rise of production chains. It slashed the cost and increased the reliability of moving freight around the world, making shipments both cheaper and more predictable.[16] It allowed for intermodal transportation: a container now glides smoothly from ship to truck and onto the factory floor. Containers also facilitated just-in-time production: companies now need only limited inventories to meet customer orders and are able to save the money otherwise tied up in inventories. For example, by the early 2000s, Walmart's massive inventory turned over 7.7 times annually—once every month and a half and up from 4.1 times in 1990. Dell's annual inventory turnover is a legendary 91.6 times, or one turnover every four days, up from only 1.7 times in 1990.

To be sure, shocks to the system, exemplified by the 9/11 attacks, have at times forced global companies to adopt "just-in-case" inventory systems—loading up on supplies in case ships are delayed. The same is feared to result from excessively tight and prolonged cargo security clearance procedures.

In world trade patterns, just-in-time meant a new stream of merchandise from Asian factories directly to retail stockrooms in North America and Europe—and became one reason that manufacturing jobs migrated from traditional industrial nations to Asia. In 2007, nearly 45 million container-units crossed the docks at U.S. ports—some 123,000 per day—or three times as many as in 1990.[17]

The Internet era yanked trade further. One study shows that a 10 percentage point increase in the growth of local Web hosts is associated with a 0.2 percentage point increase in the growth of merchandise exports.[18] So roughly speaking, doubling the number of Internet hosts could lead to a 2 percentage point increase in trade growth, hardly a trivial contribution. For an average country in the late 1990s, when the Internet was far from universal, the Web contributed to a 1 percentage point increase in annual export growth. For countries like India, where Internet-powered services have become a lifeline, the importance of good IT is decisive.

The Genius of Most Favored Nation (MFN)

Much trade would never have existed if the tremendously steep policy barriers of the Depression era had remained in place. Trade opening throughout history has come in many flavors—reducing tariffs and eliminating quotas and licensing systems, relaxing and harmonizing product standards, lowering domestic subsidies that invite retaliation, and so on. Trade liberalization has been multidimensional—unilateral, bilateral, plurilateral, and multilateral alike. By now, the liberalization landslide has engulfed just about the entire planet.

The multilateral system has been the most ingenious of the various tiers of trade policy regulation and reform. An informal multilateral system operated in nineteenth-century Europe. The system was launched by the Anglo-French Cobden-Chevalier commercial treaty of 1860, which stipulated that if either France or Britain negotiated further agreements with third parties, each principal would get the same deal as the third party or better.[19] This had an unintended effect: other European countries wanted to obtain as favorable a treatment as Britain got in the French market, and thus sought a deal with France. The German customs union known as the Zollverein joined the fray and agreed to the same terms, creating an incentive for smaller states to seek a level playing field. A domino effect ensued—nonmembers signed up so they would not lose out on preferential treatment enjoyed within the club. Treaties spread, linking countries, similar to the way that Facebook and MySpace now link one person to the friends of another.[20]

But openness withered in the interwar era, with the onslaught of the Great Depression and its grease, protection. Tariff wars spiraled, leading to duties well above the levels of 1913. The big nail in the coffin was the U.S. Smoot-Hawley Tariff of 1930, which raised U.S. tariffs on more than twenty thousand imported goods to record levels. The fever spread. In addition to tariffs, quotas, import licenses, and exchange controls confined world trade within formal and informal empires—the British bloc of Imperial Preference, the European gold standard bloc centered around France, and a Central European bloc knit around Germany. Each bloc used discriminatory trade policies to establish economic spheres of influence.[21] By 1931, tariffs on foodstuffs had shot up to an average level of 53 percent in France, more than 80 percent in Germany, and above 100 percent in Bulgaria and Poland. Between 1929 and 1932, trade in manufactured goods dropped by a whopping 42 percent, and trade in agriculture fell by 13 percent.[22]

The backlash against protectionism came from the New World. A liberal coalition in the U.S. Congress passed the Reciprocal Trade Agreements Act (RTAA) in 1934 to unwind Smoot-Hawley. The RTAA authorized the president to negotiate reductions of up to 50 percent in the existing import duties on a reciprocal basis.[23] By 1945, the United States had entered into thirty-two bilateral agreements with twenty-seven countries, under the RTAA system.[24]

The RTAA set the tone for the trade order following the Second World War. The real genius of the new order was an institutionalized multilateral system, "MFN for real." Its genesis was the General Agreement on Tariffs and Trade (GATT), signed in 1948 by twenty-three countries.[25] Created as an umbrella framework to reduce tariffs and nontariff barriers, GATT's first round yielded some forty-five thousand tariff concessions affecting some 20 percent of global trade. It led to eight subsequent multilateral trade rounds—including the current Doha Round—and expansion of the club to its current number of 152 members.[26]

At the heart of the GATT system was nondiscrimination. The agreement melded together some 123 bilateral trade agreements that were generalized to all GATT members via the MFN clause. However, the problem with the system was free-riding—countries could use the MFN clause to enjoy the preferences extended in negotiations between other countries, while doing little themselves.[27] The Torquay Round (1951) mandated that the GATT negotiations be multilateral, and the Kennedy Round (1964–1967) put multilateralism into practice. Multilateralizing reduced the free-riding problem, and somewhat limited the coordination costs of arriving in agreements that covered the entire membership. Unlike the informal MFN system that arose under the pre–World War I network of bilateral treaties, the GATT regime had no expiration date; instead, members were bound to their tariff concessions without time limit. This institutionalized system of nondiscrimination ensured that a growing roster of members could enjoy the proverbial level playing field. It was no longer a system merged from bilateral agreements. To the contrary, this was multilateralism with teeth—countries coming together to negotiate common agreements.

The multilateral agreements would also encompass more subjects as tariff barriers were lowered. Through the Dillon Round (1960–1961), negotiations centered on tariffs; after that, the talks expanded to nontariff measures and other new turf.[28] The Uruguay Round (1986–1994), the most ambitious completed round to date, went well beyond tariffs and nontariff barriers to liberalization of services, some limits on investment distortions, and protection of intellectual property, plus the reduction of barriers in two previously sacrosanct (and heavily protected) sectors, textiles and agriculture. The Uruguay Round culminated in a comprehensive agreement among the 128 GATT members and the establishment of the World Trade Organization (WTO) as a multilateral body to oversee global trade. The ongoing Doha Round was launched in 2001; the agenda has been contested and cut along the way, but the round still covers a multitude of issues, not only the customary topics but also new issues ranging from harmful fishing subsidies to trade facilitation.

Taking Stock of Openness

While much remains to be done, multilateral and unilateral tariff cuts attained in the postwar era are in many ways stunning. Average tariffs around the world have plunged to single digits, while openness—measured by merchandise exports plus imports over GDP—has surged dramatically (figure 3.3).

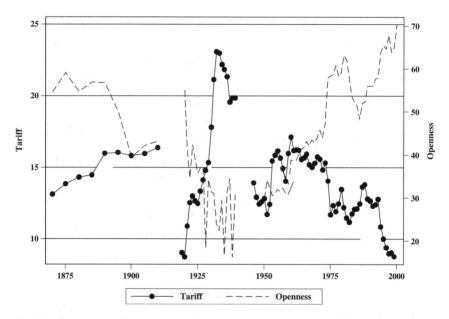

Fig. 3.3 Average Tariffs and Openness around the World, 1875–2000 (%). *Source*: Estevadeordal and Suominen, *The Sovereign Remedy: Trade Agreements in the Globalizing World* (Oxford: Oxford University Press, 2009).

Advanced nations have liberalized much more forcefully than developing countries. The United States and Europe have been the global locomotives of liberalization. The United States reduced its average applied tariffs from 20 percent in the wake of the Great Depression to 3.5 percent today, Germany from 25 percent, and Britain from 23 percent to the European Union (EU) average of 5.2 percent.

Developing countries, besides acceding to the GATT system much later than the advanced nations, often retained their highly protectionist policies through the early 1980s. Argentina's average tariffs on manufactured imports were 141 percent in the early 1960s, Brazil's 99 percent, and Pakistan's 93 percent.[29] But by 2007, the average applied tariffs for these three countries were 12 percent, 12 percent, and 14 percent, respectively.[30] Likewise, China's average applied tariff had come down to 10 percent and India's to 15 percent. The end result for these leaders among emerging nations is about the same, although their starting points and paces have varied. Much of tariff opening frenzy owes to aggressive unilateralism on top of multilateral commitments: applied MFN tariffs are generally well below the bound MFN tariffs that countries have committed to in the WTO.

Sharpening Preferential Edges

Alongside the multilateral rounds has grown a massive body of preferential trading arrangements (PTAs) and bilateral and plurilateral agreements. These are generally aimed at zero tariffs, not just tariff concessions attained in the WTO, and also seek to lower a wide range of service and investment barriers. Coming in many flavors—from free trade agreements to customs unions to economic partnership agreements—PTAs have become a dominant force in the global economy, starting with the formation of the European Communities in 1958. Depending on the calculation, some 300 PTAs are in place around the world, right alongside the multilateral trading system. The number of PTAs notified to the WTO is expected to reach 400 by 2010, and could rise even further. After all, a world of more than 190 sovereign states (this number depends on who is counting) creates the mathematical possibility of almost 40,000 bilateral PTAs.

The PTA frenzy has swept the world.[31] Today, only one country, Mongolia, remains outside the web of PTAs, and many countries have signed multiple deals—the United States has fourteen, Mexico sports twelve, and Singapore is approaching twenty.[32] About half of global trade is carried out among partners to a trade agreement.[33] For some countries such as Chile, Mexico, and Turkey, which have formed PTAs with their main trading partners, the bulk of foreign trade flows under the umbrella of their preferential trade agreements.

A quarter century ago, many PTAs were slim deals that remained as mere paper agreements; today, many PTAs are deeply liberalizing and thoroughly implemented. U.S. agreements typically drive tariffs down to zero on 95 percent of goods within ten years.[34] Not only has the number of agreements grown and their depth increased but also their content has become more complex and encompassing. PTAs have advanced beyond market access for goods to manifold "behind-the-border" issues such as investment, intellectual property rights, competition policy, and government procurement. Some pacts, like the Caribbean Community, have taken collaboration even further to address macroeconomic cooperation and labor mobility, and to coordinate positions in multilateral trade negotiations. Indeed, the fact that more business gets done and more trade is freed under the umbrella of PTAs is a key reason that countries pursue them alongside WTO talks.

The proliferation of PTAs has produced a massive debate on whether they are truly and ultimately good cholesterol for the veins of world trade. The long-standing question is whether PTAs are "building blocks" or "stumbling blocks" to the grail of multilateral free trade.[35] Extending the ruminations of Jacob Viner, who asked in 1950 whether PTAs would abet trade diversion from the world's best and lowest-cost producers, the stumbling block camp argues that PTAs largely coddle special interests that benefit from the exclusion of outsiders, and drain energy from multilateral trade talks. Indeed, the leading stumbling block proponent, Jagdish Bhagwati, sees PTAs as termites eating away at the multilateral trading system.[36] Nuno Limão of the University of Maryland finds evidence of stumbling blocks in analysis suggesting that the United States and the European Union limit their multilateral tariff concessions in goods traded with their PTA partners.[37]

But the building block camp is starting to win some of the battles. Among advanced countries and the most successful emerging countries, unilateral, multilateral, and PTA liberalization have gone hand in hand, resulting in "open regionalism"—formation of trade groups in which members liberalize not only to each other but also to all of their trading partners. Particularly in Latin America, where trade opening was a notable achievement of the Washington Consensus, multitiered tariff reduction strategies were evident.

As a result, most PTAs are found to be more trade-creating than trade-diverting. One of the more rigorous estimates by Dean DeRosa shows that some of the world's major PTAs—the EU, the North American Free Trade Agreement (NAFTA), Association of Southeast Asian Nations (ASEAN), Southern Common Market (Mercado Común del Sur, MERCOSUR), and European Free Trade Association (EFTA)—create trade both among the "insider" members and, in nearly every instance, for outsiders as well.[38] The big exception is trade diversion against "outsiders" in agriculture, not surprising in light of the extreme barriers and pervasive rent seeking in this sector. Leaving agriculture aside, an Inter-American Development Bank–World Bank–London School of Economics team shows in perhaps the most rigorous analysis yet that PTAs in the Americas have been genuine building blocks to global trade.[39] The region's deals have induced the member countries to reduce their MFN barriers more than they would have in the absence of the PTAs.

The latest evidence indicates that the advance of PTA liberalization has been accompanied by more modest liberalization of MFN tariffs than in the 1990s (a period when countries slashed their high tariff profiles). But it can also be said that the most liberal developing countries in the PTA sphere—Chile, Central America, Canada, Mexico, Peru, Singapore, and Thailand—have some of the lowest MFN tariffs and the smallest degree of tariff dispersion. The endgame of the current PTA frenzy is also plausible: in contrast to Jagdish Bhagwati, another creative thinker, Richard Baldwin of the Graduate Institute in Geneva, argues that PTAs are like falling dominos.[40] Their spread gives outsiders incentives to form new PTAs or to join existing ones, lest they see their market access erode. In Baldwin's crystal ball, this built-in logic of the PTA system will eventually culminate in a system ever closer to global free trade.

There are clear yet less-quantifiable synergies between the regional and multilateral tiers of trade opening. Understanding, negotiating, and implementing agreements on the PTA front can nourish a cadre of civil servants and political leaders with the skills and energy to push the ball forward on the multilateral front, and vice versa. For instance, negotiating an accord on telecommunications services trade in the WTO will materially strengthen the government's capacity to negotiate another services chapter in a PTA. Many a Mexican official became a cunning, world-class trade negotiator after the "apprenticeship" with the hard-charging U.S. team in NAFTA talks in the early 1990s.

PTA-mandated trade facilitation measures—such as modern customs procedures for importers or a single window for the paperwork required of exporters—deliver immediate benefits for the country's trade with *all* its partners. Preferential trade agreements are also an antidote to "free riding," the unhealthy flip side of the MFN principle. Most favored nation wards off discrimination, but it also enables footdraggers to enjoy the benefits of market opening by others and do none of their own. As PTAs expand, countries that choose to free-ride on the WTO system find they are increasingly left out when it comes to writing trade rules and enjoying access to foreign markets.

Trade Boost

Has trade followed this postwar frenzy of institutionalized cooperation? Andrew Rose, from the University of California-Berkeley, garnered fame by taking issue with WTO enthusiasts. He contended that it is not the GATT/WTO system but rather unilateral trade policy reforms that have propelled trade. In a 2002 critique, he summoned a whopping sixty-eight measures of trade liberalization to show that none of them was significantly correlated with GATT/WTO membership. Trade liberalization, when it occurs, usually lags GATT entry by many years, and the GATT/WTO often admitted new members that were closed and remained closed for years.

Refuting Rose, Arvind Subramanian, then at the International Monetary Fund (IMF), and Shang-Jin Wei of the University of Maryland argued that the WTO system has had a massive positive impact, more than doubling world trade from their counterfactual alternative.[41] According to their model, additional imports by industrialized countries were $8 trillion more than they would have been in the absence of the WTO. Bilateral trade flows among industrialized countries, which have liberalized more in the WTO context than developing countries, were 175 percent greater because of their WTO membership. These findings resonate in a number of other studies.[42]

But the debate does not end there. Theo Eicher of Washington University and Christian Henn from the IMF combine the various approaches to trade opening—WTO accession, reduction in tariffs abroad, and PTA formation—finding that once these previously omitted variables are stacked alongside the WTO variable, the positive WTO effects vanish altogether.[43] Preferential trade agreements emerge as stars in this analysis, on average resulting in trade creation of 123 percent. The good news from these dueling analysts seems to be that pulling the policy lever does generate greater trade flows—the debate is about what policy level yields the biggest bang.

Advantages of Liberalization

Today's trade policy panorama displays an unprecedented trinity of multilateral opening, liberalizing bilateral and plurilateral agreements, and an extraordinary expansion of world trade. Virtually all countries belong to a trade agreement of some kind, all but one belong to a PTA, and most belong to several agreements simultaneously. By the turn of the millennium, most of the world's 6.7 billion people lived in open economies.[44]

This is remarkable. Trade liberalization in theory should not really happen. While consumers are numerous and have plenty to gain from freer trade, they are too dispersed to assemble a weighty lobby. By contrast, import-competing producers are few and can easily coalesce in pursuit of barriers. In short, even if liberalization makes the country richer, theory says that policy will remain stuck because the political costs of opening outweigh its economic benefits. The concentrated forces of protection win out in the political battleground.

And yet, experience is completely different. Protectionist forces have surrendered ground. Exporter lobbies, Japanese-style trading firms, Walmart, and firms that buy huge amounts of industrial inputs—such as Siemens, Hitachi, and Caterpillar—have gradually captured the battleground. Michael Hiscox of Harvard attributes the long U.S. push for freer trade, starting with the Reciprocal Trade Agreements Act of 1934, to the boom of export industries and multinational corporations in the global economy, forces that overwhelmed firms hurt by imports.[45]

In developing countries, the road to free trade was paved by the failure of infant industry protection during the 1960s and 1970s and drastic macroeconomic reforms in the 1970s and 1980s. Further contributors were the end of exchange controls in many countries and the advance of democratization—from 30 democracies in 1975 to some 130 today—which brought in new and vocal *demandeurs* for freer trade and helped break entrenched monopoly strangleholds.[46]

Protrade interests today have an increasingly powerful argument in their arsenal: the global race to integrate reinforces the urgency to negotiate trade agreements in order to retain a beachhead in foreign markets.[47] Credit for the free trade mantra is also owed to vocal supporters in ivory towers, think tanks, and the news media.

The GATT and the WTO arguably facilitate the staying power of open trade. A forum for logrolling across issue areas has its advantages, and so does a dispute settlement system that gives definitive rulings. How else would countries have engaged in the immensely long horse trading of successive GATT rounds and kept their promises to lower tariffs? Why would the United States bother to comply with rulings against it in cases initiated by unfriendly nations like Venezuela (reformulated gasoline) or small states like Costa Rica (underwear) if not because of the overall benefits of the WTO?[48] Why else would so many countries have joined the WTO?

No one-size-fits-all argument exists for trade liberalization. Domestic political economy continues to be at the center of trade policy, and much of the political dynamic depends on the economic fortunes of workers and industries. Even so, the motivations to lower barriers and maintain open trade regimes are surprisingly strong.

To be sure, trade history does not move in only one direction. Some countries have joined the WTO simply to gain access to the markets of other members while erecting their own "hidden" trade barriers. It comes as no surprise that one of the staunchest liberalizers, Mexico, also sports one of the most active trade defense systems. India, with a hugely protected agricultural sector but a rather solid liberalization record in other sectors, is the number one instigator of antidumping cases.

Further, trade regimes are seldom open across the board. Hong Kong and Singapore are exceptions, but most regimes contain tariff peaks, generally in agriculture and textiles, and PTAs often provide exceptions and stringent rules of origin in these sensitive sectors.[49] In short, while opening has proceeded around the world, governments have to appease powerful lobbies. Accommodation is at least the temporary price for lower barriers. But on balance, the expansion of trade demonstrates that we have been moving in the right direction.

Is Trade a False Scapegoat?

Trade has split world opinion in half for ages. Some celebrate it as an engine of prosperity and a great equalizer, as a source of the higher quantity, quality, and diversity of products in the world economy; others see it as the dark force behind inequalities and job losses. The dark force view has gathered adherents in recent years, especially in the developed world, as we discuss in chapter 8. This, in turn, has led even staunch free traders to argue for addressing the supposed problems of trade—to balance "free trade" with "fair trade"—in order to avert a full-blown protectionist backlash. But it turns out that trade has been ascribed an outsized role by both sides.

Transforming the World Economy

The relationship between trade opening and incomes has troubled economists for decades, if not centuries. Adam Smith and David Ricardo believed that specialization resulting from trade would generate higher national income. And growing trade and income have indeed gone hand in hand for the better part of history, especially in the pre- and postwar eras.

In episodes of trade booms in the past century and a half, both trade and incomes grew, but trade grew more rapidly than income. In the forty-three years after 1870, world income nearly tripled while trade more than quadrupled. In the fifty years after 1950, however, income increased by a factor of five while trade increased by a factor of eleven! The exception was the onset of the Great Depression, when trade dropped much more sharply than output.

So does trade raise income? Many answer with a resounding "yes." In a famous and controversial 2002 piece, the World Bank's David Dollar and Aart Kraay argued that the "post-1980 globalizers" in the developing world—such as Argentina, Brazil, China, India, Nicaragua, Hungary, and Malaysia—saw growth accelerate from 1.4 percent a year in the 1960s and 2.9 percent a year in the 1970s to 3.5 percent in the 1980s and 5 percent in the 1990s (figure 3.4).[50] Rich countries had experienced a similar growth spurt in the 1960s. Meanwhile, the nonglobalizing developing countries did much worse, seeing their annual growth rates falling from highs of 3.3 percent during the 1970s to only 1.4 percent during the 1990s. The share of trade in the economies of globalizers doubled to reach 33 percent of GDP, while trade relative to GDP actually declined among the nonglobalizers.

This is by no means trivial: more than half of the developing world resides in the post-1980 globalizers. And they have benefited. The fraction of the population of these countries living below the constant $1 a day

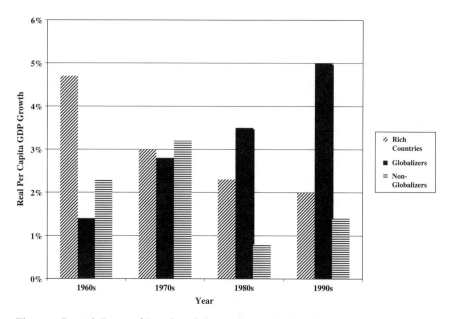

Fig. 3.4 Growth Rates of Developed Countries, and Globalized and Nonglobalized Developing Countries in 1960s–1990s. *Source*: Dollar and Kraay, "Trade, Growth, and Poverty" (Policy Research Working Paper No. 2615, World Bank, Washington, DC, 2002).

poverty threshold fell sharply between the 1980s and the 1990s: from 43 percent to 36 percent in Bangladesh, from 20 percent to 15 percent in China, and from 13 percent to 10 percent in Costa Rica. Dollar and Kraay argue that it is not the rise in trade volumes that has directly lifted the poor out of poverty, but the economic growth generated by trade. When trade rises, average incomes rise, and the average incomes of the poorest fifth of society rise proportionately.

Trade also has been good for the developed nations. In another widely cited study, a three-man band of the Peterson Institute found that the United States economy alone had gained no less than $1 trillion annually—more than $3,000 per person—due to globalization by 2003, and stands to gain from there onward another $500 billion per year from future policy liberalization.[51] Past gains amounted to about 9 percent of GDP in 2003, and potential future gains constitute another 4 percent. This is a comprehensive calculation encompassing estimates of sifting and sorting of firms so that the most efficient expand and the least efficient shrink; reduced markup margins associated with monopolistic competition that would occur in the absence of trade; stimulating laggard industries (remember autos and steel) to match the productivity of foreign competitors; and enlarging the range of choice for both producers and consumers.

The results are echoed by another band of economists and lawyers, Matthew Slaughter, Grant Aldonas, and Robert Lawrence, who argue that American families gain as much as $15,000 a year due to freer trade.[52] European analysts have figured that if no integration had taken place since 1950 in Europe, the EU's GDP per capita would be 20 percent less today.[53]

Multilateral trade rounds have delivered some of these gains. The Uruguay Round final act gave an estimated boost in annual global GDP ranging between $40 billion (assuming constant returns to scale) and $214 billion (assuming increasing returns to scale, meaning that each new unit can be produced at a lower cost than the prior one). This translates to up to 1 percent in yearly global output.[54] Econometric estimates of the benefits that Doha might deliver are unequivocally positive, although the magnitude critically depends on the ambition of the negotiated outcomes and the assumptions made with respect to economies of scale and other features of the world economy. The estimates of the direct impact for the world welfare range from $168 billion to $287 billion a year. However, studies in general do not take into account the dynamic effects that trade liberalization might induce, such as the shift-and-sort version of creative destruction. These benefits are difficult to quantify, but they could be very large.

To be sure, there are also marked differences across countries in the gains that they might score from Doha. For instance, Mexico, a country with plenty of market access to its main trading partners and a relatively open domestic market, would attain more limited gains than countries with less market access abroad and more protection at home, such as Brazil, Thailand, or Indonesia.

All the cited findings are rather coarse. Recent studies have produced more subtle, sectoral findings. In a 2008 study, Sibylle Lehmann and Kevin O'Rourke focused on the late nineteenth century, arguing that while at the time industrial tariffs were positively correlated with growth—the higher the tariffs, the more growth—agricultural tariffs were negatively correlated with growth.[55] But alas, they also find that the relationship was not necessarily meaningful in statistical terms—there was correlation, but not necessarily causality. More robustly, Antoni Estevadeordal of the Inter-American Development Bank and Alan Taylor of the University of California at Davis analyzed the past thirty years, arguing that tariffs on capital and intermediate goods retard growth, while tariffs on consumer goods have a much weaker effect.[56] Services trade, for its part, has consolidated the gains from goods trade. A fittingly all-Indian team, Aaditya Mattoo, Randeep Rathindran, and Arvind Subramanian argue that countries with fully open telecom and financial services sectors grow up to 1.5 percentage points faster than other countries.[57]

Granted, stormy intellectual battles have been waged. Francisco Rodriguez and Dani Rodrik answer the trade enthusiasts by experimenting with new openness indicators and find little evidence that open trade policies among developing countries are significantly associated with economic growth.[58] In critiquing the U.S. studies, Rodrik, a globalization skeptic, uses an entirely different calculation than the Peterson Institute team and argues that the U.S. economy would gain a mere 0.25 percent of national income, around $35 billion, if all U.S. tariffs and other barriers were abolished—well below the $500 billion estimate of the Peterson Institute group. But Rodrik's arithmetic is simple and antiquated, hailing back to the year 1927. Yet leftist economists at the Economic Policy Institute, L. Josh Bivens and Jared Bernstein (subsequently an economic adviser to Vice President Joe Biden), draw on Rodrik's calculations to claim that U.S. gains from trade liberalization are puny, ranging between $4 billion and $20 billion.[59]

Yes, there are methodological problems in these dueling studies. It is very hard to isolate the effects that trade can have out of the multiple forces that determine economic growth. Critics charge that the indicators of openness do not capture trade barriers—or that the indicators are highly correlated with other sources of economic performance, so that it is not trade but other factors that propel growth. They also have claimed that growth actually drives trade, not the other way around,[60] or that the studies are resoundingly circular—that globalizing nations decided to become globalizers because they grow more to begin with.

These comments have markedly sharpened debate as well as econometric techniques. Analysts have turned to better means to isolate the bang from trade liberalization from other factors spurring growth, and control for the multiplier effects of growth on trade. Recent findings are remarkably nuanced and robust.

Institutions and Trade

A very consequential finding resulting from the scholarly back-and-forth is that not all countries grow if the floodgates of trade are opened. Like in finance, domestic institutions intervene, and they can either distort or augment the good effects of trade. Intellectual horse races have been waged between those seeing institutions as the key to growth— such as Dani Rodrik, Arvind Subramanian, and Francesco Trebbi—and those seeing trade as the main lever to deliver growth, Dollar and Kraay.[61]

The two sides are complementary—the former suggest that institutions matter more for growth in the long run, while the latter imply that trade is more important over the medium term. They are both right. University of Maryland's Bineswaree Bolaky and World Bank's Caroline Freund break the tie by arguing that while trade does spur growth in general, it does not do so in economies with poor institutions and excessive regulation.[62] Rather, they claim that increased openness is, if anything, associated with a lower standard of living in heavily regulated economies, such as Burkina Faso, Ecuador, or Ukraine.

What does this mean? One possibility is that highly regulated, inflexible economies serve to expand trade in the "wrong" goods and services. Consider two distortions: excessive regulation and trade barriers. If trade barriers are dropped, they will also require domestic regulatory barriers to be dropped in order to spur growth. One without the other may just have pernicious effects. For example, in an economy where regulations raise the domestic price of manufactured goods while tariffs raise the domestic price of agricultural goods, once tariffs are removed, activity would move to the manufacturing sector—which, however, is only "artificially" made profitable.

Indeed, a recent study applying highly granular, firm-level data in India illustrates some of these issues.[63] While trade liberalization should result in a reallocation of output *within* firms through changes in their product mix, the analysis finds that such "product rationalization" is far less common in India than it is in the United States in response to trade opening. This is due to the role of industrial regulation in India, which, as in many other developing countries, tends to prevent an efficient allocation of resources.

These frictions, in turn, may mean that regulations cultivate the wrong sectors and perhaps fatten a few already fat cats, and reduce national income overall. Situations similar to these vicious cycles can lead to "immiserizing growth"—scenarios where current growth is bad for future growth because it eats itself from within.[64]

The main contribution of the institutional school is to demonstrate that trade does not translate into growth all on its own. Rather, domestic "complementary policies" (better institutions, good governance, training of entrepreneurs, export promotion, trade facilitation, and the like) are equally necessary as at-the-border policies (trade opening) in translating trade into growth.[65] This conclusion in turn has impacted the work of international development agencies and financial institutions. No longer are they concentrating on the fine art of coaching trade negotiators; rather, they are turning to more multidisciplinary approaches to get the most out of the trade liberalization that negotiators have achieved.

Lost Your Job to Trade—Really?

Comparative advantage is a footloose proposition. Beginning in 1850, new centers of textile manufacturing migrated from Britain to New England to the Carolinas to Mexico and now to China. Car manufacturing spread from North America to Latin America and Asia, and within Asia, the auto industry has spread from Japan to Korea to China. These shifts were facilitated both by technology innovations and policy liberalization that together abetted a vast expansion of trade. And they were in good part driven by lower wages: Mexico's hourly compensation is only 11 percent of the U.S. level and China's is only slightly more than 3 percent.[66] While these percentages are on the rise with higher productivity in the developing world, they are astonishingly low and understandably appetizing for a manufacturer looking to get an edge in global commerce.

The migration of jobs abroad has been paralleled by a giant job churn in the developed countries. According to a compilation of data from various sources, a recent study finds that on average 16.6 million American jobs were lost each year in 1992–2004, while 18.3 million jobs are created each

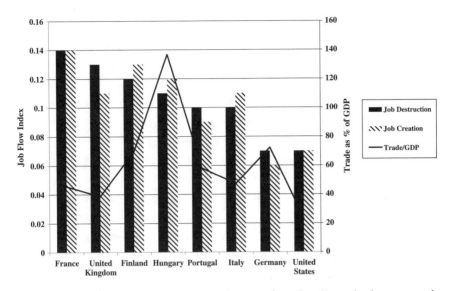

Fig. 3.5 Job Destruction and Creation in the Manufacturing Sector in the 1990s and Trade as a Share of GDP in 2007. *Source*: Haltiwanger, Scarpetta, and Schweiger, "Assessing Job Flows across Countries: The Role of Industry, Firm Size, and Regulations" (World Bank Policy Research Working Paper No. 4070, November 2006); UN Comtrade.

year.[67] Many are swirling in the whirlpool: some 15 percent of American workers change jobs every year. Overall, U.S. job creation as a share of total employment is at a par with that of many other European and Latin American countries, while job destruction levels are somewhat lower.[68] However, in manufacturing, job creation and destruction in the United States are at a par, yet the churn pales before the experience of France and Britain (figure 3.5). Notably, all three have rather low levels of exposure to foreign trade compared to some smaller European nations such as Hungary and Portugal where the churn is of medium level.

In theory, job losses can be explained by moving comparative advantage—migration of jobs abroad from developed countries and subsequent import penetration to developed country markets. In the famous Hecksher-Ohlin model, knocking down trade barriers (either through technology or policy) expands trade. This has the effect of raising the income of relatively abundant factors of production in a country, notably capital in developed economies (the so-called "North") and less-skilled labor in developing countries ("South"), while lowering the income of relatively scarce factors (less-skilled workers in the North and capital in the South).

With greater trade, labor and capital are used more efficiently as each country expands production of goods and services in which it has a comparative advantage. The expansion raises income in nearly all countries. But while total income rises, some groups are paid less and some even lose their jobs. In our example, owners of capital in the North will prosper, but less-skilled workers in the North face unemployment and falling wages. There are losers as well as winners. The Stolper-Samuelson model of 1941 rigorously spells out these consequences of the Hecksher-Ohlin account.

Other avenues exist through which globalization might lead to job destruction in the North. One is capital mobility: investment moving from high-wage to low-wage countries, shifting jobs as it goes. The dreaded "offshoring" phenomenon means that companies in the North relocate economic activity to foreign affiliates in the South, abandoning both factories and workers in the Rust Belt and Bavaria. Outsourcing, the first cousin of offshoring, means buying inputs from abroad rather than from home suppliers, and is attributed with similar effects. Still another possible means of job destruction is free immigration from the South. When labor mobility is unfettered, experience shows that workers sensibly migrate to high-wage countries, increasing labor supply in those favored locales and thus driving down wages.

Thinking purely in terms of global welfare, none of these avenues—even in the worst case—is bad for the world economy. Countries specialize in the things they do best; capital and labor both flow to where they are employed most productively.

The problem is that not everyone gains equally or at the same pace from globalization, and some lose substantially and permanently. In the North, misery may await older, unskilled workers from unfettered globalization—those who are too unschooled or too advanced in years to take up new occupations. But do these dismal visions bear out in reality? No and maybe; consider the following three facts:

First, Hecksher-Ohlin and Stolper-Samuelson are only models of trade—and not the only models of trade. Almost by definition, countries export goods and services in which they have a comparative advantage and import goods in which they have a comparative disadvantage. Extensive empirical research, however, shows that national comparative advantages and disadvantages do not closely track the abundance and scarcity of factors of production—namely, capital, labor, and land.

For example, Korea became a leading exporter of steel, a highly capital-intensive product, long before it became modestly rich and capital-abundant. India has become a major software exporter, even though the country's labor force has far more unskilled rural workers than highly skilled IT specialists. The United Kingdom remains a leading exporter of men's woolen suits (at the top end), even though it is a high-wage country. All of these exceptions, and many more, can only be explained by the dominant role of technological innovation and entrepreneurial talent in shaping comparative advantage. The real worry for the North is not that low-wage workers in the South will take all the jobs, but that the North itself will slack off as the center of technology and entrepreneurship.

Second, while U.S. and EU exposure to low-wage economies and workers has grown quite impressively, it still trails well behind their exposure to competition from high-wage countries. Trade as a share of GDP has grown across the OECD region in the past decades. But OECD trade with low-wage countries, despite growing much faster than their overall trade, still makes up less than a third of total OECD trade. The figure is higher for Japan (nearly 50 percent) due to its heavy trade with Asian economies, and for the United States (33 percent), likely for the same reason and because of intense trade with Mexico. Indeed, U.S.-manufactured imports from developing countries surpassed those from developed countries in 2004.

But importantly, much of the trade with developing countries today involves goods that the developed countries *no longer* produce. Even in 1989, it turns out, *traditional* developing country manufactured exports accounted for less than half of U.S. imports from developing countries.[69] The most striking growth has occurred in the developing country share of U.S. imports of computers and electronics. The story of fierce competition from low-wage country imports is significantly more nuanced and much less striking than commonly assumed.

If anything, there has been a great deal of staying power in manufacturing in the North. The capacity of the developed countries to adapt to the rise of the emerging markets is often underestimated. Some of this has to do with domestic policy barriers owing to the limited cross-border migration of low-wage earners to rich countries,[70] and some reflects an underestimation of business adaptation as firms climb up the technology ladder in the rich countries.

The third fact to keep in mind is that there is as much trade penetration by U.S. and EU exporters into the poorer countries of Asia, Africa, and Latin America—both in goods and services—as there is the other way around. And at least as much inshoring reaches the United States and Europe as offshoring goes in the other direction. A study by Matthew Slaughter shows that the number of manufacturing jobs insourced to the United States between 1987 and 2002 grew by 82 percent, while the number of U.S. jobs outsourced overseas grew by only 23 percent.[71] The United States is a *net exporter* of business services to India, meaning it exports more services to India than India exports to the United States. Moreover, insourced jobs are often higher paying than outsourced jobs.

Investment flows are still mostly from one developed economy to another developed economy. FDI flows, a proxy for offshoring, have surged from some 7 percent of the OECD region's GDP to more than 25 percent between 1980 and 2005, and to above 40 percent for the EU-15. But only a fraction of the flows were destined to low-income countries—less than 15 percent for most EU economies. The United States is somewhat of an anomaly with 31 percent destined to low-income countries, much of this headed to Mexico.

Is That Trade Churning Away?

In any economy, many jobs are always churning, and some jobs are permanently lost—but is trade the *main cause*? Trying to discern the causal relation between trade and jobs yields conflicting findings, depending on data and methodologies. But either way, the magnitudes are not large.

In the advanced OECD countries, the biggest identifiable adverse impact of globalization is the downsizing of manufacturing employment. The OECD estimates that trade accounted for some 4 percent of all permanent layoffs in Canada, the United States, and the European Union in 2000. In industries heavily exposed to international competition, 27 percent of jobs were lost between 1970 and 2000, as compared to 16 percent for total manufacturing.[72] This data indicates a negative ricochet from trade, more precisely from being stuck in an import-competing, uncompetitive industry. But the finding is muted by the fact that industries facing high competition accounted for less than 4 percent of total employment and all manufacturing accounted for just 22 percent of total employment in the examined economies.

Look at the United States, for example. Trade and labor analyst Lori Kletzer notes that 6.45 million workers in U.S. high-import competition industries—such as apparel, footwear, knitting mills, leather products, textiles, blast furnaces, radio and television, toys and sporting goods, motor vehicles, tires and inner tubes, and transport equipment—lost their jobs over a period of twenty years (1979–1999). This works out to around 320,000 jobs a year, some 38 percent of all job losses in manufacturing. Since manufacturing is less than a fifth of the American economy, the job losses caused by trade account for about the same 4 to 5 percent of all layoffs, as discussed in the OECD study. Josh Bivens of the Economic Policy Institute likewise reports that between 2000 and 2003, import competition and the rising trade deficit in manufactured goods accounted for 34 percent of the decline in U.S. manufacturing jobs.[73]

Head of the Trade Adjustment Coalition, Howard Rosen, gives the best statistical picture. He suggests that of the 16 to 18 million jobs lost annually, approximately 3 to 4 million are displaced workers who face serious adjustment costs, about 500,000 of whom are workers displaced by import competition. This represents approximately 3 percent of total job losses, 15 percent of displaced workers, and about a quarter of workers affected by mass layoffs. The total job gains appear to be cyclical, hinging on ups and downs in the economy, while the involuntary job losses seem to be structural, representing permanent downsizing in the affected industries.

Indeed, the primary reason for job churn is technological change. Among the fastest-declining jobs in America through 2016 will be occupations such as file clerks, order fillers, photographic processing, sewing machine operators, cashiers, packers and packagers, and electrical equipment operators.[74] This is because of innovations ranging from the Internet to digital cameras and automatic packaging machines—automatization, disintermediation, simplifications, and just plain do-it-yourself check-in and checkout.[75]

Gazing at the American landscape more broadly, the association between offshoring and sector-specific manufacturing employment has been negative, but targeted to narrowly defined sectors. Robert Feenstra and Gordon Hanson find a significant negative relationship between employment and "narrow outsourcing" (imports of intermediate inputs from the same sector), but no significant association between employment and "broad outsourcing" (imports of intermediate inputs from all sectors).[76] They also argue that foreign direct investment used for outsourcing from a low-wage country may increase the extent of wage inequality in both the low-wage and high-wage countries.[77] This happens because the tasks shifted abroad are likely to be those requiring the least skills in the high-wage country but the most skills in the low-wage country. Workers at the bottom in each country lose out: in the rich country, their jobs migrate; in the poor country, the better-trained workers move up the ladder.

Like the OECD results and much other research, this finding has happy implications for skilled workers: foreign outsourcing may have accounted for up to half of the increase in the share of total wages paid to skilled workers in the United States, Japan, Hong Kong, and Mexico in the 1980s and 1990s. Whether you are in Monterrey, Osaka, Shanghai, or San Francisco, it pays to be skilled.

The Offshoring Bogeyman

Even before the term was coined, "offshoring" was an unnamed soldier in the trade and jobs debate, rising to become lead warrior in the NAFTA battles of 1993. Ross Perot predicted that millions of U.S. manufacturing jobs would be sucked into low-wage Mexico. A decade later, offshoring fears reached service jobs once considered nontradable and thus "safe from liberalization." The age of the Internet put an end to that complacency, and the "outsourcing bogeyman" became a staple of trade skepticism.[78] In the 2004 presidential campaign, John Kerry campaigned against corporate "Benedict Arnolds" intent on shifting U.S. jobs overseas and betraying American workers.

In a 2006 *Foreign Affairs* article, renowned economist Alan Blinder caused a minor uproar—despite his assurances that no major unemployment would occur—by suggesting that offshored U.S. service positions would likely exceed the previously estimated ceiling of 3.3 million, and that American service jobs susceptible to offshoring "in the electronic future" would be two to three times the number of manufacturing jobs (which according to Blinder tallied 14.3 million in 2004).[79] Adding to fears was a new argument: skills acquired in universities and on the job may no longer serve as a secure dike against intrepid foreigners. Globalization is increasingly about "unbundling" tasks in the production process between those jobs that can be exported and those that cannot.[80]

But the figures may be off. Bradford Jensen and Lori Kletzer argue that the total number of U.S. jobs that might be outsourced to low-wage countries will be 15 to 20 million. This is a far cry from Blinder's range of 30 to 40 million services jobs, approximately 40 percent of which would be in the manufacturing sector (long considered to be at risk).[81] Skill levels are less critical; the key is whether the task can be performed remotely and the service delivered in real time via the Internet. A haircut remains untradable, but reading an MRI is not.

Here is where the bad news ends. As we noted, more jobs are inshored than offshored. As with merchandise trade, the story again is a saga of targeted negative effects amid broad positive benefits. Victims are concentrated at the lower end of service skills (for example, remote data entry clerks and IT troubleshooters), albeit more widely distributed across the spectrum of skills and geography than in manufacturing.

And as with outsourcing, several authors have detected a positive effect between offshoring and wages in general and for skilled workers in particular, in the United States, Japan, and Europe.[82] There are also positive boomerang effects on jobs at home. OECD economists find that offshoring has no effect on overall employment, but in some cases, it has a positive effect on sectorwide employment: some jobs are lost when production activities move abroad, but others are created because offshoring makes certain firms more competitive.

In Old Europe, offshoring of manufacturing jobs had little bearing on overall manufacturing employment, while offshoring service tasks often had a positive impact on overall labor demand. This is because offshoring of service tasks helped home firms improve their quality, cut their costs, lower prices, increase sales, and thus hire more workers.[83]

Catherine Mann authoritatively cuts through the clutter of debate on IT-related jobs in America.[84] She argues that the expansion of the globalization of software and computer services will drive down prices of IT goods and thus enhance U.S. productivity growth and create new higher-value, higher-paid technical jobs. New programming jobs may be springing up in India, but they are not canceling out job growth in the United States. Rather, they propel U.S. jobs by spurring productivity gains in America.

Bridging the Income Gap?

In 1942, economist Simon Kuznets, later a Nobel laureate, put forth a famous hypothesis: after a certain threshold of average prosperity, the degree of inequality would level off. Everyone would be richer, but at the same time, through various channels of causation, income earners would be more equal. The most important channel was urbanization: in the early stages, workers who left the land for the bright lights would earn much higher income, accentuating the gap with those left behind in agriculture. Much later, when 60 percent or more of the population was already urbanized, the gap between rural and urban incomes would make a smaller contribution to inequality.

Following this argument, if trade propels growth—particularly in urban areas, as we have contended—it should also work, at least in a modest way, to reduce income disparities once the Kuznets threshold has been passed.

What does the evidence say to Kuznets? Dollar and Kraay argue that trade raises incomes in the developing world. While average incomes and GDP growth rates have been on the rise in most countries, incomes have actually become less equal, although not as unequal as portrayed in the popular media. A 2008 OECD study found that over the twenty-year span, the average increase in inequality was around 2 Gini points (the Gini is the best measure of income inequality), or as little as the current difference in inequality between Germany and Canada.[85] So the OECD region became more like Canada and less like Germany in two decades.

But to be sure, the trend is there and it is vivid in some countries. Since 2000, income inequality has risen significantly in Canada, Germany, Norway, the United States, Italy, and Finland, while declining in the United

Kingdom, Mexico, Greece, and Australia. So where are we now? The IMF shows that in the early 2000s, the top 10 percent of U.S. wage earners had earnings that were 143 percent above those in the bottom 10 percent; in the United Kingdom, the gap was 122 percent; in France, 100 percent; and in Belgium, 87 percent.[86] Income inequality—measured as the ratio of the top tenth percentile to the bottom tenth percentile of wage earners— grew in most OECD nations during the period of analysis between 1994 and 2005; the only exceptions were Japan, Ireland, and Spain.[87] Trade easily gets the blame: for countries with greater wage inequality, the increases coincided with a more than doubling in trade with middle-income nations (table 3.2).

An immediate reaction to the collapse of the Kuznets hypothesis is to blame trade. If trade grew and income inequality rose, there almost has to be a link—at least, that is the argument. Even though there are multiple plausible causes of inequality—technological change, deunionization, deindustrialization, immigration, and education—the spotlight is on trade.[88] Egalitarian thinkers rushed to the barricades, demanding that trade deals be halted.

Table 3.2 Trade with Middle-Income Nations and Earnings Inequality in the 1990s and 2000s, Selected OECD Economies

	Percent of Trade with Middle-Income Countries, 2007	Inequality (90th to 10th Percentile Earnings), 2005	Percent of Change in Trade with Low-Income Countries, 1990–2007	Percent of Change in Inequality, 1994–2005
Canada	14.9	3.7	174.8	5.7
United Kingdom	17.0	3.5	145.5	2.9
France	17.6	3.1	102.5	0.0
Germany	20.5	3.1	128.6	14.8
Australia	28.1	3.1	153.3	6.9
Japan	38.2	2.9	131.9	−3.3
United States	39.7	4.9	101.4	8.9

Source: Authors, on the basis of UN Comtrade and OECD data.

For protraders, this is troubling, even more so for those free traders who welcome greater equality as a good thing.[89] Rising inequality has certainly fueled the backlash against free trade and globalization. But is this a fair rap?

In developing countries, evidence in the 1980s and 1990s revealed no connection between more trade and more inequality. For example, the famous World Bank duo, Dollar and Kraay, found that in Malaysia, the average income of the poorest fifth of the population grew at a robust 5.4 percent annually, and even in China, where inequality did increase sharply, incomes of the poorest 20 percent of the population still grew at 3.8 percent annually. Inequality went up in some countries (such as China) and down in others (such as the Philippines), but there was no systematic link to globalization. Better explanations were found in domestic education, taxation, and social welfare policies.

Fresh research suggests that the rise of China and India as major exporters did in fact hurt the income of low-skilled workers in the developed world. Robert Lawrence argues that increased trade probably played a part in causing greater U.S. inequality in the 1980s—for it was during that decade that U.S. imports of manufactured goods from developing countries boomed.[90] By the 1990s, however, the impact of greater trade on inequality was much smaller, as many imports from developing countries were no longer made in America. More imports of items no longer made at home could not possibly undermine wages in the United States. Lawrence finds extremely little pressure from import price competition on U.S. inequality: from 1981 to 2006, without trade, blue-collar labor in the United States might have earned 1.4 percent more than they did, and most of that would have come before 2000. Most inequality, as with job churn, is caused by factors other than trade—technological change, business cycle developments, and competition among domestic firms.

Further, the gaps are tough to measure: Lawrence shows that about 60 percent of the U.S. income gap reflects measurement problems, importantly the use of different price deflators to measure output and wages in real terms, and the omission of benefits in reporting take-home pay. An additional 10 percent is attributable to the rapid acquisition of skills by white-collar workers—their productivity grew even faster than the productivity of blue-collar workers. That leaves just 30 percent of the gap that can be attributed to the rise of "conventional" wage inequality. So studies are explaining only a third of the action.

An IMF global study in 2008 found that increasing trade liberalization and export growth actually *reduced* income gaps.[91] The contribution of trade to equalizing incomes is about 10 percent of the change. Meanwhile, technological change, especially the rise in the use of IT, propels income inequality, explaining about 35 percent of the change. In the developing world, the shift in employment away from agriculture and better education contributed another 10 percent to reducing income gaps. Disconcertingly, the IMF team also finds that increased financial openness—especially to FDI—is associated with higher inequality and basically neutralizes the inequality-reducing effects of trade. Here, the explanation is simple: FDI generally creates good jobs at good wages, and that process enlarges the degree of income inequality in urban areas. You could call this a twenty-first-century version of the Kuznets hypothesis—not higher wages as workers move from rural to urban settings, but rather higher wages as they move from domestic to foreign firms.

The spatial effects of trade integration within countries are more complex. Regions with greatest integration in the world economy often see clusters of industries and an agglomeration of manufacturers and services providers in one place. The case of Mexico is emblematic: Inter-American Development Bank's Ernesto López-Córdova finds that the four northern Mexican states bordering the United States saw a massive inflow of investment and manufacturing activity following NAFTA, and accounted for 60 percent of Mexico's trade boom in the decade following the deal.[92] With five additional states, the figure rises to 90 percent. In the meantime, the other sixteen central and southern states remained by and large disconnected from integration, contributing less than 1 percent to Mexican export growth during the period.

Unsurprisingly, much of the lack of connectivity can be traced to variables other than sheer geographical distance. Poor infrastructures in Mexico's southern states impeded access to the U.S. market, and worse educational standards and credit availability undermined the competitive strength of firms in the south and their ability to reach the U.S. market. Uneven integration, in other words, split Mexico into two different countries, much like the case with Italy's productive north and laconic south.

But interestingly and echoing the IMF's findings, the states with greatest participation in global trade saw a decrease in inequality among households, while inequality deepened in states that remained disconnected from global trade.

What does this wealth of research mean to trade, jobs, and wages? First, it means that trade is good for growth and appears to be good for equality, at least in the developing world; second, that FDI and technological progress increase the premium on higher skills.[93] Humans doing nonroutine cognitive tasks cannot be outsmarted by machines, at least not yet.[94] Third, it means that trade integration requires national complementary policies to bring together regions disconnected from globalization to enjoy its fruits.

Most important, even if globalization did produce income inequalities, trade barriers are not a remedy, but rather a false solution. For example, one study suggests that prohibitive trade barriers against China and India would be very costly for the rich countries. Barriers against the Asian giants might cost the developed countries as much as 17 percent of their projected output by the year 2100, and reduce the incomes of *high-skilled* workers by around 25 percent in comparison to a free-trade scenario.[95] If equality is the goal, better strategies than trade protection are plain to see: more and better education, additional and improved infrastructure, more available low-cost credit, and so on.

Conclusion

Global trade has soared to heights that probably even the most enthusiastic GATT founders would not have envisioned. Trade opening has delivered growth, propelled prosperity, and lifted millions out of poverty. But its effect on jobs and wages is strongly—at times, harshly—contested. Globalization compels shifts in employment, inducing people to move to different positions in their companies, to other companies in the same sector, or to a new sector altogether. Such shifts are generally but not always positive, entailing sharper specialization, higher productivity, and bigger paychecks. But opportunity favors the prepared worker and the educated mind.

One lesson to take home from recent decades is that technology has created more of the action in income gaps and job churn than trade. The negative employment effects of trade are targeted, not widespread. Certain regions, sectors, or classes may be hard hit, but in general, the adverse effects are temporary. By contrast, the positive effects are broad and durable.

The future global economy will not be a world of complete specialization where each country finds its niche and sticks to that task. Comparative advantage will remain footloose—which means that countries will compete with one another in the same industry. Fragmentation of production will enable even "new" jobs in the developed world to migrate to developing countries—witness the skill-intensive production of microprocessors, now assembled in China, Malaysia, and the Philippines. As long as there are wage differentials among countries, there will be offshoring, outsourcing to low-wage countries, and human migration to high-wage countries.

But given the hunger of consumers for variety, the tens of thousands of distinct goods and services in a modern economy, and the resulting expansion of intraindustry trade, countries do not have to go head-to-head; they can also exchange goods and services with one another in the same industries. Furthermore, in today's global economy, the migration of comparative advantage is not a one-way street. Skill-intensive chunks of the production chain—everything from aircraft production to software design and medical research and development—are doing very well in the developed world, inviting inshoring investment from countries like China and attracting bright migrants from countries like India. Japan, the United States, and Europe remain at the cutting edge of innovation, pulling other countries up the ladder with them. The world trading system is an arena of constant competition and specialization, but unlike sporting events, it is an arena where everyone can come out a winner.

4

MIGHTY MULTINATIONALS

Investment abroad is a very old phenomenon that can be traced at least to the Hudson Bay Company, founded in 1670 by English capitalists to gather furs from Canada. The modern term is foreign direct investment (FDI), where the word "direct" implies controlling ownership by the mother corporation. Today, the mother corporation or parent firm generally carries out headquarters functions for subsidiary corporations spotted around the world. The controlling ownership is generally 100 percent for each subsidiary, but it can be as low as 10 percent if a block of shares that small still delivers control to the parent. The whole group is generally called a multinational corporation (MNC), even though the parts are incorporated in different countries; to get around this inconvenience, the group is sometimes called a multinational enterprise (MNE). Other common terms are transnational corporation or transnational enterprise.

Foreign direct investment has been on a tear since the 1970s. Statistical data distinguish between annual flows of new investment money (whether debt or equity) to subsidiaries abroad and the accumulated stock of investment (including retained earnings) in the foreign enterprises. FDI flows reached a peak of $1.8 trillion in 2007 (figure 4.1), and the FDI stock at the end of that year had a historical (or book) value of $15.6 trillion.

Firms based in advanced countries generally supply around two-thirds of the total FDI flows and stocks, with American, British, French, Canadian, and Dutch MNCs leading the pack. Advanced countries are also the dominant recipients of FDI. Thus, contrary to popular mythology, most

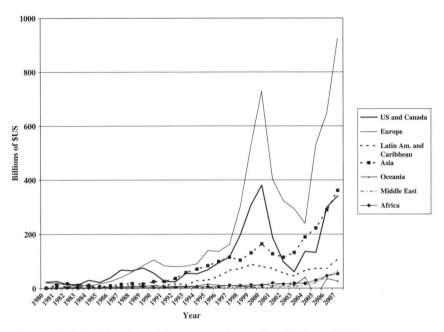

Fig. 4.1 Global FDI Inflows in 1980–2007, by Region (billions of $US).
Source: United Nations Conference on Trade and Development (UNCTAD).

foreign investment is not a matter of rich countries seeking out cheap labor in poor countries. Indeed, FDI inflows to developing countries, which were tiny and confined to natural resources in the 1950s, reached a record figure of $500 billion in 2007 that was spread among services, manufacturing, and some natural resources, with Asia leading the pack as a top destination.

Like trade, FDI has become hugely important in the global economy, as well as for individual countries. The ratio between inward FDI stocks and global gross domestic product (GDP) is now 27 percent; for Europe, the ratio exceeds 40 percent of GDP; for developing countries as a group, the ratio is 30 percent of GDP; and for the United States, 15 percent. In dollar terms, FDI stock placed in the United States is massive, some $1.5 trillion at the end of 2007, more than double the size of FDI in Germany and more than ten times FDI in Japan.[1]

Small countries, however, rely particularly heavily on MNCs to supply capital and create jobs. Averaging four aspects of exposure to foreign investment—FDI inflows as a percentage of capital formation, FDI inward stocks as a percentage of GDP, value added of foreign affiliates as a percentage of GDP, and employment of foreign affiliates as a percentage of total employment—the numbers show that small countries such as Luxembourg, Belgium, Hong Kong, and Singapore are more than 60 percent "transnationalized." The figure for Trinidad and Tobago and Estonia is more than 40 percent, and for Chile, Jamaica, the Netherlands, and various Eastern European countries, it is above 30 percent.[2] The transnational dimension in large economies is considerably lower, but still important: 10 percent for Germany, 7 percent for the United States, and less than 5 percent for India.[3]

The Rise of Grand Globalizers

In 1998, there were 53,000 MNCs with 450,000 foreign subsidiaries; by 2007, there were about 80,000 MNCs and 800,000 affiliates.[4] Multinational companies are no wallflower in the globalization game. They contribute a third of the planet's output, with total sales of $31 trillion in 2007.[5] They employ at least 82 million people, equal to the population of Germany. And they account for an astonishing two-thirds of world trade. Half of that (or a third of total world trade) is *intrafirm* trade between branches of the same company.[6] As much as 90 percent of U.S. trade is estimated to flow through multinationals of all nationalities operating in the United States.[7] The Bureau of Economic Analysis calculates that U.S. MNCs alone account for more than 50 percent of U.S. exports and more than a third of American imports—as well as for a quarter of U.S. GDP and 20 percent of private-sector jobs.[8] The worldwide operations of U.S. MNCs account for half of all profits in the United States. In China, MNCs are estimated to account for a third of output and half of exports.

Leading the top-ten list of MNCs by sales are household names: Walmart, ExxonMobil, Royal Dutch Shell, British Petroleum, Chevron, Toyota Motor, Total France, ING Group, General Motors, and General Electric (GE). Collectively, their sales amounted to some $2.5 trillion, about a fifth the size of the entire U.S. economy. Walmart's sales in 2007 were $379 billion and profits were $13 billion (retailers, after all, have tight margins); Exxon sold $360 billion of petroleum products and earned $41 billion in profits, or $6 billion more than Canada's entire budget.

Multinational companies play their investment cards in two decks—one for cross-border mergers and acquisitions (M&A), taking over existing firms abroad, and the other for brand-new, "greenfield" investments. When good times are rolling, M&A deals keep investment bankers shuttling across oceans to iron out deals. Mergers and acquisitions constitutes the bulk of global FDI, and is the favored mode for expanding in advanced economies; greenfield is more common in developing countries. Almost twelve thousand greenfield projects were launched in 2007, a good year. Multinational companies commonly enlarge their foothold in host economies by reinvesting their earnings. In fact, some 30 percent of all FDI today represents reinvested earnings, and MNCs typically reinvest around half their profits made abroad and repatriate the other half as dividends to the mother corporation.[9]

New Multinationalization

The MNC ecology has become dramatically more complex in recent years, at least in three ways. First, the world of MNCs is diversifying well beyond manufacturing and petroleum. The bulk of new FDI now flows into service sectors—banking, retail, transportation, infrastructure operations, tourism, and the like. While financial services firms have long been prominent global players, the list of the top one hundred services firms now includes some twenty nonfinancial giants such as Walmart and Germany's retail operations, Metro AG and Bertelsmann.

Second, MNC mother ships are sprouting up in new home countries. Alongside their traditional base in advanced countries, MNCs are now flowering from Latin America and Asia. Foreign direct investment outflows from developing countries grew from 5 percent of the world total in 1990 to some 8 percent in 2007.[10] The United Nations Conference on Trade and Development (UNCTAD) reports that the one hundred largest MNCs based in developing countries in 2007 held $570 billion in foreign assets. With foreign assets of $71 billion, Hutchison Whampoa of Hong Kong tops the list of emerging-market MNCs, followed by Petronas (Malaysia), Samsung Electronics (Korea), Cemex (Mexico), Hyundai Motor (Korea), and Singtel (Singapore).

Some of these companies are highly globalized: Cemex operates in thirty-five countries and Samsung in thirty-two. And they have swallowed some big deals. In 2005, Chinese computer firm Lenovo, now the world's fourth-largest computer manufacturer, made waves by purchasing IBM's $11 billion personal computer (PC) business. In 2006, with the takeover of Arcelor (Europe's biggest steelmaker), India's Mittal Steel leaped to first place among the world's steel companies.

Third, this "colonialism in reverse" is complemented by investment going back and forth among the main emerging markets. "South-south" corporate investment more than tripled between 1995 and 2003, and currently hovers around $50–60 billion annually.[11] Consider the Indian companies now conquering Latin America. Infosys, TCS, Genpact, and Sasken have set up facilities in Mexico, Argentina, Brazil, Chile, and Uruguay. In 2005, Indian pharmaceutical giant Dr. Reddy's paid $61 million to acquire Industrias Quimicas Falcon de Mexico, a steroids manufacturer. In the auto industry, Tata has joined forces with Fiat to manufacture "new-generation" pickup trucks in Argentina. Brazilian MNCs are perhaps the most potent response to Asian firms: Brazilian aircraft manufacturer Embraer set up its initial China operation in May 2000 and produced the first airplane outside Brazil at its Harbin factory in 2003. Among planes with thirty to one hundred seats, Embraer now holds more than 40 percent of the mainland China market, topping its Canadian-based rival, Bombardier.

Emerging market MNCs arguably enjoy a special springboard that enables them to rise quickly to the global arena: domination of their own large and rapidly growing domestic markets. Brazilian Grupo Positivo controls almost a fifth of the domestic computer market, more than Hewlett-Packard and Dell combined. Tata's empire has tentacles across India, and its $2,500 Nano car will be hard for foreign car companies to match in the battle for the 200 million–strong and growing Indian middle class. If Nano succeeds in India, Tata can easily take the car into other emerging markets.

Firms like Tata, Lenovo, Cemex, and Embraer arguably have another special advantage in each other's markets: instinctive understanding of business is the chaotic context of developing countries. Antoine Van Agtmael, the investor who coined the term "emerging markets," predicts that firms based in these countries will be more numerous than those based in today's advanced countries by 2030, when the combined size of emerging economies is bound to overtake their Western counterparts.[12]

Notwithstanding the hive of ascendant MNCs, a relatively few big players—termed "The Happy Few" by Thierry Mayer of the University of Paris and Gianmarco Ottaviano of the University of Bologna[13]—will continue dominating the MNC world. Of the American nonfinancial companies in the Standard & Poor's top-1,500 list, the top 10 percent, or 150 firms, account for 84 percent of sales. The same story is repeated internationally. And only a handful of MNCs are genuinely global. Truly big fish, like GE, which operates in more than 100 countries, and IBM, which has set up shop in 170 countries, are the whales of the MNC aquarium. The same holds for firms based in Europe and Japan, and certainly for firms based in emerging markets. But the exploding number of MNCs shows that many companies find profit in applying their expertise to markets outside the home country.

What Moves Companies?

Why are companies spanning borders? What are the benefits of going multinational? The most powerful force underlying the global reach of MNCs is the ability of a company to profit by applying its "firm-specific capital"—all that costly expertise tied up in patents, brands, production techniques, distribution systems, and management skills—outside its home sandbox without duplicating the expense of creating those assets a second or third time.

Go back in time when trade rules were critical to the expansion of foreign ventures. Nineteenth-century international companies were simple hub-and-spoke networks that created and controlled international trade routes and thrived on open markets at home and abroad, importing raw materials from the colonies, manufacturing them at home into finished products, and subsequently exporting those products both to the colonies and other foreign markets.

In recent decades, FDI, like trade, has naturally gravitated to size and growth—which is why investments in China, India, and Brazil are so popular today. Surveys of chief executive officers (CEOs) resoundingly show that a driving reason to go abroad is to access big markets with lots of middle-class consumers. Foreign direct investment in the service sectors has boomed because the service economy in emerging markets is expanding to encompass some two-thirds of GDP on average.

From Jumping Tariffs to Seeking Efficiencies

Growth is not the only driver of multinationalization; policy has also powerfully shaped it. Matthew Adler and Gary Hufbauer calculate that roughly 30 percent of the U.S. inward FDI stock growth and 18 percent of U.S. outward FDI stock growth can be attributed to policy liberalization in 1982–2006.[14] Since policy liberalization for inward FDI generally goes together with policy liberalization for imports, this finding stands on its head a traditional explanation for FDI that became popular after the First World War, namely to leap over trade barriers. According to the old story, rigorously analyzed by Thomas Horst in 1969,[15] "market-seeking" firms face tariffs or other barriers on their export sales, making it more costly to export than to "jump" the trade barrier and produce locally in the protected country's market. When tariffs are liberalized, such incentives disappear, and the foreign company may decide to pull its tariff-jumping plants out and centralize operations in one country. In a way, then, tariffs are like high transportation costs—to avoid them, a company may just relocate abroad altogether.

This was a good story in its day. When the First World War was followed by a global protectionist spiral, the hub-and-spoke import-export operations metamorphosed into a tariff-jumping business model with real on-the-ground operations abroad. General Motors and Ford built auto plants in Europe and Asia, allowing them to sell in important markets. Fears of a "Fortress Europe" in the 1970s and 1980s prompted many U.S. companies to establish operations in the European Union.

But in recent decades, evidence shows that *reducing* trade barriers does more to boost inward FDI than maintaining a protected local market. In fact, "efficiency-seeking" FDI happens *because* of open trade. One reason is that companies prefer to locate where they can bring inputs free of tariff barriers. Another reason is that companies prefer to locate in countries that have market access to other countries, so they can easily export part of their output. Low barriers around the home market are often associated with low barriers around foreign markets through preferential trade agreements. Still another reason is that the same forces of political economy that enable low trade barriers usually go hand in hand with forces that relax impediments to inward FDI—a phenomenon in the background of findings reported by Adler and Hufbauer.

In fact, one hypothesis that explains developments in some markets is that the height of trade barriers shapes the type of MNC organization: high trade barriers promote a horizontal style, with a parent's subsidiary firms producing the same goods and services in each location; low trade barriers promote a vertical style in which related subsidiaries slice the production process geographically into different stages. Low barriers are thus also key to global production chains.

The classic modern-day trade agreement resulting in vertical MNC organization is the North American Free Trade Agreement (NAFTA). The deal modestly lowered U.S. tariffs on Mexican goods (U.S. tariffs were already fairly low, so going to zero duties was not a big leap) and, more significantly, lowered Mexican tariffs to U.S. goods and barriers to inward FDI from all sources. This led to a huge inflow of FDI into Mexico from around the world. Japanese car and appliance manufacturers set up plants in Mexico to produce cars, TVs, and much else in Mexico for sale in the domestic market and for export to the United States. U.S. apparel firms headed south to hire cheaper Mexican labor and send their finished goods back to the U.S. market. In short, improved market access to the United States, coupled with short distance and a welcome mat for foreign investors, made Mexico hugely attractive for MNCs seeking to use the country as an export platform for the U.S. market. Studies back up these ideas. An Inter-American Development Bank team showed that tariff liberalization for two-way Mexican trade with the United States and Mexico's liberalization of FDI inflows under NAFTA were key determinants of surging FDI inflows.[16]

The Mexican case is not a mere anecdote. Empirically, the tariff-jumping explanation has proven less robust than the argument of a complementary relationship between trade and FDI. For instance, one study projects that the removal of bilateral tariffs between the United States and Britain would increase U.S. flows of FDI to the United Kingdom.[17] A complementary relationship is also found for India.[18] A veteran of FDI studies,

Bruce Blonigen of the University of Oregon has found that tariff jumping is an option for only a few firms based in advanced countries.[19] In a recent analysis, Dean DeRosa found that among U.S. free trade agreement partners, inward FDI stocks tend to be directly and very strongly related to trade openness.[20]

In the developing world, multiple domestic policy reforms during the 1980s and 1990s—raising permissible levels of foreign ownership, relaxing capital controls, reforming regulation, guaranteeing against expropriation, and improving the investment climate—made the countries far more attractive to foreign investors, thereby adding fuel to the global FDI boom (figure 4.2). Foreign assets of U.S.-based MNCs grew about 8 percent faster in the years following liberalization, starting around 1982.[21] Countries set up investment promotion agencies to tap into FDI, and perhaps surprising

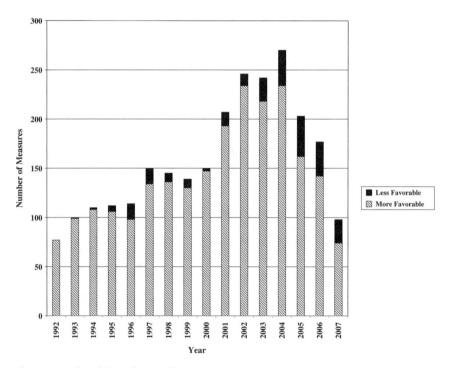

Fig. 4.2 National Regulatory Changes on FDI, 1992–2007. *Source*: United Nations Conference on Trade and Development (UNCTAD) World Investment Report 2008.

to skeptics, these agencies often succeeded.[22] Doctrines pronounced in the Washington Consensus inspired a privatization spree across emerging markets and the Eastern bloc in the 1990s, providing more fuel for FDI as foreigners gobbled up telecom companies and utilities across Eastern Europe, Latin America, and Asia. New financial instruments to hedge against currency risks and insure against political risks also helped foreign investors feel more comfortable.

Multiple Tools of Trade

The liberalization tide was advanced and codified by bilateral and multilateral investment pacts. Bilateral investment treaties (BITs) are the staple instrument, proving mutual guarantees for investors between the partner countries. The number of BITs has skyrocketed since the mid-1990s, to more than 2,600 today among no fewer than 179 countries.[23] Germany has sixteen BITs today; China has fifteen, and Morocco twelve. More than 250 of the bilateral and regional free trade and economic cooperation agreements, like NAFTA, also carry sturdy provisions to liberalize and protect investment. Multilateral investment agreements are lagging, and only since the Uruguay Round (concluded in 1994) has investment been formally addressed in the World Trade Organization (WTO), under the auspices of the trade-related investment measures (TRIMs) agreement—designed more to prevent trade-distorting practices than to promote investment.

Bilateral investment treaties are found to increase FDI flows between the partner countries, even though the independent effect is often hard to isolate from other variables that propel investment.[24] But the bilateral flows may also go up when one of the countries signs a BIT with a third country. For example, if the United States and Thailand have a BIT, investment flows between them go up—and again when Thailand signs a BIT with China. Bilateral investment treaties apparently have a signaling effect—signing a BIT with one country indicates to the rest of the world that the signatory respects the property rights of *all* foreign investors.

There are also some 2,730 double-taxation treaties (DTTs). These agreements lower withholding tax rates and increase tax certainty for MNCs operating abroad. But they also tighten the surveillance of abusive transfer pricing practices and in other ways discourage tax evasion.[25] These features could dampen FDI. On balance, however, the positive effect wins. The average odds of FDI occurring between any one pair of countries in the world are 0.6 percent. A tax treaty between two countries raises the chances to 0.7 percent, a big increase on a small number.[26]

On top of the various bilateral and regional agreements are multilateral investment codes. However, these have never been very successful or far-reaching. Several multilateral initiatives have tried to incorporate investment: the 1948 Havana Charter, the OECD Draft Convention on the Protection of Foreign Property (drafted in 1962, revised in 1967), the United Nations Code of Conduct on Transnational Corporations in the late 1970s and 1980s and, more recently, the initiative to forge a Multilateral Agreement on Investment (MAI) by the Organization for Economic Cooperation and Development (OECD) in the mid-1990s.

The WTO also has been involved. As a result of the Uruguay Round, investment is addressed to a limited extent in the Agreement on Trade-Related Investment Measures (TRIMs); more importantly, in the General Agreement on Trade in Services (GATS); and less directly, in the Agreement on Trade-Related Intellectual Property Rights (TRIPs) and the Agreement on Subsidies and Countervailing Measures (ASCM). But the coverage of these deals is far from comprehensive. In fact, there has been little success at institutionalizing multilateral investment provisions owing to strident divisions among countries over the extent of protection, the depth of liberalization, and whether to address the development dimensions of investment. As a result, developing countries that want to burnish their image but not sign on to the full plate of U.S. and EU demands have pursued BITs and DTTs as a means to gain credibility in the eyes of investors—through commitments to property protection, stability, predictability and transparency.[27]

Technology also plays a role in the spread of multinational corporations. There is a rise in the talent pools around the world such as in Bangalore, not only in Silicon Valley and Route 128 near Boston. Studies have found that knowledge and other rather intangible assets drive foreign investment—patents, trade secrets, copyrights, trademarks, marketing skills, and the like. These days, the combination of trade and investment liberalization facilitates FDI, but technical progress makes it happen.

IBM's CEO, Samuel Palmisano, has made this point in concrete terms. He argues that today's MNC is quite unlike the export-import company or the centralized corporation of yesteryear, with a smattering of production and sales abroad. Today's companies are not "multinational," he argues, but "globally integrated enterprises" whose components, from back office to manufacturing to product development, are dispersed around the world in a vast smart grid. We are no longer talking about companies with a giant mother ship and brain that sits in a first-world city, deploying into third-world countries for the sole reason of selling products or operating low-end assembly plants, call centers, and the like. Rather, the integrated enterprise is a global web of activities where some nodes come together to form a final product and other nodes sell that product. Even the most basic Dell computer ordered by a Malaysian journalist comes in two dozen pieces from fifteen different countries on three continents, gets assembled in Jakarta, Indonesia, and is subsequently exported to Kuala Lumpur.

Even sophisticated operations, such as research and development and product design, may no longer have to be centralized; rather, local talent will be tapped wherever possible. Now R&D can be performed in Palo Alto, St. Petersburg, or Bangalore. In short, multinationals are gradually moving from an efficiency-seeking model of labor cost arbitrage to a brains-pursuing hunt for global talent and ideas.

But we have not yet reached the world of free-flowing FDI and free-ranging MNCs. This is not a buyer's market: many countries impose steep demands on foreign investors, such as prescribed requirements on local content or employment in the executive suite, or on joint partnership with local firms. Many countries still wall off "priority sectors" from foreign investors. As we explore in chapter 9, national security and public safety are the explanations (and mostly excuses) *du jour* around the world for blocking foreign firms.

Service sectors are often closed to FDI in emerging countries. India, for example, allows foreign retailers to own 51 percent of outlets, but only if they sell just a single brand of goods—like Ralph Lauren clothing. In Mexico, foreigners may offer banking services through the local subsidiaries of foreign financial institutions, but only if Mexico has signed a free trade agreement that includes a financial services chapter. China limits foreign investment in real estate. The restricted list goes on to include electricity and gas supply, medical and educational services, media, and transportation.

A few countries are still engaging in old-school populist nationalizations, particularly in the resource sector. In 2007, Bolivia's state-owned oil company, YPFB, reclaimed full control of two main oil refineries from Brazil's Petrobras. Venezuela has taken over a number of oil projects—including properties owned by ExxonMobil, Norway's Statoil, and Italy's ENI—in the Chavez government's drive to nationalize private companies, both domestic and foreign. Against the evidence, but with the prompting of President Correa, Ecuador is seeking damages against Chevron that could amount to $27 billion.[28] The fifteen-year-old class-action case was filed on behalf of thousands of indigenous Ecuadorians, even though Petroecuador, not Chevron or its predecessor Texaco, was responsible for harm to the environment. Less-blatant actions include Bolivia's decision to hike taxes on mining companies and Kazakhstan's review of all contracts relating to natural resources.

Another sensitive field of direct investment is farmland, where the buyers are typically based in countries like Saudi Arabia and China, and the sellers are developing countries in Africa, the former Soviet Union, and Latin America.[29] The goal of this investment is both to ensure food for the home country and to raise agricultural productivity. One deal in Madagascar has already toppled the local government, and given the scale of the land rush and frequent hints of corrupt dealings, more blowups seem certain.

Some countries have turned their back on FDI by conspicuously escalating political risk, but even established and steady players have room to liberalize. According to one estimate, if the United States adopted the same low level of FDI restrictions prevailing in the United Kingdom—including screening requirements, foreign shareholding requirements, nationality of management, and visa limitations—U.S. inward FDI stock would increase by some 20 percent.[30]

Indeed, right in the OECD club, the effect of completely removing idiosyncratic FDI restrictions would make the group's FDI inflows go up by 80 percent, that is, almost double.[31] If just the "national interest" screens were eradicated, average OECD inward FDI stocks would have been 20 percent higher in 1980–2000 than they were, and if nationality tests for management personnel were relaxed, average OECD inward FDI stocks would have increased by roughly 10 percent. These are simple fixes with big payoffs.

Another study of developing countries calculates that complete removal of controls on the repatriation of export earnings would have increased annual FDI inflows as a share of GDP by as much as 1 percent annually in the 1990s; that capital account liberalization would have about the same effect; and that a unitary exchange rate would have increased inflows by about half of 1 percent.[32] Cumulated over twenty years, the stock of inward FDI would have increased by the same amount as in the OECD, or 20 percentage points in the ratio of FDI to GDP.

How to Get Investment?

Almost all countries around the world, states within such federal countries as India, the United States, and Brazil, and towns within states are engaged in efforts to catalyze investment, both domestic and foreign. Jurisdictions large and small have granted special treatment to foreign investors—a single window for foreign investors to do their paperwork for investment and profit repatriation guarantees; tax advantages, such as tax holidays, reduced rates, and investment allowances; and industry parks and export processing zones (EPZs), geographically bounded areas aimed at attracting foreign investment through sweeteners like duty-free imports and exports, infrastructure investment, good safety, and reduced regulatory interference. Governments from Ohio to Norway and Kuwait advertise in the leading newspapers their various benefits for investors, from superior transport infrastructure to educated workforces and opportunities for weekend canoeing for battle-worn executives. Derogative terms are tossed about to denigrate rivals—Massachusetts in the United States, for example, is famously called "Taxachusetts."

Yet, the global distribution of FDI is far from even. Big, growing countries naturally draw in more in absolute dollars. And many small, vibrant economies such as Hong Kong, Bulgaria, Malta, the Bahamas, Jordan, and Singapore get markedly more FDI than could be expected given the size of their economies. But others, like many poor sub-Saharan African countries, seldom get a knock on the door except to sell their oil or farmland.

How do MNCs pick their sites? Survey after survey shows that the locational choices are based on size and growth potential of the market, quality of labor (particularly critical for companies aiming at standardization across markets), good communications and transportation infrastructure for shipping inputs and outputs, and in the more unruly environments, rule of law and safety (companies do not want their executives robbed on the way to work).[33] "Soft" variables, such as tailored incentives, tend to be secondary to the "hard" dimensions of economic size, growth and stability, human capital, law and order, and solid physical infrastructures.

UNCTAD's 2007 survey of the reasons for MNCs to invest makes the point.[34] More than half of the surveyed CEOs saw access to large and growing markets (China, India, Russia, and the United States) as the most important driver of their FDI, followed by access to resources (17 percent of respondents), especially skilled labor. Access to low-cost labor was an enticement to only 9 percent of the firms. On the risk side, geopolitical and financial instability were mentioned as the main uncertainties that could hamper FDI, followed by an increase in protectionism.

In another UNCTAD survey, CEOs of foreign affiliates ranked macroeconomic and political stability, quality of telecommunications, and the supply and cost of skilled labor at the top of their investment prospectuses, followed by corporate taxes and the quality of banking and other financial services.[35] Corporate income taxes are regarded as particularly important by foreign affiliates in manufacturing and services, while incentives seem to be of the greatest importance for those in manufacturing.

The World Bank's investment climate unit Foreign Investment Advisory Service (FIAS) echoes these results. In a November 2007 survey, 304 senior executives of European, North American, and Asian MNCs cited low labor costs and flexible labor policies as key competitive advantages, and political instability and inadequate infrastructure as key impediments to increased FDI flows. A 2002 survey of 101 companies by a World Bank body, Multilateral Investment Guarantee Agency (MIGA), found access to customers was the most important factor (ranked as "very important" by 77 percent of the companies),[36] followed by stable social and political environment, ease of doing business, and reliability and quality of utilities.

Races to the Bottom—Or Top?

In March 2009, the U.S. Congress started hounding international tax havens and secret bank accounts for hiding money that really
ought to flow into U.S. government coffers. Switzerland was incensed,
but Gordon Brown, the British prime minister, showed up in Washington
calling for international, concerted closure of tax havens.

This spirited uproar—motivated to a good extent by public outrage
over the buried treasures of Bernie Madoff and other con artists, and Sir
Allen Stanford's Ponzi schemes—was the mere tip of a giant iceberg of
long-standing debate on tax lures in the global economy. In the 1980s and
1990s, the rise of MNCs led many an analyst to conjecture that countries
seeking to attract investors would strive to sweeten the deal with conditions better than their neighbors. Collectively, countries would engage in
a race to the bottom, each seeking to attract multinationals with ever-
lower taxes and regulatory exceptions. The underlying notion of leftist
scholars like Susan George was that global capital is mobile and MNCs
are free to exploit third-world countries.[37] Capital could vote on its feet
and could only be attracted if pampered; taxes would thus be pushed onto
labor because it is stuck to a fixed location. Soon enough, a regulatory free
fall would get under way, corporate taxes would plunge to zero, and MNCs
would rule the world. In this line of thinking, sovereignty becomes irrel-
evant and the welfare state fades into history.[38]

Granted, there are tax havens and hiding places for money, from Vanu-
atu to Bermuda to Monaco. And yes, countries around the world have
devised incentives, changed regulations, and created export processing
zones to draw MNCs. Certainly, there is abusive transfer pricing to reduce the revenue claims of high-tax countries like Germany, Japan, and
the United States. For MNCs with the entire globe as a playground, there
are multiple legal and quasi-legal strategies for reducing domestic corporate taxes, such as borrowing in high-tax countries to take advantage of
interest rate deductions, or charging foreign affiliates in low-tax countries
favorable prices on inputs and bargain royalties to shift profits in their direction.

But it turns out that these patterns are not all bad—and that a giant race
to the bottom is not exactly how the game plays out, for four reasons.[39]

First, in 1980, the top personal income tax rates in OECD countries aver-aged some 67 percent, and corporate rates averaged nearly 50 percent; countries also sported extra layers of tax on capital, including dividend taxes, capital gains taxes, inheritance taxes, and wealth taxes.[40] With the Reagan-Thatcher revolution, these rates—which hurt savings and invest-ment and stifled growth—came down to an average of 40 percent for personal income taxes and 27 percent for corporate taxes, respectively.[41]

These cuts, tax literature argues, were in part spurred by race-to-the-bottom logic. Tax competition prevails between municipal governments within states or provinces, between state and provincial governments within countries, and between national governments in the global economy.[42]

Be that as it may, the tax cut spree has not necessarily been bad for gov-ernment kitties. True, in the United States, the collection of corporate in-come taxes has fallen significantly as a *share of total global profits* for U.S. companies. But Michael Devereux of the Center for Economic and Policy Research (CEPR) shows that revenues from corporate taxes in the OECD region are higher than at almost any time in the last four decades.[43] This is in part due to the very tax reductions. Devereux concludes that "only at low rates of tax does [further increases in the tax] rate have a positive im-pact on tax revenues. Above moderate rates, further increases in the tax rate may actually reduce revenues." He suggests that the optimal rate from a revenue-raising standpoint might be 31 percent, similar to the optimal 33 percent rate advocated by Kimberly Clausing of Reed College.[44] Joel Slemrod, another fiscal expert at the University of Michigan Business School, has reached similar results. Openness to FDI, he finds, is nega-tively associated with statutory corporate rates (more open means lower tax rates), but not with revenues collected as a fraction of GDP. Tax *collec-tion* has gone up despite (or likely because of) the lowering of tax *rates*.[45]

These findings suggest that moderate tax rates invite more MNC activ-ity, which then provides more tax revenue than would be collected with higher tax rates. This, in turn, could explain why the presumed tax race to the bottom has not dented the welfare state. Indeed, as UCLA's Geoff Garrett argues, the relationship tends to be positive: more multinational-ization and globalization means bigger government.[46]

Contrary to the expectations of the race-to-the-bottom school, Geoff Garrett of UCLA and Deborah Mitchell of the Australian National University, like Michael Devereux, find that in the 1990s, FDI was associated with higher effective rates of taxation but lower tax rates on labor. Rather than shifting the burden of taxation from mobile capital to immobile labor, governments show greater reliance on capital and less reliance on labor for public revenue.[47]

This seems to indicate that globalization increases the supply of "compensation" to labor to offset the "efficiency" pressures from companies. As market integration increases economic insecurity in the advanced industrial countries, governments need to spend more, not less, to cushion workers. And here is the kicker: taxes on corporations and spending on welfare may not necessarily be detrimental to the interests of industry, but actually may invite companies to locate. Why? Because a larger welfare state softens antiglobalization pressures, helps maintain public support for openness, and if done right, can promote productivity and competitiveness.[48]

Even if corporate taxes have been dropping, we are far from the bottom—and unlikely to keep going further down. Richard Baldwin and Paul Krugman offer a game-theoretic argument: economic integration among countries produces centers of industrial concentration that are highly attractive to MNCs, and thus allows the involved regions to extract more tax revenue from their MNCs than they could without such industry agglomerations. They contend that, with globalization, the tax gap between countries widens at first—with integration there is initially a race to the bottom—but then the gap narrows as integration advances. Ultimately, agglomeration may produce a semblance of tax harmonization.[49]

There is also little evidence of a global race to the bottom in environmental regulations to attract polluting companies, or that environmental regulations actually affect firm location. Rather, many firms employ the same production techniques abroad as they do at home. If anything, there are races to the top. Unlike in the tax realm, it appears that some degree of global coordination under the Kyoto framework will induce an upward climb with respect to limitations on greenhouse gas emissions.

The existence of race to the bottom on labor rules is also dubious. For-eign direct investment may actually raise the bar: the OECD finds that openness to FDI has led to better labor standards.[50] In some cases, em-ployers actually prefer to have standards imposed because they constrain the behavior of some of their less-scrupulous competitors.[51] Within MNCs, labor practices in foreign plants tend to be broadly similar to their domes-tic labor standards.

Daniel Drezner of Tufts University points out that while some countries—Pakistan, Bangladesh, Panama, and Zimbabwe—exempt their export pro-cessing zones (EPZs) from labor regulations, other counties have not followed that lead and instead have introduced new labor standards in their EPZs. Some governments have established higher minimum wages for EPZs in the hope of establishing a more stable and productive work-force.[52] Keith Maskus argues that firms have an incentive to put on their best behavior in an EPZ, for example, by paying a wage premium or pro-ductivity incentive bonus to attract workers.[53] Firms that operate in EPZs tend to be larger, and research shows that pay scales and working condi-tions are positively correlated with firm size. Products made in EPZs are generally intended for export to developed economies where the demand for product quality is high, which in turn implies the need for above-average workers.

In fact, standards and regulations are most vexing to MNCs when they differ sharply across jurisdictions. Companies operating in many coun-tries want either vanilla rules or chocolate rules across all countries, but not a mix of flavors—or a flavor of the month.[54] Companies also have an inter-est in the "one rule" approach for competitive reasons. In her award-winning book, Wellesley's Elizabeth DeSombre shows that multinational firms may oppose stiffer environmental regulation in their home countries, but once such regulations are enacted, these firms often will switch their posi-tion in favor of global regulatory standards. Companies want other pro-ducers to face the same regulatory constraints that they must meet.[55]

More generally, these findings reveal another fallacy in the race-to-the-bottom claim—that the state is the servant of mobile capital and does not respond to other constituencies, such as voters, lobbies, and bureaucra-cies.[56] This is a Marxian proposition. Will every rule be tailored to attract the unknown foreign player who has yet to arrive on the scene? Political science renders one skeptical about the power of foreign players to over-shadow their domestic rivals in jousting over national policies—or in the ability of a "benevolent" government to attract FDI in the face of opposition from domestic monopolies. Multinationals often have smaller incentives than domestic producers to lobby in any one country because they have smaller stakes in any single national market. Developing and developed countries devise regulations to protect their homegrown firms from the competitive pressures that foreign investment can engender.

Are Regulations a Magic Bullet?

There is a second reason why race to the bottom is not the wave of the future. It is not the golden wand for countries to draw multinationals. As surveys resoundingly show, taxes are important, but they are not the main determinant of location choices. This has exposed another fallacy in the race-to-the-bottom story—that government taxes and regulations are the be-all and end-all. Rather, what matters is the balance between taxes and regulations on the one hand, and labor productivity, infrastructure quality, educational opportunities, and character of governance on the other. The importance of this balance often creates a race to the top, as countries improve their local investment climate through better training, stronger rule of law, leaner bureaucracies, less corruption, and better logistics—even as they raise taxes and strengthen regulations.

In the 2007 UNCTAD survey, CEOs of foreign affiliates were quite happy with attitudes toward foreign investors, corporate income taxes, and double taxation treaties in countries around the world. But many developing countries were sorely lacking on some of the factors most coveted by the corporate leaders—rail and road infrastructures, reliable natural resource supplies, good real estate, and international sea links.

What is more, some incentives may even be redundant. A McKinsey Global Institute survey of thirty foreign executives who have moved operations to India reveals that financial incentive—such as a waiver of the 35 percent tax on corporate profits for companies moving back-office processing and information technology jobs to India—was the least-important factor in their decision.[57] In fact, given India's prowess in information technology (IT), the companies likely would have hired locals even in the presence of the tax.

The same holds true for some of the constraints imposed on foreigners. The surveyed foreign automakers in India said they would have sourced components locally even without local content rules because of the cost and time required to import parts, rising import prices, and the large supply of relatively low-wage, technically trained labor in the local component industry. Consider Mexico or Brazil: neither has joint-venture requirements in the retail or retail banking sectors, yet foreign players have generally come in through joint-venture operations. Local market knowledge is crucial to success in service industries, and that is what the local partner provides. China and India might not need to impose such rules either, since local partners often furnish foreign players with government contacts required to cut through the bureaucracy and make a deal.

In general, such requirements can be bad economics. Theodore Moran, Edward Graham, and Magnus Blomström, some of the world's most seasoned FDI analysts, argue that countries should steer clear from domestic-content, joint-venture, or technology-sharing requirements on foreign investment because these rules neither increase the efficiency of local producers nor produce host country growth. Rather, they argue, such provisions merely interrupt intrafirm trade, a potent source of host country growth, and cut off the potential for FDI to streamline production processes, update technology, and add to host country resources. The costs of forcing MNCs to link with locals are often higher than the benefits.[58]

The third problem with the race-to-the-bottom argument is that it assumes that once a company relocates overseas and finds an attractive bottom, it will vanish from sight and no one at home will know what it is doing. But it is certainly the case that hoards of domestic lobbies are quick to scream foul if they find domestic companies operating sweatshops or polluting abroad. As a result, firms often use domestic standards in their foreign operations to avoid the critique that they are shopping abroad for low standards.[59]

Nongovernmental organizations (NGOs) around the world monitor and rank corporations by their adherence to global standards. Even less-passionate consumers have become more alert to odious labor practices, environmentally hazardous production methods, and the failure to observe "fair trade" practices. In response, companies go to great lengths to be good citizens—even changing their brands to connote a high-minded regard for social and environmental responsibility.

This "good citizen" mentality carries over when MNCs choose places and ways to do business. PepsiCo left Myanmar in 1997 to disassociate itself from the repressive regime.[60] General Electric pushed for the OECD Anti-Bribery Convention in order to bring all units of its global, sprawling enterprise under a single set of good rules. A multitude of companies are turning green to please consumers. Deere & Company, the farm equipment manufacturer, practices the same low-emissions paint process in China as in the United States.[61] Motorola in 2007 committed all of its worldwide manufacturing sites to reducing greenhouse gas emissions (some were already covered under the Kyoto Protocol or the EU's Emissions Trading Scheme).[62] The thirteen members of the U.S. Private Equity Council have pledged to apply responsible investment guidelines, tailored after the UN's Principles for Responsible Investment, to cover environmental, health, safety, labor, governance, and social dimensions of their projects.[63]

Besides observing and raising standards, companies and investors have *en masse* adopted corporate social responsibility (CSR) programs. According to some estimates, by now about 61 percent of companies have CSR charters, and some 11 percent of all $25 trillion of investments under management in the United States are subject to a social responsibility clause.[64] These codes are an exemplary form of aid: they are designed to do good both for the recipient country and for the company. A few illustrative examples are: Chevron has allocated $30 million to battle AIDS, tuberculosis, and malaria—diseases that have devastated communities in which the company operates—and among other things, the company has distributed fourteen thousand malaria nets.[65] Deere & Company has invested almost $500 million in wind energy to assist rural economies produce electricity. Microsoft's Unlimited Potential Plan strives to double the number of people who are currently online from 1 to 2 billion by 2015, in part by manufacturing computers priced at $100. While MNCs are not knights in shining armor, their actions signal a race to the top.[66]

Still another problem with the race-to-the-bottom argument is the assumption of footloose companies ready to depart at the first sight of a tax incentive elsewhere. To be sure, there is empirical evidence that MNCs are more mobile than domestic companies,[67] and that they respond to tax differentials,[68] but the response takes place over a period of years, not months. It seems doubtful that a prospective host country should curtail the entry of particular MNCs just because they might be more footloose than other firms. Studies show that new jobs created by MNCs tend to persist—longer than new jobs created by domestic firms.[69] That is a worthwhile benefit; let's examine further benefits next.

The Crowding In Effects of FDI

Countries presumably have engaged in reformism and improved business climates because they covet foreign investment. But does multinationalization impart the expected benefits?[70]

Answers to this question are contested, although the argument is less politically charged than the race-to-the-bottom debate. The more negative view is that MNCs do more harm than good—outcompete and crowd out local firms and simply establish foreign oligopolies and monopolies, produce nonessentials for the host country, and set up only a part of a productive process, affording few opportunities for the creation of supply and distribution linkages with local firms. Antitrust goes bust.

The more upbeat side argues that MNCs provide fresh capital, create jobs, expand opportunities for selling and buying local companies, transfer technology and research and development, and create backward and forward linkages with local firms that transmit operational, managerial, marketing, and exporting skills to locals.[71] The entry of MNCs, discriminating clients that they are, also will impart "demonstration effects" and raise the bar and standards among local firms aiming to do business with the MNC. Also, there are good sparks between the MNC mother ships and their foreign affiliates. Ted Moran argues that once an affiliate is linked into the headquarters supplier network—and the MNC competitive position in international markets depends on such affiliates—these best practices are upgraded continuously on a real-time basis. He quips that the MNC–foreign affiliate relationship is akin to good "parental supervision," where the outcome is a hugely dynamic movement along the industry frontier.[72]

As such, MNCs stimulate competition among the local firms, boosting their efficiency and development. A further hypothesis is that FDI does not crowd out local firms, since MNCs often enter industries where entry barriers for local firms are high. To the contrary, MNC entry may "crowd in" domestic investment. This, if happening, would validate the many analysts who predict that the entry of foreigner giants like Walmart in India's retail sector will generate investments by local suppliers and distributors.

So, which side is winning? The latter, quite handily.

In 1999, Brookings scholars Barry Bosworth and Susan Collins found that FDI in fifty-eight developing countries during 1978–1995 led to a one-to-one crowding in—each dollar of FDI generated a dollar in domestic investment.[73] A 2007 Federal Reserve Bank of Dallas study similarly showed that between 1990 and 2005, a percentage point rise in the ratio of FDI to GDP in emerging markets led to an increase of half a percentage point in domestic investment and three-quarters of a percentage point in domestic savings.[74] Such crowding in increases the recipient's productive capacity and thus has direct effects on economic growth.

Export-oriented FDI has particularly positive effects on trade, as the foreign entrants churn out exports and import new inputs. This is a familiar sight across the Chinese eastern seaboard and south of the U.S.–Mexican border. FDI in the service sectors—especially business services, communications networks, and financial services—has a similar complementary effect, especially when the "commercial presence" of foreign players increases.[75] Foreign direct investment also can provide a path for emerging economies to extend their range of exports into products customarily sold by advanced countries—and evidence suggests that greater diversity and sophistication of exports are closely linked with economic growth.[76]

There are nuances, however. For one, the benefits from greenfield investments differ from mergers and acquisitions. Greenfield FDI implies an infusion of large amounts of capital—production facilities, distribution centers, and possibly research labs, along with skilled management. The result is an identifiable increase in the host country's stock of physical and intellectual capital. By contrast, M&A or "brownfield" investment usually brings only a limited increase in the stock of physical capital, but intellectual capital may increase sharply. Either way, there could be knowledge spillovers to local firms and budding entrepreneurs.[77] Further, horizontal spillovers and externalities are most prevalent in FDI in developed countries—but there is also growing evidence on vertical spillovers and externalities for FDI in the developing world.[78]

As in trade and finance, the positive spillovers from FDI are not automatic. Again, absorptive capacity becomes an issue—high technological capability and labor skills, strong local competition, and a policy of free trade all help countries "use" MNCs.[79] Like trade, FDI can harm the economy in a country with highly protected and distorted systems. Conversely, countries with low barriers to trade, clear regulations, and few restrictions on business operations can tap MNCs to score efficiency gains and higher income. These circumstances require diligent homework for the prospective host country, but the benefits of fixing trade regimes, education systems, and infrastructure are immense, much beyond the improved odds for attracting MNCs.

The preconditions also play out at the firm level. The more productive firms tend to "self-select" into becoming suppliers to MNCs. This, in turn, means that prior good performance is what attracts MNCs to partner with local firms, and a partnership in turn improves performance further.[80] Research also suggests that being a supplier admits a firm into a network of high-performing companies, since knowledge flows are particularly strong among foreign MNC subsidiaries located in the same country.[81] Local firms aiming to supply MNCs have strong incentives to shape up beforehand.

A potential problem with this virtuous cycle is "adverse selection": multinational companies pick the local stars as partners, while their domestic competitors get stuck with the duds. In addition, so the argument continues, MNCs poach the best workers from domestic firms. Even if this is true, these arguments are not reasons for a *country* to be skeptical of MNCs: these side effects should be seen as Schumpeterian creative destruction—less-productive firms are closed and more-productive firms are enlarged. Only when the local government ties itself to the fortunes of local competitors of MNCs will these side effects be viewed in a negative light.

As discussed earlier, market size and growth potential matter a great deal in attracting MNCs and FDI. Fast-growing large markets are more attractive than small island nations far away. Small countries are disadvantaged by these economic realities, but they can shrink their handicap with open trade regimes that give their firms better access to markets abroad. Rigorous studies have found that the more fluid the linkages between the various potential host countries, the more FDI they receive.[82] Seamless spatial units like the EU, NAFTA, and ASEAN create zones of free movement for goods and investment, resulting in genuinely regionwide manufacturing operations. North American auto production is a prime example: thousands of vehicles produced in the North American market cross borders no less than seven times before a finished car emerges.[83]

Finally, what also matters to the ultimate impact of FDI is the same factor that arbitrates the effects of financial or trade flows: local institutions. Ted Moran summarizes a vast swath of literature on FDI and development, arguing that while FDI in natural resources can generate revenues for public services, economic diversification, and social development, it can also be a source of corruption, upheavals, and economic stagnation; while FDI in infrastructure can bring electricity, water, and other services to ever-larger numbers of businesses and households, it can also impose lopsided economic and foreign exchange burdens on the beneficiaries; and while FDI in manufacturing can help the host economy move from low-skilled to higher-skilled economic activities, it can also lock the host in inefficient operations.[84] The key to determining the outcome in any of these sectors is the policy environment established by developing country host governments, and reinforced by developed country authorities, as well as multilateral lending institutions and civil society organizations. Good behavior gets rewarded in the world economy, as it does in many other spheres of life.

Are MNCs Too Far from Home?

How do MNCs benefit their home countries, and how much have they benefited from their forays overseas?

The transmission of valuable industrial know-how through the arteries and veins of multinational corporations is a controversial phenomenon. This transmission is sometimes likened to the loss of blood, much to the detriment of workers and communities in the home country. But research has shown—as IBM chief Samuel Palmisano points out—that MNCs often locate abroad to tap local expertise.[85] Knowledge spillovers from home to host country also travel the other way around, from host countries to home countries, also vectored by MNCs. Multinational operations are in many ways like legal industrial espionage that benefits all sides. One may contest who monetizes the knowledge most in the end. But from the point of view of global economic productivity, such two-way knowledge diffusion is very good news indeed. It means that the people of the world do not have to reinvent the wheel two, three, or more times.

The proof is in the pudding. Firms that engage in international transactions outperform domestic firms in several dimensions, such as product variety and output per worker. A recent study finds that Chinese firms with more than 50 percent of foreign ownership introduce on average more than twice as many new varieties of goods as purely domestic firms.[86] This reflects the reservoir of product know-how that MNCs bring when they go abroad.

The benefits that MNCs bring to their home economies are more contested. In some developed countries, MNCs produce heartburn when they manufacture overseas rather than at home. Workers protest that MNCs ship jobs abroad; legislators argue that MNCs exploit tax havens overseas and do not pay their fair share at home. What do the numbers say?

In the United States, the Bureau of Labor Statistics confirms some of these effects. From 2000 to 2005, U.S. multinationals cut more than 2 million jobs at home, even as employment in the rest of the private sector grew. U.S. operations of foreign multinationals also shrank by five hundred thousand, as foreign investors cut costs and sold off U.S. companies. And U.S. MNCs do not create massive job numbers relative to their sales. In 2006, the top 150 U.S.-based non-financial multinationals generated 47 percent of jobs (home and abroad) attributed to the Standard and Poor's top fifteen hundred nonfinancial companies, while accounting for 57 percent of the sales and 62 percent of the profits. Further, MNCs paid less in taxes as a share of global corporate profits than in the past.[87]

But a closer look reveals a more positive picture. Looking just at recent events, multinationals have cut jobs less aggressively in some industries than comparable domestic firms. In the United States, for example, overall employment in manufacturing fell by 18 percent between 2000 and

2005, but U.S.-based multinationals cut jobs by only 12.5 percent. As a rule, multinationals retain their R&D and headquarters jobs in the United States to serve the global market.

Taking a longer view, rigorous research shows that multinationals are more productive, pay more, and are better managed than their domestic counterparts. Andrew B. Bernard of Dartmouth's Tuck School of Business and Bradford Jensen of Georgetown University estimate that plants operated in the United States by U.S. multinationals are far larger (149 percent), older and more established (by 4.6 years), and more productive (6 percent) than nonmultinational plants, and that they are substantially more capital intensive (by 89 percent) and pay higher wages (14 to 20 percent more).[88] Some 50 percent of multinational plants export, as opposed to 17 percent of nonmultinationals. Matthew Slaughter argues that U.S. multinationals pay up to 24 percent more in wages in the United States than domestic companies, and that they purchase as much as 90 percent of their inputs from the United States, not overseas.[89] In Europe, Mayer and Ottaviano find big differences, too. Exporting firms pay a wage premium on 10 to 20 percent above the wages of purely domestic firms, and MNCs pay an even larger wage premium.[90] They also find that MNCs have a higher value added, employ more capital per worker, and have more skilled workers and higher productivity than domestic firms and even exporting firms that are not MNCs.

Dinosaur MNCs cannot be faulted for shedding jobs. The real job boost to national economies comes not from established behemoths but from the formation of new multinationals. In their initial period of hypergrowth, these firms can create a massive amount of employment. General Electric and Ford hired enormous numbers of American workers in their growth years; today, Microsoft, Apple, and Google have added some 110,000 service jobs to the U.S. economy. Mayer and Ottaviano argue that policy makers should not "waste time helping the incumbent superstars," but rather "nurture the superstars of the future."

Conclusion

The global company is for real. The number of MNCs spanning the world has multiplied in the past two decades, and the biggest ones have become genuinely global, operating in a multitude of countries and earning revenues that rival the size of major OECD economies. But the global company is not king. Marxist-inspired views about MNCs eviscerating national policy officials and the welfare state have been turned on their head. "Bidding wars" appear an exaggeration; attracting FDI involves much more than the offer of lower taxes. An educated population with reliable work habits, a capacity for innovation, an open trade regime, political stability, good infrastructure, and even a sturdy social safety net are all important. These factors also are the ones that enable a country to entice its homegrown MNCs to retain the most valuable parts of production at home. FDI is where global and domestic meet; as it turns out, what is good for home is generally good for host and for the global company straddling the two harbors.

5

SOUTHBOUND

Year 2008 left an imprint on world history. It was the year when the global economy took a terrific hit and globalization got a punch in the face. This was not a hit in popularity contests; this was a hit in hard numbers.

The world economy started to slide in mid-2008, but the reality check came in the last quarter of the year. Comparing the fourth quarter to the third quarter, real gross domestic product (GDP) in the United States and the United Kingdom dropped by 1.6 percent,[1] in Germany by 2.1 percent, and in Japan by a depressing 3.3 percent. More than five hundred thousand Americans lost their jobs during those three months, and the rest worried about losing theirs. China's growth was still positive at 6.8 percent, far below the 2007 figure of 9 percent, and not enough to stop a tide of mass layoffs.

This only heralded worse to come. Analysts repeatedly downgraded their gloomy forecasts for the fate of the world economy in 2009. In October 2008, the International Monetary Fund (IMF) predicted that world output would increase by 2.2 percent in 2009; in November 2008, the IMF dropped its figure to 1.7 percent; and by January 2009, the forecast came tumbling down to just 0.5 percent, the lowest rate since the Second World War. The latest estimates at the time of writing put 2009 global growth at negative 0.8 percent (table 5.1).

Advanced economies fared badly, with growth dropping by 3.2 percent into the freezing zone. Real activity in 2009 contracted by 2.5 percent in

Table 5.1 Economic Growth in 2007–2011, Select Economies (as projected in January 2010)

	Year over Year					Q4 over Q4		
				Projections		Estimates	Projections	
	2007	2008	2009	2010	2011	2009	2010	2011
World Output[1]	**5.2**	**3.0**	**−0.8**	**3.9**	**4.3**	**1.3**	**3.9**	**4.3**
Advanced Economies	2.7	0.5	−3.2	2.1	2.4	−0.7	2.1	2.5
United States	2.1	0.4	−2.5	2.7	2.4	−0.3	2.6	2.4
Euro Area	2.7	0.6	−3.9	1.0	1.6	−1.8	1.1	1.8
Germany	2.5	1.31.2	−4.8	1.5	1.9	−1.9	1.0	2.5
France	2.3	0.3	−2.3	1.4	1.7	−0.5	1.6	1.6
Italy	1.6	−1.0	−4.8	1.0	1.3	−2.4	1.3	1.1
Spain	3.6	−3.6	−3.6	−0.6	0.9	−3.1	0.1	1.2
Japan	2.3	−1.2	−5.3	1.7	2.2	−1.8	1.8	2.5
United Kingdom	2.6	0.5	−4.8	1.3	2.7	−2.8	1.9	3.1
Canada	2.5	0.4	−2.6	2.6	3.6	−1.6	3.6	3.5
Other Advanced Economies	4.7	1.7	−1.3	3.3	3.6	3.0	2.7	4.0
Newly Industrialized Asian Economies	5.7		−1.2	4.8	4.7	5.8	3.1	5.4
Emerging and Developing Economies[2]	8.3	6.1	2.1	6.0	6.3	4.3	6.4	6.9
Africa	6.3	5.2	1.9	4.3	5.3	...	...	...
Sub-Sahara	7.0	5.6	1.6	4.3	5.5	...	...	...
Central and Eastern Europe	5.5	3.1	−4.3	2.0	3.7	1.2	−0.2	5.9
Commonwealth of Independent States	8.6	5.5	−7.5	3.8	4.0	...	...	...
Russia	8.1	5.6	−9.0	3.6	3.4	−6.2	2.4	4.3
Excluding Russia	9.9	5.3	−3.9	4.3	5.1	...	...	...

(continued)

Table 5.1 *(Continued)*

	Year over Year					Q4 over Q4		
				Projections		Estimates	Projections	
	2007	2008	2009	2010	2011	2009	2010	2011
Developing Asia	10.6	7.9	6.5	8.4	8.4	. . .	. . .	. . .
China	13.0	9.6	8.7	10.0	9.7	10.7	9.3	9.4
India	9.4	7.3	5.6	7.7	7.8	5.9	9.6	8.3
ASEAN-5	6.3	4.7	1.3	4.7	5.3	3.6	4.8	5.5
Middle East	6.2	5.3	2.2	4.5	4.8	. . .	. . .	. . .
Western Hemisphere	5.7	4.2	−2.3	3.7	3.8	. . .	. . .	. . .
Brazil	5.7	5.1	−0.4	4.7	3.7	3.1	3.9	3.7
Mexico	3.3	1.3	−6.8	4.0	4.7	−3.0	3.2	5.4
Memorandum								
European Union	3.1	1.0	−4.0	1.0	1.9	−1.9	1.3	2.2
World Growth Based on Market Exchange Rates	3.8	1.8	−2.1	3.0	3.4	. . .		

Notes: Real effective exchange rates are assumed to remain constant at the levels prevailing during December 8, 2008–January 05, 2009. Country weights used to construct aggregate growth rates for groups of countries were revised.

[1] The quarterly estimates and projections account for 90 percent of the world purchasing power parity weights.

[2] The quarterly estimates and projections account for approximately 76 percent of the emerging and developing economies.

Source: IMF, World Economic Outlook Update (released September 22, 2009, and January 26, 2010).

the United States, 3.9 percent in the European area, and 5.3 percent in Japan. Emerging markets and developing economies, while endowed with larger foreign exchange reserves and greater economic resiliency than in previous downturns, are estimated to have grown by only 2.1 percent in 2009. China, fueled by the government's stimulus programs, did well at estimated 8.7 percent growth, but India's growth fell to 5.6 percent, well below the near-double digit growth rates of the past. Amid the crisis, the World Bank sternly warned that each 1 percent drop in global growth would trap another 20 million in poverty.

Officials frantically denied a rerun of the Great Depression. But the trajectories in the stock market and manufacturing output were not at all reassuring (figures 5.1A and B). The greatest investor of modern times, Warren Buffett, characterized 2009 as an economy in "shambles."

Jobs were lost—many of them. Some 4.1 million American jobs, equivalent to the population of Los Angeles, vanished between February 2008 and February 2009, and unemployment climbed to 7.6 percent, a twenty-seven-year high. As the crisis turned into a recession, many more jobs were lost. Unemployment surpassed 10 percent in October 2009, and mainstream analysts agreed that a jobless recovery was in the cards. In Germany, Europe's economic engine, unemployment rose to 8.1 percent in December 2009, twice the forecast level, French unemployment soared to 10 percent by the end of 2009, and almost a fifth of Spaniards were out of work, and in Japan, the land of stability, unemployment flirted with 5 percent.

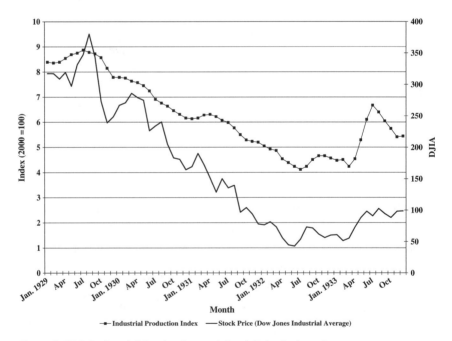

Fig. 5.1A U.S. Industrial Production and Stock Price Indexes in 1929–1933.
Sources: Board of Governors of the Federal Reserve System; Yahoo! Finance.

Equity markets collapsed. On March 9, 2009, the Dow Jones closed below 6,600, its worst showing since 1997, and well below the last bear market bottom in 2002. Stocks plunged in Asia and in Europe, spooked by the dismal economic prospects of Eastern Europe. The European Union faced economic "disintegration," haves against have-nots, with Czech and Polish governments paying higher interest rates than Brazil or Thailand. World Bank president Robert Zoellick took it upon himself to drum up support across Western Europe for rescuing the Eastern half. Southern European economies were also in a death spiral, and the spread between German ten-year bonds and comparable Greek bonds ballooned to nearly 300 points in January 2009, heralding worse times to come for Greece.

The loss of asset value was massive and global. The four dozen main global equity markets on Standard & Poor's "Global Broad Market Index" lost a combined $17 trillion in 2008, some $4 trillion more than the annual output of the entire American economy, and hit a low of about

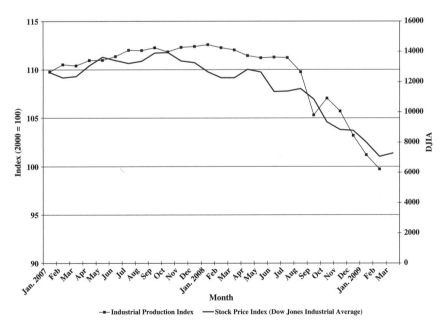

Fig. 5.1B U.S. Industrial Production and Stock Price Indexes in 2007–2009.
Sources: Board of Governors of the Federal Reserve System; Yahoo! Finance.

80 points in the first quarter of 2009, after nearing 200 points in mid-2007. Emerging market equities fell 55 percent and developed markets dropped 43 percent for 2008. Ireland fell by 70 percent, Greece by 67 percent, and Norway by 66 percent. Japan posted a return during the year at minus 29 percent, while the United States lost 39 percent.[2] Even the juggernaut BRICKs crumbled: Brazil's equity market dropped by 57 percent, Russia's by 74 percent, India's by 65 percent, China's by 53 percent, and Korea's by 56 percent.[3]

The worst sector was finance; shares lost 54 percent of their value on average, and a few giants—like AIG, Citigroup, and Royal Bank of Scotland—were almost wiped out.

The equity market's loss is often the bond market's gain; and that was true in 2008 and 2009, but only for the very safest bonds. The global safe play was U.S. Treasuries, and yields on ten-year notes dropped to a record low of 2.08 percent set in December 2008.[4] Luo Ping, director-general of the China Banking Regulatory Commission, made revealing comments in a February 2009 speech in New York: "Except for U.S. Treasuries, what can you hold? Gold? You don't hold Japanese government bonds or UK bonds. U.S. Treasuries are the safe haven. For everyone, including China, it is the only option."[5] Investors next decided to park their money in top-rated municipal bonds, which yielded almost double the Treasury bonds.

But with the economy in shambles, investors were wary of corporate debt, and by January 2009, the average yields on investment-grade corporate bonds reached 10 percent, far above the 6.5 percent rate prevailing in 2008. Lower-rated corporate debt was traded at yields between 15 and 20 percent.

Not surprisingly, spreads between emerging market debt and U.S. Treasuries widened sharply. Consider three leaders among emerging nations. In January 2007, Ukraine's debt, expiring in June 2013, was priced only 1.35 percent higher than U.S. government bonds of the same duration; South African debt was only 0.97 basis points more; and Russia's debt, set to expire in March 2030, was only 100 basis points more than the U.S. Treasuries.[6] By November 2008, Ukraine's debt was 18.13 percent more than U.S. Treasuries, and South African and Russian debts soared 6.61 percent and 5.45 percent, respectively, above Treasuries.

The housing boom, which was in many ways the start of the crisis, was unquestionably over. By March 2009, U.S. housing prices had dropped 18.2 percent below levels of the previous year. Britain's housing values were down by 17.6 percent, Hong Kong's by 14 percent, and Iceland's by 9.8 percent.[7]

Hard Times for Globalization

The global recession was bad news for national economies and workers. But also globalization, one of the engines of the worldwide growth and prosperity of the twentieth century, was hit, as the crisis wiped out many of its gains.

Finance

"Bank Earth" shut its doors. Net private capital flows to emerging markets plunged from $929 billion in 2007 to $667 billion in 2008 and further to $435 billion in 2009 (figure 5.2). Emerging European nations faced the biggest drop: the volume of $20 billion for 2009 was less than a tenth of the level of $267 billion in 2008, and one-twentieth of the level of $393 billion in 2007. Emerging Asia attracted $164 billion in 2008, well below $315 billion in 2007, even if recovering decently to $236 billion in 2009. Latin America netted $131 billion in 2008 and $135 billion in 2009, after $184 billion in 2007. The good news is that the 2009 tally was far better than expected at the start of the year in Asia and Latin America, in particular.

With governments and firms in the G10 rich economies vacuuming up available loans, borrowers based in emerging markets faced a crowding-out effect in global bond markets. Emerging market bond sales nearly shut down in the fourth quarter of 2008 (figure 5.3 and table 5.2). With the G10 financing requirement scheduled to triple from $1 trillion in 2008 to more than $3 trillion in 2009, the Brazils and Indonesias of the world were left with crumbs.

Global foreign direct investment (FDI) flows also fell, from a level of $1.98 trillion in 2007 to $1.7 trillion in 2008 and further to $1.04 trillion in 2009.[8] The richest economies took the worst hit, with FDI flows falling by 41 percent in 2009, after the already bad 2008.[9] Particularly

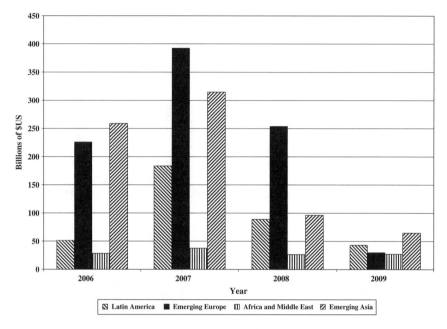

Fig. 5.2 Net Private Capital Flows in Select Economies, 2007–2009.
Source: Institute for International Finance.

affected were the United States, the United Kingdom, Spain, France, and Sweden.

On the whole, cross-border mergers and acquisitions (M&A) back-pedaled, falling by 31 percent year-on-year between 2007 and 2008 (table 5.3). German M&A activity fell 23 percent, and French activity was decimated to less than a sixth of 2007 levels. The better news was that US M&A activity held firm, and emerging East Asia and Brazil saw gains. India's cross-border M&A deals doubled and China's increased by a quarter.[10] Overall, however, year 2009 delivered cold water practically everywhere.

Even remittances, a resilient financial flow that exploded by more than 2.5 times from $100 billion in 1995 to a record $265 billion in 2008, would be hit. Remittances in 2009 were projected to fall around 6 percent. Living was now tougher for migrants to the rich countries—if it was worthwhile for them to come at all. In January 2009, unemployment among Mexican immigrants was 9.7 percent, up from 4.5 percent in March 2008.[11]

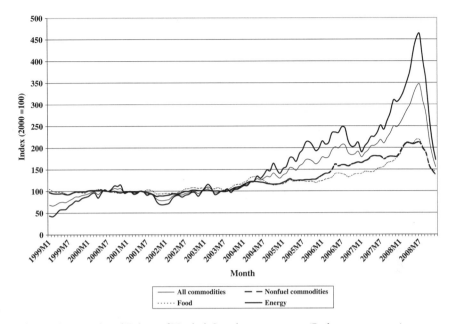

Fig. 5.3 International Prices of Traded Goods, 1999–2008 (Index 2,000=100).
Source: International Monetary Fund.

As many as 3 million Mexicans were expected to return home from the United States in the early months of 2009.

The only uptick in the charts came on development and balance of payments finance. The World Bank planned up to $100 billion in new long-term loans between 2009 and 2011. The IMF busily plugged financial holes with billions in short-term emergency loans—for example, $7.6 billion for Pakistan, up to $2.4 billion for Latvia, and $800 million for El Salvador—and asked creditors for more mortar.

Trade

The crisis had far-reaching implications for global trade. The first casualty was trade finance—the credit required to move as much as 90 percent of traded goods across borders. Rates on trade finance loans shot up by 3 percentage points in the fall of 2008, prompting the World Trade Organization (WTO) to convene a special meeting and the World Bank to create a new trade finance fund.

Table 5.2 Quarterly International Bonds and Notes by Residence of Issuer (announced

	Q1 2007	Q2 2007	Q3 2007	Q4 2007	Q1 2008
All Countries	1,577.2	1,656.4	1,018.3	1,036.7	1,170.4
Developed Countries	1,345.0	1,389.9	882.0	914.7	1,056.2
Australia	32.8	37.6	17.0	19.7	39.6
Austria	31.4	11.8	11.3	14.4	17.6
Belgium	11.3	21.1	10.4	7.8	6.3
Canada	25.0	26.4	18.6	23.5	28.0
Cyprus	0.2	3.1	0.1	0.1	-
Denmark	10.2	8.7	1.4	3.9	3.6
Finland	1.8	10.1	0.6	1.2	2.0
France	76.2	85.5	39.6	69.9	67.9
Germany	136.7	113.5	76.7	65.1	137.8
Greece	14.2	11.6	2.0	-	19.6
Iceland	4.5	4.1	1.9	3.2	3.4
Ireland	78.1	106.0	77.1	62.7	61.5
Italy	42.3	59.5	17.2	33.1	32.8
Japan	6.6	8.1	5.8	7.6	5.1
Liechtenstein	0.0	0.2	0.0	0.0	0.0
Luxembourg	24.8	27.2	24.5	33.2	13.6
Netherlands	120.3	94.6	66.3	77.9	67.5
New Zealand	0.4	0.6	0.4	0.3	0.0
Norway	12.9	10.9	8.5	9.8	15.4
Portugal	3.0	17.1	3.3	45.0	7.9
Spain	87.6	88.8	55.2	30.3	17.1
Sweden	23.6	31.1	10.7	13.6	14.1
Switzerland	1.8	1.9	0.2	0.4	0.6
United Kingdom	234.9	252.5	161.9	157.7	118.5
United States	353.0	358.1	271.1	274.5	374.9
Offshore Centers	150.5	178.7	80.9	57.2	41.3
Bahamas	0.7	0.6	1.0	0.5	0.9
Bermuda	5.1	4.7	0.6	1.7	1.1
Cayman Islands	130.2	146.0	66.1	38.2	31.4
Hong Kong SAR	2.1	5.0	1.6	1.6	1.0
Lebanon	1.0	1.0	0.6	0.7	0.9
Mauritius	0.2	0.1	0.1	0.3	0.1
Netherlands Antilles	6.3	10.7	9.1	8.6	3.6
Singapore	3.0	5.7	1.2	1.5	1.6
West Indies, UK	1.5	2.1	0.2	3.5	—

issues), 2007–2009

Q2 2008	Q3 2008	Q4 2008	Q1 2009	Q2 2009	Q3 2009	Q4 2009
1,878.9	1,008.7	1,340.1	1,719.2	1,675.0	1,197.6	1,150.2
1,737.1	927.3	1,271.9	1,602.0	1,500.5	1,072.1	1,019.7
28.6	18.2	15.1	26.2	27.5	34.4	55.2
11.8	6.6	10.8	21.2	19.1	12.0	4.5
41.0	7.1	23.0	28.1	25.2	8.0	8.8
67.1	34.3	13.8	26.2	38.9	27.2	32.3
2.3	0.1	-	-	3.6	0.7	0.0
10.4	7.7	4.6	18.4	18.8	7.4	10.9
9.3	3.6	0.9	15.8	9.7	3.0	8.9
136.1	62.6	83.0	131.8	183.6	95.4	92.4
108.4	71.7	135.3	136.7	94.5	84.0	66.0
9.6	0.5	4.0	35.0	22.5	0.8	13.6
5.0	0.6	0.0	0.0	-	0.0	0.0
76.7	39.4	110.0	74.2	62.5	65.8	41.6
75.1	39.2	90.7	47.9	44.4	64.1	51.6
8.0	2.1	1.0	1.0	3.7	2.9	8.1
0.3	-	-	-	-	-	-
25.7	12.6	19.7	12.9	19.3	37.2	19.1
130.6	51.1	84.5	143.5	135.3	66.1	67.0
0.8	0.4	0.4	-	-	0.2	1.8
23.2	8.1	3.3	12.1	11.4	9.6	11.6
21.1	8.4	3.3	18.1	15.3	10.2	9.1
87.9	32.9	50.0	85.1	89.5	59.4	54.2
33.6	23.3	17.2	36.2	43.6	33.1	22.3
2.3	1.3	0.3	0.2	0.7	0.8	2.1
316.1	294.6	400.6	175.2	187.0	176.5	164.1
506.1	200.9	200.3	552.6	441.6	268.6	283.8
49.1	33.5	19.1	29.7	39.1	35.7	36.4
0.2	0.3	0.1	0.1	1.6	0.1	0.8
8.6	2.5	-	7.8	2.5	2.8	4.2
29.3	23.1	13.8	15.8	27.2	22.0	21.8
1.7	1.6	2.4	1.0	3.4	2.3	1.9
0.9	0.5	-	2.1	-	0.2	0.5
0.0	0.1	-	-	-	-	-
4.8	4.7	2.7	2.4	2.8	5.0	2.0
1.6	0.6	0.1	0.0	0.5	2.7	3.1
1.1	0.2	0.0	0.2	0.4	0.7	0.1

(continued)

Table 5.2 (*Continued*)

	Q1 2007	Q2 2007	Q3 2007	Q4 2007	Q1 2008
Developing Countries	55.1	57.8	23.1	28.6	22.0
Africa & Middle East	6.0	10.28	5.67	6.7	3.8
Egypt	0.8	-	1.06	-	-
South Africa	0.6	5.82	1.78	0.5	-
United Arab Emirates	3.2	3.58	1.51	4.8	3.2
Asia & Pacific	14.4	21.10	7.46	12.3	8.7
China	1.2	2.85	0.83	-	1.1
India	4.9	3.10	3.56	2.5	0.7
South Korea	4.3	10.45	2.21	7.3	3.1
Europe	16.42	13.50	3.17	4.1	4.7
Russia	6.1	5.79	0.62	0.3	0.3
Latin America & Caribbean	18.2	12.87	6.81	5.5	4.9
Argentina	0.7	4.82	0.47	0.2	0.0
Brazil	3.9	3.19	2.21	1.5	2.3
Mexico	2.2	1.58	2.16	1.6	1.6
International Organizations	36.7	30.01	32.30	36.3	50.9

Source: Bank for International Settlements (BIS), *BIS Quarterly Review*, June, September, and December 2009, March 2010.

As it sank the real economy, the crisis slashed demand for imported goods and services. After July 2008, prices of internationally traded commodities plunged, forcing many exporters of soybeans, iron ore, and oil to search for plan B. Global commerce stagnated and started collapsing in late 2008, and shrunk by 12.2 percent in 2009 (figure 5.4). This was the first decline since 1982, when developing countries were buried in debt and the United States wrestled with double-digit inflation, and the largest drop since the Second World War.

The buyers of last resort, American consumers, abandoned their malls, and the U.S. trade gap shrank to a monthly figure of $36 billion in January 2009, the lowest level in six years. Europeans also cut their purchases. As a result, the global money wheel slowed and Asian export-dependent

Q2 2008	Q3 2008	Q4 2008	Q1 2009	Q2 2009	Q3 2009	Q4 2009
45.6	19.4	5.3	27.7	51.3	53.9	63.8
9.2	2.0	0.2	2.3	14.0	7.7	9.5
0.1	-	-	-	-	-	-
0.5	-	0.1	0.1	2.4	0.6	-
6.3	2.0	-	0.2	6.2	4.8	1.9
12.6	6.4	3.0	10.9	15.7	20.4	13.6
0.1	2.6	-	-	1.0	2.2	1.4
0.0	-	1.0	-	-	1.2	2.8
9.1	2.8	2.0	6.1	12.7	9.2	3.9
15.7	9.1	0.1	6.3	12.1	8.9	12.3
3.3	5.7	-	-	3.0	0.7	1.0
8.1	1.9	2.1	8.3	9.5	16.8	28.5
0.1	0.2	0.0	0.1	0.1	0.1	0.1
1.9	0.9	0.1	1.5	4.1	5.1	6.8
1.1	0.3	2.0	3.7	3.7	5.0	8.8
47.0	28.6	43.7	59.6	84.1	35.9	30.2

nations suffered. The Japanese trade balance turned $1.8 billion negative in January, the biggest drop since the mid-1980s, when American imports from Asia dwindled. China's trade surplus, under $5 billion in February 2009, was down from $40 billion in each of the three previous months, and fell by nearly a third in 2009 from the 2008 levels. Global imbalances shrunk in 2009 to less than a half of the historical 2006 figures.

From Markets to Policies

The economic debacle would have profound effects on policy—domestic and international alike. But there would be a grand paradox. On the one hand, hard times underlined the importance of policies

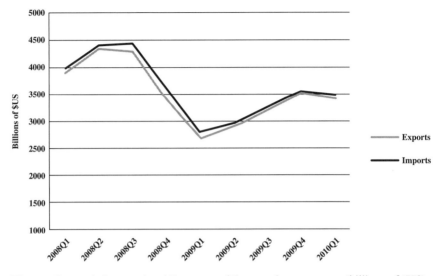

Fig. 5.4 Quarterly International Exports and Imports in 2008–2010 (billions of $US).
Source: World Trade Organization.

conducive to globalization as a means of reviving the world economy. In the past, trade and financial integration have served as powerful engines of growth and prosperity, as our prior chapters show, and this seems like a reasonable bet for the future. Globalization is not a magic bullet, but it has been an anchor during bad times; on many occasions throughout the postwar era, countries have dug themselves out of deep difficulties by exporting to world markets and borrowing from international banks.

On the other hand, the crisis, like any other turmoil of this scale, tempts a turn to isolationism, nationalism, and protectionism. It threatens the very policies that could jump-start recovery by drawing on the forces of globalization. In the precrisis period, some skeptics were already voicing their doubts about globalization; these skeptics now see the crisis as validating their suspicions. Job losses, industrial bankruptcies, and bank failures spark demands to severely regulate financial systems, and tempt policy makers to adopt protectionist measures ranging from higher tariffs to buy-domestic procurement. They also sap enthusiasm from trade liberalization.

Table 5.3 FDI Flows and M&A Activity in Select Economies, 2007–2009
(billions of $US)

Region/Economy	FDI Flows		Cross-Border M&As		
	2007	2008	2007	2008	2009
World	**1,978.8**	**1,697.4**	**1,031.1**	**706.5**	**239.9**
Developed Economies	**1,358.6**	**962.3**	**903.4**	**581.4**	**195.4**
Europe	899.6	518.3	557.5	273.3	127.1
European Union	842.3	503.5	526.5	251.2	109.6
Austria	29.6	13.6	9.7	1.3	1.8
Belgium	110.8	59.7	1.0	2.5	12.1
Czech Republic	10.4	10.7	0.1	5.2	2.7
Denmark	9.4	10.9	5.8	6.1	1.6
Finland	12.4	−4.2	8.3	1.2	0.5
France	158.0	100.7	28.2	4.6	1.3
Germany	56.4	24.9	44.0	31.9	2.4
Hungary	6.1	6.5	0.7	1.6	1.9
Ireland	24.7	−20.0	0.8	2.9	1.4
Italy	40.2	17.0	23.6	−2.4	1.1
Netherlands	118.4	−3.5	162.3	−8.2	22.6
Poland	22.6	16.5	0.7	1.0	0.5
Romania	9.9	13.3	1.8	1.0	0.0
Spain	37.0	65.5	51.7	33.7	31.5
Sweden	22.1	43.7	4.6	18.8	1.0
United Kingdom	183.4	96.9	171.0	147.7	24.9
United States	232.8	316.1	179.2	227.4	39.9
Japan	22.5	24.4	16.1	9.3	−5.9
Developing Economies	**529.3**	**620.7**	**97.0**	**104.8**	**37.7**
Africa	69.2	87.6	7.9	21.2	5.7
Egypt	11.6	9.5	1.7	15.9	1.6
Morocco	2.8	2.4	0.3	−0.1	0.3
South Africa	5.7	9.0	4.1	6.7	4.2
Latin America and the Caribbean	127.5	144.4	20.6	15.5	−4.4
Argentina	6.5	8.9	0.8	−3.3	0.1
Brazil	34.6	45.1	6.5	7.6	−1.4
Chile	12.6	16.8	1.4	3.2	0.8
Colombia	9.0	10.6	4.3	−0.1	−1.6
Mexico	27.3	21.9	3.7	2.3	0.1
Peru	5.5	4.8	1.1	0.3	0.0
Asia and Oceania	332.7	388.7	68.5	68.2	36.5

(*continued*)

Table 5.3 (*Continued*)

Region/Economy	FDI Flows		Cross-Border M&As		
	2007	2008	2007	2008	2009
West Asia	77.6	90.3	23.0	16.3	2.3
Turkey	22.0	18.2	16.4	13.2	1.6
South, East, and Southeast Asia	253.8	297.6	45.3	52.6	34.1
China	83.5	92.4	9.3	5.4	11.2
Hong Kong, China	54.4	63.0	7.0	8.7	2.1
India	25.1	41.6	4.4	10.4	6.2
Indonesia	6.9	7.9	1.7	2.1	1.3
Malaysia	8.4	8.1	3.9	2.8	0.2
Singapore	31.6	22.7	7.4	14.2	9.7
Thailand	11.2	4.6	2.4	0.1	0.3
Southeast Europe and the Commonwealth of Independent States	**90.9**	**69.3**	**30.7**	**20.3**	**6.8**
Russian Federation	55.1	41.4	22.8	13.5	5.0
Ukraine	9.9	4.8	1.8	5.9	0.2

Source: United Nations Conference on Trade and Development (UNCTAD) and UNCTAD Global Investment Trade Monitor No. 2, 19 January 2010, World Investment Report 2009.

In the wake of the crisis, economic policy making is no longer about fine-tuning the business cycle or boosting growth rates by a percent. The whole design of the economic system is now up for grabs. This is hardly reassuring, and opens many doors for new obstacles to global commerce and capital flows. Although economies will recover, unintended consequences await. Companies going under and governments taking over is not the best recipe for globalization.

How do we resolve the paradox that protectionism gains steam right when it is most destructive? That is our subject in the next four chapters. We are not in the business of advocating whole-scale repeal of globalization; economic integration is a positive force, quite unstoppable anyway and even better when allowed to flourish. But something will have to give; anxieties need to be addressed, some compromises should be struck, and some upgrades installed. We focus on key policies needed to get globalization back on track and to keep it there: revamping the global financial system, reigniting the Doha Round and reforming the creaky WTO, preempting hidden protection from trade to finance to investment, and reducing worker anxiety about the world economy.

6

A DANGEROUS TIME IN GLOBAL FINANCE

The financial crash in 2008 shattered global economic growth and many a worker's hope for early retirement—or stable employment. Mortgage overdrive was joined at the hip with a housing bubble, triggering a global financial crisis that obliterated lending and investing around the world. Equity and property markets slumped, trade collapsed, economies ground to a halt, and emerging economies from Pakistan to Hungary clamored for International Monetary Fund (IMF) assistance. The Great Crisis became the number one issue for prime ministers and presidents, business leaders, politicians from all parties, and policy makers across the spectrum from economics to national security.

The challenges before us are formidable: jump-starting the global economy while installing fire walls against future bubbles, and fashioning a new architecture of global finance to cope with future shocks. The challenges are inherently multilateral and thus bewilderingly difficult because many proposed fixes—in fiscal policy, monetary policy, financial regulations—pierce the heart of national sovereignty and threaten social contracts. Solutions do not easily lend themselves to multilateralism, tricky balancing acts are required.

The Drivers of the Debacle

Crises have been with us at least since the bursting of Tulip Mania in 1637 and the South Sea Bubble in 1720. But now we face a new problem— unprecedented speed and reach of contagion.

If finance is global, so are crises and so must be the responses. However, while it spurred some common action, the latest crisis prompted a lot more international finger-pointing—at Washington. It is common to say, and China has said it, that the root of the crisis was lax U.S. regulation and easy money during the Greenspan years.[1] While blaming America is politically opportune, it is only partly justified. The causes were more complex. Getting at the right answer will be critical for preventing future crises.

Thus far, four main hypotheses have dominated the back-and-forth debate about the origins of the Great Crisis; a full answer would probably combine these forces into a perfect storm.

The first hypothesis holds that the bubble was created by a U.S. money glut—low interest rates and low taxes—fashioned to safeguard the economy from panic after the September 11, 2001, terrorist attacks. Money glut theorists assert that well-intentioned policies paved the way to economic hell—heavy borrowing, low savings, a housing boom, and then a crash.

Led by Alan Greenspan—crowned the "greatest central banker in history" by economist Alan Blinder—central banks around the world placed an almost religious faith in efficient-market theory. They refused to consider whether asset bubbles might be driving stock and housing prices, let alone that central bankers should do anything.[2] The world economy clearly did need stimulation after 9/11, but many now say that the stimulation should have been channeled into productive public infrastructure and private investment, not poured into a consumer-driven buying spree, particularly of outsized homes and vacation condos. After all, in the wake of the Asian crisis of the late 1990s, China pursued the alternative path of productive infrastructure with great success, laying the foundation for a decade of rapid growth.

Instead, in America, mortgage loan originations ballooned more than 50 percent per year for three years, from $1.05 trillion in 2000 to $3.95 trillion in 2003. When the Federal Reserve finally woke up and began raising the federal funds rate in May 2004, the twenty-city Case-Shiller housing index had gained more than 15 percent during the preceding twelve months. It is the consumer-driven flavor of the 2005–2008 bubble that differentiates it from the earlier dot-com bubble and other financial crises. Steven Gjerstad and Nobel laureate Vernon Smith contend that when consumer debt is concentrated at the low end of the wealth distribution, crises can be transmitted fast and forcefully into the financial system.[3]

The second hypothesis points to global forces that inflated the bubble beyond all reason. Federal Reserve chairman Ben Bernanke and *Financial Times* columnist Martin Wolf argue that the Asian savings glut engendered an influx of foreign investment into the United States, which in turn kept real interest rates low and abetted the boom in U.S. asset prices.[4] China's export-generated dollar reserves (a trillion dollars by November 2006), high savings rate (more than 40 percent of gross domestic product, GDP), and low consumption (less than 50 percent of GDP) found a perfect match in low U.S. savings (practically zero at the height of the housing boom), an insatiable appetite for consumer goods, and world-class asset markets.

This lopsided pattern, wherein Asia sells and lends and America buys and borrows, was fostered by the Asian financial crisis. The crisis not only drove global capital to the world's safe haven, the United States; it also compelled the Asian nations to build their reserves through exports—often destined for the U.S. market—in order to cushion themselves against future shocks. During the decade beginning in 2000, Beijing and Tokyo invested their dollars in U.S. Treasury debt and quasi-government securities (Fannie Mae and Freddie Mac), allowing Americans to buy more and bigger houses. The Asian savings glut found its natural release in America.

The third hypothesis ascribes the bubble to unscrupulous lending practices, especially in the United States. Flimsy underwriting standards enabled mortgage loans to be extended in massive volume to subprime borrowers—Americans with a history of loan delinquency, outright bankruptcy, or insufficient income. By 2006, this shoddy segment grew to an astonishing one-quarter of the mortgage market.[5] Seeing a quick chance for the American Dream, Main Street accompanied Wall Street into exuberant overdrive.

Contemporary studies predicted that one in every five subprime loans would go into foreclosure, affecting more than 2 million homes.[6] Adjustable-rate subprime mortgages, the bulk of subprime lending, represented less than a tenth of all mortgages outstanding in the United States, yet they ended up accounting for more than 40 percent of foreclosures.

The fourth and now the most-favored hypothesis about the transformation of a housing bubble into a crisis of global proportions puts a heavy emphasis on the confluence of regulatory vacuums and financial engineering. In an effort to extricate itself from any responsibility for global financial imbalances, the IMF tries to argue that regulatory failures, along with money glut, were central to the story.[7] Financial innovators sliced risky housing loans into tranches and repackaged them into supposedly low-risk securities. This sausage machine had two defects: One, the total price of all the slices often exceeded, by a wide margin, an appropriate value for the underlying and still risky assets. Two, there was a severe disconnect between the package of slices and the originator of underlying loans—the mortgage originator was insulated from any penalty for creating bad assets after selling the loans into a pool and walking away.

Six years before the crash, Warren Buffett warned that derivative securities are financial "weapons of mass destruction."[8] And yet, at its height in 2007, the $55 *trillion* world market for derivatives went unregulated, even though the market was then bigger than world GDP. The derivatives market was dominated by credit default swaps, instruments that are essentially insurance policies for investors who lend money to corporations or buy mortgage-backed securities, although there were plenty of other financial instruments in the derivatives zoo. Self-regulation on Wall Street was only a nameplate. Risk managers were brought into the executive suite, but they were denied the power or the incentive to say no. Financial executives suspected they were building sand castles, but the guiding philosophy was to grab this year's bonus and move on before the waves washed in. For their part, central banks had scant idea about the leverage and risk that the top two hundred financial firms were concealing on their balance sheets.

Asset watchdogs, also known as rating agencies, failed on two important scores: objectivity and accountability. Moody's and Standard & Poor's relied on statistical databases from an earlier era of housing finance to award double- and triple-A ratings, while buyers of engineered securities understood nothing beyond the letter grade. Ratings agencies faced no legal liabilities for misleading assessments and had every incentive to give easy grades, since issuers gladly paid the agencies for inflated ratings.

Meanwhile, excessive leverage was used to enhance profits on rising asset values. False confidence was the flavor of the day.

Ultimately, the speculation in exotic financial instruments came to tears. Risk that had been buried surfaced quickly once the housing bubble began to deflate; confidence evaporated and assets were dumped. Consumer debt crashed and the consumption binge came to an end. The great global deleveraging was on its way. Credit evaporated and economies contracted.

The Crisis Response

The global financial free fall in the fall of 2008 prompted British Prime Minister Gordon Brown to call for Bretton Woods II, a full-fledged revision of global economic governance. Both to keep control of the ball and to recognize the weight of emerging countries, President George W. Bush convened an emergency meeting of G20 leaders, on November 15, 2008. The list of participants—including such emerging nations as China, India, Brazil, Indonesia, and Mexico—was far more momentous than the agreed action plan. For the first time, twenty heads of state, rather than the usual seven or eight, debated the financial issues of the hour, a watershed.

The G20 action plan called for financial market transparency, complete and accurate disclosure by firms, and no more "excessive risk taking" by banks and financial institutions. An international "college of supervisors" was supposed to ensure implementation. The plan also asked finance ministers to craft a list of financial institutions whose collapse would endanger the global economy. The final call was a standstill on protection, including export controls and trade barriers.

Simon Johnson, former chief economist of the International Monetary Fund, complained, "[T]his is plain-vanilla stuff they could have agreed on without holding a meeting."[9] Nor were global equity markets much impressed. The Dow fell more than 200 points (or 2.3 percent) from the Friday before the summit, the United Kingdom's FTSE 100 was down 1.1 percent, Germany's DAX fell by 0.9 percent, and France's CAC-40 fell by 1 percent. The luster of the G20 was tarnished when the World Bank reported in March 2009 that seventeen of them had breached their commitments not to create new trade barriers.[10]

Stimulus vs. Super-Regulators

The second G20 summit in April 2009, convened in London, fell far short of Prime Minister Gordon Brown's ambitious aspirations for a Bretton Woods II conclave that would re-create the multilateral trade and financial systems of the twenty-first century. The preparations were clouded by stark differences on the fundamental issues between two camps. The Obama administration, along with the United Kingdom and Japan, argued for more stimulus from the other governments, while the Europeans and Chinese—in part fearful of inflation and fiscal deficits, in part happy to free ride on U.S. stimulus—balked at the idea. The Europeans sought sturdy, global financial regulations and global supervision, while the United States instinctively wanted to keep regulatory policy in the hands of national officials.

The G20 declaration quite expectedly struck a middle ground. The three proxies for global stimulus sought by the Obama administration were to restock the IMF with $500 billion in new lending capacity, to create $250 billion of new Special Drawing Rights (SDRs, a sort of international money), and to provide fresh trade finance on the order of $250 billion (circulated and recirculated over two years). The language on global regulatory coordination was agreeable enough to the French. The summiteers also pledged to oppose protectionism and to conclude the eight-year Doha Trade Round, albeit without a date certain. Along with the concurrent European Central Bank's interest rate drop, the communiqué elated markets and encouraged consumers. The Dow rose 1.2 percent; Britain's FTSE 100 closed up 4.3 percent; Germany's DAX swelled 6.1 percent; and France's CAC 40 jumped 5.4 percent. A week later, as Obama was finishing his European tour, U.S. consumer confidence was up for the first time in weeks.[11]

The third G20 in Pittsburgh defied doubters. Besides resolving to clamp down on bonuses earned on Wall Street and concluding the Doha Trade Round by the end of 2010, the summit produced two major results. The first was a pledge to expand the say and sway of emerging markets in the IMF by increasing their quota by 5 percentage points to 48 percent of the total. The U.S.-sponsored idea will go some way toward addressing the grudge held by China and India vis-à-vis the IMF's founding fathers and dominant members, Europe and the United States.

The second result was the "framework for strong, sustainable and balanced growth," code for macroeconomic policy coordination among the main economies, with some degree of peer review by the lead countries themselves, and oversight by the IMF. While purported for the longer haul, the initiative is aimed at propelling domestic demand in China, Germany, and Japan in lieu of their dependence on U.S.-bound exports—a pattern that the Obama administration has deemed unsustainable given the twin facts of growing U.S. external debt and dampened U.S. consumer demand. This idea for rebalancing global growth is strikingly similar to that pursued in the mid-1980s, with the main difference being that instead of China, the main source of U.S. trade deficits was the other Asian dragon, Japan. The renowned 1985 Plaza Agreement succeeded at committing the United States—also then the world's consumer of last resort—to tighten its fiscal policy, compelling Japan to boost private demand through tax reform, and persuading Germany to stimulate its economy by cutting taxes.

Delivering the Goods

In light of high anxiety levels, divergent agendas, and shared incentives to safeguard national prerogatives, the G20 summits produced a decent working agenda. The immediate test for the G20 is to live up to its commitments—to channel new funding to the IMF, revamp financial regulations, avoid a protectionist tide, restart the Doha Round, and retire America's burden to propel the world economy. These measures would show the world and the markets that G20 is a body that can do the world's business. The acid test for the G20 is black-and-white: will the agreed measures revive and rebalance the global economy?

It will be a challenge to pull off the commitments, and perhaps a greater challenge to restart the engine of world economic growth. The U.S. Congress and other parliamentary bodies have to deliver more than $1 trillion of new money to the international financial institutions (IFIs), especially the IMF. The Obama administration along with European, Japanese, Chinese, Indian, and Brazilian leaders must step up to the plate to arrest the spread of protectionism and resume global trade talks. And the G20 faces the very same issue that has shackled the G system throughout its multiple incarnations from a G4 to a G8, and now G20: implementing the internationally agreed macroeconomic policy changes when they may clash with domestic political imperatives.

The G20 summitry reflects two fundamental propositions about multilateral economic governance. First, domestic political economy equations rule on fiscal policy. Except for Plaza, the subsequent Louvre agreement, and a few occasions in the late 1970s, the G system has self-censored strong commitments for policy changes, and instead focused on information sharing and debate on global policy issues. German voters still recall the hyperinflation of the 1920s as an era that hurried in Hitler; and they dread inflation, even if its prevention comes at the expense of growth. This stifles the Merkel government's hand in enacting heavy countercyclical measures. China seemed to take U.S. warnings more seriously, and Beijing issued forceful stimulus programs. But the motivator is primarily a domestic one: China's reckoning that exports to the American market can no longer be the only solution to the question of how to deliver jobs to an army of marginally employed and restive workers who now live in the impoverished Western provinces.

The second proposition about global economic rule making is that financial oversight remains a sovereign prerogative right alongside the power to print money. Finance has always been an oasis of national protection, an area where supranationalism is difficult to attain.[12] Even if sharing a common currency, European states are only now amenable to turning oversight and supervisory functions over to new EU-wide bodies—and even then the national regulators and other agencies still play an important role.[13] So, on the regulatory side, full global convergence is hard if not impossible to achieve. But positively, there is the genuine likelihood that, by allowing distinct regulatory models to bloom, better practices will be discovered. Monocrop global regulation would likely be watered down to reflect the lowest common denominator; by contrast, higher standards can be shaped to the contours of national circumstances. To be sure, there are vexing issues where greater coordination should be accomplished in order for global finance to flow unobstructed. The existing tools for cross-border crisis management are blunt at best. The lack of common rules on ways to deal with bank failures can entice countries to seal themselves off from cross-border finance, lest their taxpayers face the awful experience of a foreign bank going bust on home soil.

Going Forward

In the midst of crisis management, it is natural to put aside the underlying problems confronting the world economy. But certain issues must be addressed going forward, ensuring the solvency of the global financial system and preventing future tragedies.

Gatorade to the System

The chain of events in the fall of 2008 was a setback for the proponents of global financial liberalization. "Why should we not insulate ourselves," many are asking, "from the reckless greed of Wall Street?" The most immediate temptation is to impose strict controls on the movement of portfolio capital in order to combat financial panic and to stave off speculator sprees, on the argument that one encounter with Wall Street's toxic waste is quite enough. When emerging countries in an earlier time imposed their own capital controls—Chile in the 1980s and Malaysia in the 1990s—clucks of disapproval were voiced in financial circles. After the United States started a financial avalanche, such criticism has had less force.

Capital controls are a controversial and polarizing subject. As we discuss in chapter 2, some scholars—perhaps most notably Harvard's Dani Rodrik—think controls help developing countries flatten their boom and bust cycles. To cite just one example, Morocco, a moderately prosperous nation in North Africa with close economic ties to Europe but also with strict capital controls, was little affected by the 2008 crisis. Other scholars emphasize the cost of capital controls. Not only can they dampen inward foreign direct investment (FDI)—contrast the difference between India and China over the past fifteen years—but also the prospect of tighter controls can discourage foreign investors from bringing money to the country when times are tough, for fear that funds will be frozen when political winds change course. This was exactly what happened in Thailand in 2006, when leaders briefly flirted with capital controls to stop foreigners from pushing up the value of the baht: stocks plummeted 15 percent virtually overnight. Late in 2009, Brazil experimented with a 2 percent tax on inward portfolio investment to arrest the upward drift of the reais; the consequences of this latest episode remain to be seen.

Looking forward over the next decade, the widespread reinstatement of controls would quell flows to emerging countries at the historical moment when they are positioned to absorb large quantities of foreign capital in their debt and equity markets—and at a time when lower consumer spending in the United States and other rich nations needs to be balanced by higher capital outlays in developing countries. Given the vast funding needs of the United States and a few other advanced countries, simply to finance fiscal deficits, emerging markets already risk being crowded out in international financial markets. Adopted on a wide scale, national policies aimed at taming inward flows would send the wrong message, compounding the injury.

Rather than bright line limits on flows, regulated financial institutions should be subject to tough internal risk standards, information requirements, and detailed quarterly disclosures of their portfolios. The scope of regulated financial institutions should include banks and thrifts that gather deposits, broker dealers in securities markets, insurance companies, money market funds, and big issuers of short-term commercial paper.

Two key goals should guide these endeavors: First, to ensure that loans extended and assets acquired by regulated financial institutions are matched by reliable earnings streams or ready assets on the part of borrowers and issuers. Second, to make certain that the equity capital base and liquid assets held by the regulated institutions are adequate to weather a significant downturn in the business cycle. For example, while the "normal" equity capital base (assuming the asset side of the institution's balance sheet is marked to market) might be 10 percent, it should be lowered in bad times and increased in good times in order to counter procyclical lending behavior. Minimum liquid assets—meaning government debt akin to Treasury bills—might be set at 10 percent of total assets.

Standards that carried out these simple prescriptions have so far eluded the best and brightest among our financial regulators. For example, under Basel II, any commercial lending by banks would be subject to an 8 percent capital requirement, regardless of the creditworthiness of the borrower. The figure may or may not be too low for normal times, but more importantly, there is no requirement that banks hold adequate liquid assets, and most significant, the Basel II standards did not apply to broker dealers, insurance companies, and other financial institutions. Even as applied to banks, Basel II was full of holes when the crisis hit, not worth 251 pages of complex text. Large banks were allowed to use their own internal ratings to assess risk and measure capital. U.S. banks were only scheduled to start implementing it. Nonbank financial institutions such as AIG, GE Capital, and broker dealers were not covered by the system. Liquidity requirements as distinct from capital requirements were not articulated. This is a serious problem: capital is one thing—an accountant's guess as to the difference between assets and liabilities, both marked to market—but liquidity is quite different, ready cash in the form of Treasury bills or deposits with the Federal Reserve.

To the limited extent it had an effect, Basel II worked in a procyclical fashion. Capital requirements did not rise in the asset boom, and internal rating systems were rigged to indicate lower rather than higher risk. As housing and other asset prices rose, it seemed that everyone could get rich by participating in the credit boom, either by borrowing heavily to buy an "investment home," packaging and selling mortgage-backed securities, or writing credit default swaps. Once the financial crisis struck, everyone tried to unload assets—and, of course, that guaranteed a plunge in asset values. Institutions suddenly became wary of extending new credit because the next borrower might default just like the last one.

New Rules of the Game

The laissez-faire spirit of Basel II made for bipolar finance: the highs are truly high, but the lows are really low. The roller coaster not only accentuates the business cycle domestically, but also curtails the provision of credit and trade finance to foreign borrowers when the global economy turns sour. A new Basel accord, if it is written, should remedy this fault by "through-the-cycle" rating methodologies that filter out the impact of the business ups and downs.[14] More importantly, a new accord should cover the full range of regulated financial institutions, require much better internal risk assessments, and impose tough capital requirements and liquidity standards.

We are not optimistic that the Financial Stability Board (FSB), given a new name and a fresh mandate by the G20, will be up to the task, at least not in the near future. Much will have to be done by national regulators, perhaps working in tandem with the FSB. In his landmark book *Manias, Panics and Depressions*, first published in 1978, Charles Kindleberger concluded that financial crises are "hardy perennials" of the world economy. This is a gloomy thought, but at the very least, our challenge is to ensure that the next crisis does not just copy 2008.

Both the European Union nations and the United States have issued proposals for comprehensive regulatory reform. With varying degrees of rigor, the plans center on consolidated regulatory power in order to avoid the current overlap and fragmentation of authority, and to ensure sturdy oversight of financial markets. In Europe, the mechanisms for doing this are now increasingly regionalized. On both sides of the Atlantic, entities that previously escaped regulation altogether, like hedge funds and private equity firms, would be subjected to registration requirements, and their risk-management practices would be scrutinized. The standards on capital and risk management for systemically important firms would be increased; the U.S. plan also calls for a "systemic risk regulator," possibly the Federal Reserve, to second-guess the operations of large bank holding companies like Citigroup or JPMorgan Chase and insurance conglomerates like AIG and Chubb. And pressed by the more populist parts of the U.S. and European governments, the reformers also have vowed to clamp down on executive pay and on financial derivative instruments, like credit default swaps.

Regulatory changes will have major international extensions. The crisis laid bare the fact that while financial regulations are still national, financial firms are global. Although banks operate across borders, cross-border crisis resolution—particularly methods to resolve an ailing, systemically important bank—remains a national affair, even within Europe. The fact that each country has its own resolution laws and entities sets the stage for a massive coordination problem among national regulators when parts of a financial conglomerate scattered across many countries start to fail. Confidence in the conglomerate can be lost quickly if confusion and chaos reign, rather than a clear and unified stance among the various regulators either to preempt the impending failure or to unwind the financial institution altogether.

We are thus at a fork in the road; the choice is between either an expansion of the regulatory prerogatives of national governments over foreign banks (and thus potential disincentives for full-blown globalization) or more coordinated global regulation and crisis management principles (paving the way for global expansion of financial institutions). The most immediate moves may be down the first path.

Over the Top

Enacting any meaningful reforms will entail major political battles—battles that are still brewing at the time of this writing. But an equal if more distant challenge is avoiding regulatory overstretch, and undoing a clampdown if it occurs. The risk of regulatory excesses runs high now that voters are livid. The shift in power toward national capitals will invite legislative exuberance. The road is short from the politics of crisis management to the politicization of crisis management.

Much has already happened without government action: financial service firms, duly chastened, are getting better at self-regulation. In July 2008, an industry association, the Institute of International Finance (IIF), issued its own 170-page blueprint of best practices, which proposed multiple reforms for capital market players, ranging from risk management (give boards an oversight role) to valuation (use sensitivity analysis) and ratings (scrutinize with internal and external reviews). The IIF dedicated 2009 to monitoring the implementation of these measures among its membership. Ratings agencies have sought to mend their ways by demanding that originators and underwriters provide more detailed information and by seeking standardized collateralized debt obligation (CDO) ratings.

Official regulators have not yet finalized their own reforms. But two issues need to be managed going forward. The first is to avoid curbing financial innovation. In the 1970s, when futures and options were making their appearance, they were widely regarded as dangerous bits of engineering. Going back in time, in the nineteenth century, stock exchanges were equated with gambling parlors. To be sure, recent innovations such as CDOs and constant proportion debt obligations (CPDOs) have brought enormous grief.[15] But more often than not, financial innovations that were accepted in the marketplace have proven useful over time. They link savers with investors, hedge against commodity and currency fluctuations, and foster cross-border trade and investment. Since the minds of financial innovators will forever outpace the imagination of regulators, rigid approval processes will generally prove counterproductive. Prosperity, dynamism, and job creation all depend on financial risk taking.

Second, regulators should be wary of legal obligations that would trigger civil penalties when ignored. *Caveat emptor* should not be killed. Class action litigation in the securities markets has already become big business. In 2008, a total of 210 federal securities class actions were filed, 9 percent above the 192 filed on average for the years 1997 to 2007. Financial companies were defendants in 103 of the crisis-related cases filed in 2008. The maximum potential dollar liability hit an all-time high at $856 billion.[16]

Public policy will not necessarily be served by further expanding the scope of legal obligations. The legislative response to accounting gimmicks at Enron, WorldCom, and other posters of corporate fraud is instructive. In July 2002, Congress enacted the Sarbanes-Oxley Act, which came to be known as Sarbox or just SOX. The legislation reformed standards and reporting requirements for all U.S. public company boards, management, and public accounting firms. It aimed at tightening auditor independence, improving corporate governance, inserting rigor to internal control assessments, and enhancing financial disclosure. SOX also made senior executives individually responsible for the accuracy and completeness of corporate financial reports, and established corporate fraud and records tampering as criminal offenses.[17]

In short order, SOX was widely criticized for expensive reporting, and was blamed for sending young companies needing equity capital to financial centers other than New York—London, Hong Kong, and Shanghai. Marshall Carter, chairman of the New York Stock Exchange (NYSE), claimed in congressional testimony that only 5.7 percent of the money raised by non-U.S. initial public offerings (IPOs) was raised on U.S. exchanges in 2005, compared to 46.8 percent in 2000, and that only thirty-five foreign IPOs were listed on U.S. exchanges in 2005, compared to 100 IPOs in 2000.[18] A Wharton study counted 198 companies that delisted from U.S. exchanges in the year after SOX was passed, three times the figure of the previous year.[19] In 2006, Russell Reynolds Associates reported that 70 percent of the European companies not listed on U.S. exchanges would be dissuaded by SOX from seeking a U.S. listing.[20] The London Stock Exchange advertised that because of SOX, non-U.S. companies find London a more attractive listing than New York.[21]

To be sure, SOX may have averted new Enrons in the financial crisis of 2008–2009. And while SOX certainly inflicted disclosure costs on U.S.-based companies—and brought happiness to countless college graduates searching for a safe and lucrative career in auditing—it was not the only cause of the migration from U.S. financial markets.[22] SOX also may have inspired enhanced financial reporting, strengthened auditor independence, and reformed corporate governance around the world.

The lesson from the SOX episode of the not-so-distant past is clear: new regulations can have unintended consequences, both good and bad, and rules must be weighed and reconsidered in light of experience. Rules that make good politics today may not stand the test of time, particularly in the fast-changing world of finance. Automatic sunset requirements should be written into crisis-inspired regulation to ensure a review after five or ten years.[23]

Balancing the World's Accounts

Besides new regulations, global financial crisis prevention requires a sharp reduction in global financial imbalances. As Ben Bernanke and Martin Wolf have argued, imbalances were among the drivers of the crisis, not only by keeping real interest rates low in the United States, but more importantly by pushing cash into the hands of U.S. consumers who proved unable to "just say no."

But persistent global imbalances do not just happen by accident; they are caused by deliberate forces. The U.S. dollar has long served as the world's reserve currency, a role that practically guarantees structural deficits in the U.S. balance of payments. How else can foreign countries acquire dollars except by selling more to the United States than they buy?

The great lesson for developing countries coming out of the Asian financial crisis in the late 1990s was to build vast war chests of foreign exchange reserves as insurance against the next crisis. And build they did: the combined foreign exchange reserves of just the five main emerging markets—China, India, Russia, Brazil, and Korea—rose tenfold between 2000 and 2008, from some $300 billion in 2000 to more than $3 trillion in 2008.[24] China was the leader, with a hoard of $1.9 trillion at the end of 2008, followed by Russia, India, and South Korea. The main way for

China and others to acquire these massive stockpiles was to run large trade surpluses with the United States, since Japan was also in the business of building up its foreign exchange reserves, and the European Central Bank managed the euro in a fashion designed to avoid large trade deficits.

Besides the quest for foreign exchange reserves, global imbalances have another cause: the "glut of savings" (a phrase coined by Bernanke), meaning that productive investment opportunities around the world are less abundant than the desire of individual households to acquire financial claims. Thrifty households are not the norm in America, but they are common in China, India, Korea, Japan, Germany, and many other nations. In a capital-starved world, where the average per capita GDP in 2007 ranged from $1,000 in less-developed countries to $11,000 in upper-middle-income countries and compared to $46,000 in privileged America, why can't more opportunities for productive investment be found?

There are many reasons, but foremost are two obstacles. Around the world, vast investment opportunities are reserved to public corporations which, as a political matter, are required to operate as money-losing operations in the name of universal access. This description applies to water, electricity, highways, urban roads, universities, schools, and hospitals. Beyond these lost opportunities, other investment avenues are foreclosed by the government's inability to overcome local opposition to the construction of valuable infrastructure. This curse bedevils electric transmission lines, gas pipelines, nuclear power plants, highways, ports, and airports.

The clamor for foreign exchange reserves coupled with the global savings glut practically guarantees that the United States will run large trade deficits, year after year. To be sure, the economic slump curtailed America's epic trade gap to an annual rate of about $375 billion in 2009, a little more than half the precrisis norm. The slump also cut the Chinese trade surplus approximately in half. And yet, the imbalances seem certain to rebound.

Despite the vigorous spending and lending in China to stave off the shocks of dampened global demand, one is hard-pressed to identify structural changes that might herald a new equilibrium in the world economy. After the Great Crisis, more urgently than before, countries will want to enlarge their foreign exchange war chests. And we do not see any grand opening of investment opportunities that are now foreclosed by government action and inaction. Instead, many countries, particularly China and India, seem ready to return to their export-dependent growth strategies once the global economy recovers. Currency values reflect these underlying forces. Neither China, nor Japan, nor the European Union wants its currency to appreciate strongly vis-à-vis the dollar. Rather, it seems that Asians and Europeans are waiting for America to resume importing and to carry the world economy with renewed enthusiasm for private consumption and public deficits.

This pattern, whereby America buys and borrows and Asia sells and lends, is in theory nothing bad, but it may not be sustainable from an economic standpoint as it presupposes sustained inflow of money to America from foreigners. Continued imbalances are also politically problematic and they are bad for trade policy. Congress has long, if erroneously, flagged the U.S. trade deficit with China as a leading cause of job losses. Huge imbalances that are absorbed by consumer borrowing and public debt are a long-term recipe for financial crisis; in the meantime, they spawn bad policy.

While all key players—the United States, the European Union, Japan, and China—must be on board to address global accounts, particularly critical are Washington and Beijing. The United States and China are not only interdependent economically; their bilateral relationship critically shapes world trade and finance. Michael Pettis of Beijing University points out that China is now playing the role the United States played in the 1920s.[25] The U.S. economy then ran large trade surpluses, equal to 0.4 percent or more of global GDP, about the same as China does today. The 1929 crash cut off funding for countries with trade deficits, eliminating the ability of foreign markets to absorb U.S. export capacity, and therefore required a corresponding U.S. adjustment. The United States either had to increase domestic consumption or cut domestic production. As the 1930s unfolded, cascading policy errors forced the United States to cut production. A similar rendezvous with history is now in the making, but the players have changed sides.

While the comparison between China today and the United States in the 1930s may be flawed, avoiding a rerun of the 1930s is the imperative of our times. The new Strategic and Economic Dialogue between Washington and Beijing, first launched by the George W. Bush administration, is a step in the right direction for taming what many call China's currency mercantilism—encouraging domestic consumption instead of recycling profits within state-owned industrial behemoths in China, and promoting savings and fiscal frugality in the United States.

Two further items could be added to an already full agenda: discussing a supplement to the dollar (per China's demands), and opening investment opportunities that have been blocked too long by government action and inaction (per U.S. demands).

Supplementing the Greenback?

After the G20 meeting in London, Zhou Xiaochuan, governor of China's central bank, in a snub to the United States, argued that financial crises resulted when the domestic needs of the country issuing a reserve currency clashed with international needs for stability. Zhou called for a reform through the creation of a supersovereign reserve currency managed by a global institution both to create and control global liquidity. Clearly his model was the Special Drawing Right (SDR), ledger entries on the books of the International Monetary Fund.[26]

While the dollar will continue as the premier money for years to come, the issue of alternative arrangements should be on the agenda. One of the main reasons is the future expansion of global commerce. By the end of 2008, global official foreign exchange reserves amounted to about $7 trillion, of which 64 percent were denominated in U.S. dollars. China held about a third of the total. The figure was slightly more than a tenth of the global GDP, and around 40 percent of global imports. In the aftermath of the Great Crisis, countries will want to maintain or even increase their reserve-to-import ratios as insurance against the next Great Crisis.

Now look into 2020: a "back of the envelope" calculation shows that just to keep up with global import growth—which at least in previous years was almost 10 percent annually—official global reserves should grow to around $20 trillion, meaning another $13 trillion on top of present levels. If the United States adopts responsible fiscal policies, limiting its external current account deficit to no more than 2 percent of GDP annually over the next decade, and if it grows at a very robust 5 percent a year, the maximum net addition of dollars to foreign official reserves would be about

$4.5 trillion.[27] That leaves a yawning gap in demand for official reserves of about $8.5 trillion.

Alternatives exist for creating these reserves, but all the alternatives require extreme levels of political commitment. The SDRs are one alternative, but even after the G20 pledged to issue a new round of SDRs worth $250 billion, the total will be under 5 percent of all official reserves. Conceivably, the great powers of international finance—the United States, the European Union, Japan, and China—might permit the IMF to acquire the trappings of a world central bank and issue SDRs in sufficient quantity to satisfy rising world demand for official reserves. This solution—attractive as it might be to ivory-tower academics—seems far off. But more SDRs, if not $9 trillion, perhaps as much as $1 trillion, might be part of the answer. In fact, since SDRs are bound to become more political the bigger they grow, a complementary role for them in the global currency picture seems more viable than making SDRs the core solution.

Other answers can be contemplated as well. The currency giants alongside the United States—namely the European Union, Japan, and China—seem unlikely to engineer macroeconomic policies that would deliver current account deficits, rather than current account surpluses that have long been in their DNA. With different policies, these three currency giants together might contribute half as much as the United States to the global pot of official reserves—maybe $2 trillion. But first they need to wake up to the fact that this time deficit problems are really serious in America. And countries around the world must be willing to stuff euros, yen, and yuan in their official foreign exchange holdings.

Another answer might be the old hat trick—currency swaps between central banks, whereby each party counts the swap line *received* as a *foreign exchange asset* and the swap line *extended* as a *domestic liability*. Voila! Both central banks can record an increase in their foreign exchange reserves, but neither country needs to show rising external liabilities on its books. China could be a leader: in April 2009, the Middle Kingdom completed a series of currency swaps with Argentina, Hong Kong, Indonesia, Malaysia, South Korea, and others. These supplied Chinese yuan on the order of $95 billion to the other central banks. If the European Central Bank and the Bank of Japan follow suit, perhaps the old hat trick can be scaled up to fill the gap in demand for foreign exchange reserves.

If all else fails, there is always the option of resurrecting the official role of that most-enduring currency—gold. Today, the G20 countries collectively hold about 1,000 million ounces of gold in their central banks. Valued at the "official price" of around $42 per ounce, these holdings are worth less than $50 billion. If the central banks agreed to a new official price near today's market price, around $1,000 per ounce, they could create reserves worth about $1 trillion. But to make a real difference, gold would have to be massively revalued from the current market price of about $1,000 per ounce to about $5,000 per ounce. That would suddenly create $5 trillion of new official reserves—to be sure, distributed in a very lopsided manner between countries. But $5 trillion, on top of the other answers we have sketched earlier, might just balance the supply of official reserves against the growing demand in a flourishing world economy.

There is another side to the pursuit of rebalanced world economy: investment barriers. American and other foreign businesses seeking to invest in developing countries often incur serious headaches. As we catalog in chapter 9, one of the most open developing countries, China, has tightened its scrutiny over investment inflows and expanded the discretion of regulators to interpret competition rules in order to favor state-owned companies that are "relied upon by the national economy and national security."[28] China has arbitrarily blocked or complicated a number of deals. In March 2009, it rejected Coca-Cola Company's $2.3 billion bid for China's Huiyuan Juice Group Ltd. for obscure reasons. Resolving these issues before new investment barriers boomerang around the world will be good for America and China alike.

Learning the Lessons

Assuming that human beings continue to be entrepreneurial optimists with short memories, bull market euphoria will one day return, regulators will fall behind the curve, and new excesses will emerge. However great our success in delaying the next crisis, eventually it will strike; meanwhile, the policy tool kit needs to be updated. Academics will have to analyze three questions just as carefully as the Great Depression has been studied, and deliver their answers to the crisis managers of the future.

The first is the size of response and the division between monetary and fiscal measures. Keynesians, whose ranks swelled amid the crisis to claim many a fiscal conservative, argue that public spending on a vast scale may be needed to forestall outright depression. But as the Great Crisis unfolded, many, including the authors, felt an attack of vertigo when it appeared that the gaping U.S. deficit would gobble more than 10 percent of GDP and that it might take years to squeeze deficits down to 3 percent of GDP. Much of the $787 billion Obama stimulus package passed in February 2009 will spread money around to green energy, education, and state budgets, along with "shovel-ready" infrastructure projects. Expensive health care and energy security programs are waiting in the wings, alongside the relentless growth of Medicare and Social Security entitlements. Unless arrested, lavish and prolonged budget deficits could undermine the U.S. economy and America's standing in the world. Indeed, countries that have so far financed America's fiscal excesses, including China, might eventually call a time-out.[29]

The U.S. answer to the Great Crisis embraces a heavy dose of monetary expansion along with fiscal deficits. Eagerness to pump liquidity in the system stems from lessons learned in the 1930s, when Treasury secretary Andrew Mellon famously declared, "liquidate labor, liquidate stocks, liquidate farmers." Mellon's approach helped turn a bad recession into the Great Depression. What was needed was not liquidation but liquidity. Japanese policy makers, however, failed to provide liquidity when the country's real estate market collapsed in the early 1990s; and policy shortcomings helped ensure a decade of stagnation. A big advantage of the liquidity approach is that money pumped into the system can be pumped out later, as the economy recovers. In fact, the subsequent sale of assets acquired by the central bank in a crisis can help moderate the next asset bubble. But rapid and convincing monetary responses that reassure markets and enable troubled financial institutions to stay in business are almost certain to infuriate voters, who can only see fat cats being rescued. One way to alleviate the tension that became popular in the Great Crisis, is to fire the officers and directors of failing institutions and put a tight cap on salaries and bonuses. The real benefits of this are questionable.

If liquidity remains the central answer, even if supplemented by public spending, the second issue to resolve is the proper target of financial rescue packages. Bank bailouts emerged in a good light following the example of Sweden's rescue of its banking system in 1992, at the tail end of a property boom. The Swedish government took over bad debts and nationalized the banks. Sweden initially acquired assets equivalent to 4 percent of GDP in the rescue process, but ended up footing a fiscal cost of only 2 percent of GDP. The fiscal cost was low because, in the end, the government received solid returns when it later took the banks public.

In the Great Crisis, the United States took a different tack. The government injected capital into banks and insurance companies, guaranteed the debt of Fannie Mae and Freddie Mac, and provided incentives for well-heeled private firms to buy "toxic" real estate–related securities held by banks on their crumbling balance sheets. Keeping score is hard, but in terms of capital at risk, the amount comes to around 10 percent of GDP, when actions by the Treasury, the Federal Reserve, and the Federal Deposit Insurance Corporation (FDIC) are combined. In the end, as in Sweden's example, the fiscal cost could be far less if bank shares are ultimately sold at a profit, if guarantees are not called, and if "toxic" assets ultimately pay out at 60 cents on the dollar rather than 25 cents. The political catch-22, if roses come up, is that many of those who caused the mess will benefit from fixing it.

At the time of this writing, the U.S. government has bailed out not only financial service firms but also car companies; this has inspired other sectors to put out their begging bowls. Japan, Korea, Germany, France, and Canada also have poured billions into their car companies. Unless a sick entity can sink wide swaths of the economy, this approach makes less sense than letting the market pick the survivors. But politically it is tough to say no to a sector that directly and indirectly employs millions, supports hundreds of thousands of retirees, and tells the public that it only needs a bridge loan to weather the moment.

The third issue going forward concerns the management of bailout and support processes. Who regulates that? There are two dimensions— checks and balances in the government and conditions on the beneficiaries. The secretary of the U.S. Treasury was given broad discretion to spend and manage the initial $700 billion bailout package (known as the Troubled Assets Relief Program, or TARP).[30] Many Americans viewed this as usurpation of power, and the broad mandate had the unfortunate effect of creating uncertainty in the markets: where would the money flow, and who would get bailed out?[31] Subsequent off-budget crisis measures by the Federal Reserve raised the same problems, with many accusing it of venturing into the congressional territory of fiscal policy. Later, the proposal that the Federal Reserve be made the systemwide monitor of health and stability for all financial firms raised fears that it would acquire too much power, and might be conflicted in its roles of safeguarding price stability and warding off financial collapse. This debate rages in Congress, and we can only ask, when the next crisis erupts, whether a happier balance will be found between oversight and accountability on the one hand, and the need for rapid and decisive responses on the other.[32]

One way to bypass politics and checks and balances issues is by creating an independent, prestigious "shadow cabinet" that issues thought-out, weighty, and attention-grabbing pronouncements about economic matters. Such a council could be tasked with raising red flags about emerging bubbles and making recommendations on raising (or reducing) margin requirements on shares and bonds, initial margins on regulated commodity exchanges, down payments on houses and other real estate, and so forth. Thus far, this job has been discharged in an ad hoc, decentralized fashion by independent analysts with a penchant for doomsday scenarios, rather than in a centralized and authoritative fashion. Even without powers of implementation, the usefulness of such an advisory board—perhaps structured as a semiofficial and decidedly bipartisan body—could be great.

The fourth conundrum is what makes a firm "systemically important" and "too big to fail," and, more radically, whether companies of such size should exist to begin with. Economists agreed that the collapse of certain giants—AIG, Citigroup, Washington Mutual, and Wachovia—would trigger a financial tsunami. There also was the realization that while size mattered, it was the interconnectedness of the major firms to each other and to other market players (like hedge funds) that rendered them systemically risky. In hindsight, it seems that Treasury secretary Paulson's great mistake was not recognizing that Lehman was, in fact, too big and too interconnected to fail. By driving it to the ground on September 15, 2009, the secretary turned a $100 billion problem into a $2 trillion problem. In the future, as in the past, officials may be reluctant to announce a clear definition of "systemically important," for fear they will disadvantage firms outside the charmed ring and inspire moral hazard for firms inside. In our view, official reluctance must give way to clear and present danger when the crisis strikes. If the line is not clear, panic can engulf the strongest and biggest players—in the recent episode, these included General Electric, JPMorgan Chase, and even Fidelity. Moral hazard is no reason to stop the fire trucks when the whole neighborhood is burning, even if residents never paid their property taxes.

A radical answer, advocated by Paul Volcker among others,[33] is to break up financial giants into smaller parts, none of them too big to fail. Many politicians seized on the idea—blithely ignoring that when there is a common cause for failure (for example, subprime mortgages), the collapse of ten small institutions can exert the same shock on the economy as the failure of a single large institution. Perhaps anticipating just this nostrum, in October 2009, the Dutch megabank ING went ahead and broke itself up, selling its insurance businesses and divesting the American arm of its online-banking unit, thereby shrinking its balance sheet by more than 50 percent. Whether the ING example heralds a trend or a policy direction is not clear and, in our view, certainly not advisable—for the same set of reasons that Treasury secretary Morganthau's prescription to deindustrialize Germany after the Second World War was rejected.

A less-radical idea was proposed by the governor of the Bank of England, Mervyn King, who has argued that the bread-and-butter "utility banking" (savings and loan entities) should be distinguished from "casino banking" (more-speculative firms) when making decisions on which kinds of entities warrant government support. Utilities would be saved, casinos might not. A related answer would be to charge fees from risky firms that could be drawn down in case one of these ventures needed a government lifeline. This would effectively make the risky part of the financial industry internalize the pain, rather than shipping the pain to the taxpayers.

Overall, when it comes to deciding which firms are "too big," "too interconnected," or "too risky," the Group of Thirty, led by former central bankers, has offered a sensible checklist: criteria such as size, leverage, and connections with the financial system and real economy.[34] Breaking up such entities is not the key answer and could prove counterproductive; a better approach is to require more capital and more liquidity, use novel market-based insurance mechanisms, and to scale both capital and liquidity requirements to the extent of risk, independently assessed.

The fifth question concerns the structure of international governance to ward off future crises and their globalization. It seems that the G system—flexible coordination without heavy obligations—is well-suited for the world of international finance where circumstances change rapidly, uncertainties abound, and the treasured prerogatives of national policy making are at stake.[35] That the countries are coordinators rather than rule makers has allowed for easy expansion beyond the initial core of six nations. And nothing precludes smaller countries within the G20 system, notably the G2 between the central couple of global finance, the United States and China, as advocated by C. Fred Bergsten.

But the strength of the G system is also its weakness: no overarching system of surveillance, no real-time whistle-blowing that danger lies ahead. Is sturdier architecture needed to warn of crises ahead, to evaluate the effectiveness of G system commitments, and to calibrate the world economy when a failure in one area threatens the entire enterprise? And if so, is the IMF the right and only tool for the job?

IMF: Back in Business

As the crisis started to unfold, the IMF leaped back onto the map of global finance. Iceland, devastated by bank failures with liabilities that exceeded 600 percent of the country's GDP, sought a lifeline from the IMF. So did Ukraine, Hungary, Belarus, and Pakistan, and others in the waiting room. During 2007, shortly before the crisis struck, the IMF was winding down to a lightly staffed body charged with issuing periodic comments on the world economy and rescuing wayward countries. The policy consensus shifted rapidly once the crisis erupted, and the IMF was recalled to the frontlines of financial firefighting. The G20 commitment, yet to be realized, was to restock it with a fresh $500 billion in new lending capacity.

According to the new G20 consensus, besides reviving the IMF as a lender of last resort, the international financial system needed an international watchdog. For this purpose, the Financial Stability Forum (a talk shop that completely missed the crisis) was renamed the Financial Stability Board (FSB), with enhanced but still vague powers. The true role of the FSB, how it relates to the IMF, and whether it can be more prescient than its predecessor all remain to be determined.

Rough Going for the Fund

The IMF has not enjoyed its best days of late. Its fall from grace can be traced to the 1997–1998 Asian financial crisis, when it imposed tough conditions before dispensing emergency funds. Its insistence both on tight money and deep budget cuts to clamp down on inflation and shrink external deficits was seen in Asia as delivering extreme austerity. The way the crisis was handled created a deep-seated loathing of Washington mavens. It also inspired an army of IMF bashers, led by Nobel laureate Joseph Stiglitz.[36] As its most lasting contribution, the episode sparked a regionwide drive to build huge foreign exchange reserves, and prompted Asian nations to devise their own swap system, the Chiang-mai initiative. To this day, regional leaders harbor plans to launch an Asian Monetary Fund to displace the IMF on their turf.

The Argentine crisis of the early 2000s dealt another blow. The IMF was battered with sharp criticism for persisting in its support of the Argentine currency board, a mechanism that tied the value of the peso to the U.S. dollar, but also required the Argentine central bank to run down its foreign exchange reserves in defense of the local currency. To be sure, the Argentines were the foremost culprits, with runaway spending and a hyperactive printing press. But the episode affirmed a view that the IMF took too long to acknowledge that the currency peg could not be defended.

One outcome of these failures was the so-called Meltzer Commission, sponsored by Congress in 2000 and headed by economist Allan Meltzer. The commission came down hard on the IMF and the World Bank, and called for major change to their structures and *modus operandi*.

Further undermining the IMF's credibility was the belated discovery that it lacks teeth to clamp down on misdeeds of big players. Between 2003 and 2006, the IMF was powerless to affect the growing U.S. fiscal deficit and the undervalued Chinese yuan. Global imbalances grew ever larger, with the huge U.S. current account deficit mirrored by enormous current account surpluses in Asia, and a flood of foreign money into mortgage-backed securities, all combining to set the table for the Great Crisis.

A related malady was growing skepticism of the IMF's relevance. The macroeconomic conditions during the first few years of the millennium were stellar in the IMF's erstwhile clientele. Asian nations built reserve armories on the back of export-led development strategies; Latin American commodity producers were buoyed by insatiable Asian demand for their soy, wheat, iron ore, copper, and oil, along with the rising prices for all these commodities. Many a frontier market could access capital in the private markets. The IMF shed hundreds of economists as the demand for its rescue medicine plunged. Even supporters questioned its relevance.

The Governance Question

The International Monetary Fund received another bad rap for its initial response to the Great Crisis, but this was undeserved. In the spring of 2008, the IMF issued stern warnings about the U.S. housing bubble, well ahead of the financial chaos, raising eyebrows on Capitol Hill and in the Treasury. The IMF would have been a good soldier, if asked. But until everything fell apart, no one asked, largely because emergency cash was available elsewhere, including Chinese loans to Africa and a bizarre Russian lifeline to Iceland.

Come 2009, the IMF's *raison d'être* was revalidated. Richly replenished by the G20 summit in London, the IMF was back on the map of financial governance. And so were long-standing pressures by emerging market leaders, notably China and India, to make the IMF more representative of the G20 world. The vexing hurdles to this goal, as with so many financial issues, relate to power and money.

Governance of the IMF is practically frozen in the 1940s. The key sticking points are what the Peterson Institute's Ted Truman has called "chairs" and "shares," namely, representation at the IMF board and voting power as determined by national quotas. The United States can veto important decisions that require an 85 percent supermajority, since it holds 17 percent of the voting power.[37] While the U.S. share is not outsized relative to its GDP—some 25 percent of the world total at market exchange rates—the veto vexes other members. China and India hold 3.5 and 2 percent of the voting power, respectively, while generating more than 8 percent of

the world's GDP at market exchange rates, and almost 18 percent at purchasing power parity (PPP) exchange rates.[38]

The crisis compounded this disparity. Critics claim that the subprime
fiasco swept the United States off its high horse; no longer can the U.S.
Treasury use the IMF to tell emerging countries how to manage their
economies. But it is the Europeans who hold a truly outsized representation. EU members plus Norway and Sweden occupy eight of the twenty-
four chairs on the board (the United States has one) and claim 35 percent
of the voting power (thus, a veto as well), plus the tradition of naming the
IMF's managing director.

Rearranging chairs and shares would "flatten" the power structure in
the IMF, giving emerging countries greater voice in the institution. The 5
percent increase in the emerging markets' quota agreed upon at Pittsburgh was good progress. A similar step was made at the IMF/World
Bank Annual Meeting in Singapore in September 2006, when China,
Korea, Mexico, and Turkey were awarded tiny increases in their voting
power. The underlying assumption behind the push for a greater say by the
Indias and Chinas of the world is that IMF effectiveness requires a closer
alignment between economic power and political weight. A further argument, made by former Australian prime minister Paul Keating, is that a
power shift might make the Asian countries more responsive to the IMF's
suggestions, and perhaps take more kindly to the idea of reducing their
current account surpluses.[39] Both arguments can be questioned, but they
reflect the pressures for reform.

A reallocation of voting power that was more meaningful for the
emerging nations would likely entail a grand bargain in which the United
States gave up its veto right and the Europeans gave up shares and chairs.
Attention could then turn to the reallocation of freed-up voting power
and board representation.

Ways to slice the power in the IMF is a long-standing and vexing issue,
not only politically but also technically. There have been countless proposals, including one from the IMF's own "quota formula review group,"
a panel of outside experts with the inaccessible acronym QFRG, chaired
by Harvard's Richard Cooper. The QFRG's 2000 report put forth a linear
formula based on each country's GDP measured at market prices and exchange rates and the variability of its current receipts and net long-term

capital flows.[40] Like other proposals, the QFRG found that the status quo was far out of line with the suggested formula. Ultimately, the QFRG recommendations were deemed unacceptable by the IMF's Executive Board, for the cited reason (to be taken with a teaspoon of salt) that the formula would transfer voting power away from developing countries.[41]

The ivory towers tried to square the circle with new variables and formulas. Vijay Kelkar, a former IMF executive director, together with scholars Praveen Chaudhry and Marta Vanduzer-Snow propose to redistribute voting power by valuing GDP at PPP exchange rates.[42] This results in lowering the advanced economies share from 62 percent to 51 percent, and increasing Asian, Latin American, and African shares. The European Union and the United States would still retain their veto. Another of the many approaches, advocated by the former head of the IMF's China Division, Eswar Prasad, now of Cornell University and the Brookings Institution, would shrink the share of existing members to 80 percent of the total, and then auction the "new" 20 percent with the condition that no country can acquire a share that would give it veto power.

In the end, a redistribution of voting power will result from political horse-trading. If an academic formula is used at all, it will simply be invoked to justify an agreed political solution—much the same as tariff-cutting formulas devised at the World Trade Organization (WTO). And the political solution will be intimately related to the money question.

The money question has two aspects: the size of the IMF's lending capacity, and which members will supply the cash. The G20 communiqué promised to triple the IMF's lending capacity. Even at that size, the IMF's coffers would be but a fifth of the $4 trillion that the United States had committed by April 2009 in the form of direct spending, loans, and guarantees to arrest the financial crisis.[43]

While the United States is a very large economy, it is only one-quarter of the world total. It is easy to imagine a shock that embraced a group of countries (say East Asia) that totaled roughly the same economic size but, unlike the United States, do not issue the world's reserve currency.

Yet the commitment of $500 billion new IMF resources was seen as a watershed. It is hard to envision another large boost in the IMF's armory anytime soon. Thus far, Japan, the European Union, and the United States have each agreed to commit some $100 billion in fresh resources, China has promised $40 billion, and Korea $18 billion. Even these sums may be difficult to secure, since legislatures are wary of sending money to faraway foreign nations. At the time of this writing, the debate over American contribution turned sour in Congress just on those bases. Meanwhile, other IMF members have yet to commit the "missing" $160 billion. However, this hole might be filled by subscriptions on the part of developing countries to a new issue of IMF bonds. Since the game is pay to play, those insistent calls for greater representation on the board will have to be matched by hard money commitments, and the bond issue could do the trick.

Going forward, limitations on the International Monetary Fund may be accentuated if regional financial systems consolidate. The European Union launched a facility in 2002 whereby it can assist members outside the euro area in response to their balance of payments problems. Nothing much was heard from this initiative when Central Europe collapsed in 2009; however, Europe might get its act together now in the wake of the Greek crisis. In Asia, the Chiang-mai network of bilateral swap arrangements now totals $120 billion among thirteen countries. Fashioned after the Asian financial crisis in direct response to the IMF's heavy-handed conditionality and boosted in May 2009 in response to the Great Crisis, Chiang-mai is an instrument of coordination without a heavy bureaucracy. The urgency in Asia to boost it has accentuated with the Great Crisis and the region's hefty reserves. But it is still small and remains to be tested by a major crisis.

A moderately stocked IMF, backed by regional funds and bilateral swap lines, may turn out to be best for policy. For one thing, no one knows today how much money will be needed to get to the other side of the Great Crisis, much less the next crisis. The $500 billion figure, like much else in 2009, was drawn from the wind. For another thing, a bigger pot of crisis insurance money creates its own perverse incentives. Countries might talk the talk of better financial regulation, but not walk the walk, confident that "mother Fund" will come to the rescue if things go wrong.

We come back to the enduring tension between moral hazard and adequate insurance. Inadequate insurance, we now know, is a problem: as the Great Crisis demonstrates, financial havoc in New York or London can devastate well-managed countries located far away. Even Chile and Brazil, star students of the Washington consensus, saw their stock and property markets sink and economic growth turn anemic.

Conversely, the more money the IMF has at its disposal, the greater the odds of moral hazard—excessive risk taking by investors and countries, knowing the IMF will dash to their rescue. Research is divided about the existence of moral hazard, but recent findings show that it cannot be dismissed.[44] Even if moral hazard was not always present, it fuels domestic opposition to further allocations to the IMF. In the wake of the U.S.-backed IMF loans in the Asian financial crisis, the U.S. Congress launched a tirade against rescues, arguing that they ate up America's precious fiscal resources and only created moral hazard problems across the developing world. This reasoning guided the first few years of policy making in the George W. Bush administration, which initially refused to bail out Argentina when it collapsed in 2001. While correct in striving to preempt Argentine-style repeated boom and bust fiscal management practices, the decision, some now say, paid off in the form of a decade of irresponsible populism in Buenos Aires.

Citibank vice chairman William Rhodes suggests one way to balance the enduring tension between moral hazard and adequate insurance: create contingency funding facilities along the lines opened during the Asian crisis.[45] These are lines of credit for members with sound policies yet embroiled in a payments crisis not of their own making. Such a mechanism, apart from fighting future fires, could encourage good governance. In fact, contingency funding of this sort might have rescued Argentina in 2001, since for most of the period in the 1990s (if not in 2000 and 2001), Buenos Aires ran rather responsible fiscal policies.

Balancing Act

The International Monetary Fund has a long-term future as the global insurance agency. Its other functions—as a fire alarm and police patrol—should be sharpened. The IMF provided early warnings in the run-up to the crisis, and it is uniquely equipped to sound alarms about excessive debt, both public and private, and rising inflation on a global scale.

The IMF scored a victory in Pittsburgh, where it was recruited as the referee of the G20 pledges to coordinate policies in the interest of a balanced world economy. This is a good idea in light of the IMF's readily available armory of capable PhDs, something the leading powers in the organization should now fully harness. The big powers might also go further—employ the IMF's good offices to police exchange rates and to hash out further agreements between Washington, Frankfurt, Tokyo, and Beijing on imbalances. These tasks fall well within the IMF's mission,[46] and it has the technical apparatus to discharge its responsibilities. The problem is foot-dragging by the member states. That venerable scholar of global finance, Morris Goldstein, has called on the IMF to issue a semiannual report on member country exchange rate policies, based on calculations of "reference" exchange rates, and to make frequent use of its existing powers to conduct special consultations.[47] This is the right prescription; agreement is needed among the players that they will permit the IMF to play a meaningful role in balancing the world's accounts and delegate to it, in word and deed, the power to knock heads and the heft to shame shirking players.

It is an open question whether the IMF will, should, or ever could become the world's central bank, creating reserves (through the SDR or another vehicle) so that massive global imbalances need not be the logical counterpart of national efforts to build war chests of foreign exchange. There are many political and technical hurdles in the path of an alternative currency. The United States would not be enthusiastic about such an arrangement, since the clear implication is an erosion of Washington's "soft power" in world affairs. Agreeing on a wider basket of currencies on which to base the SDRs would be complicated, since Brazil, China, and India would probably all want their currencies represented. The governance of such a system would be fiercely contested.

Moreover, if the new currency is not widely adopted for invoicing international transactions and for denominating private international capital flows in the form of loans, bonds, and deposits, the whole construct would have a phony feel. The shift to an alternative international currency, if it comes, seems likely to evolve in a bottom-up fashion, led by market forces and decentralized national decisions, not by the grand design of a conclave of central bankers meeting in Basel, Switzerland.[48] Until that happens, the dollar will remain the default currency, both for central banks and private corporations.

The Leadership Issue

The fundamental issue with global economic governance, even with a more potent International Monetary Fund as the hired manager, is that someone has to coordinate the play. The G20, regional arrangements, and a recalibrated IMF may accommodate China, India, and the other rising powers that are calling for a multipolar world order. But enlarging the table to accommodate more countries hardly guarantees that the world will be safe for globalization. Disagreements in the core group have time and again resulted in deadlocks at the United Nations on important security issues (such as Iran) and in the Doha Round over meaningful liberalization (agriculture and services). A flattened governance structure is more democratic, but it easily can be dysfunctional. Representativeness does not equate to effectiveness. Leadership still counts.

In the critical 1945–1948 period, multilateralism happened through American strength, vision, and leadership, not because it was the vogue and everyone had a say. The Bretton Woods system worked precisely because the United States was the most powerful player at the table. Charles Kindleberger famously argued that a global hegemon, a single country that is willing and able to provide collective goods regardless of contributions made by others, is necessary for successful multilateralism.[49] Several trade analysts have blamed declining U.S. leadership in the General Agreement on Tariffs and Trade (GATT) and the WTO for the rise of regional trading blocs.[50] In the wake of the Great Crisis, the same criticism might be leveled at U.S. support for financial globalization.

The outcome of the second G20 summit reflected the Obama administration's effort, during its first extensive foreign tour, to appear sensitive to the politics of Europe and to hone its multilateral credentials. The American delegation was in a listening mode, and with its humble demeanor inspired columns upon columns about the end of *Pax Americana* and the rise of a genuinely multipolar world economy. In our view, such pronouncements underestimate the central role of U.S. leadership in world affairs and overestimate the money and market commitments that China and other emerging countries are willing to put on the table to ensure that globalization prospers—let alone have the legitimacy to lead other powers.

The United States is indispensable for the world economy. Washington can assert global leadership through the style and persuasion of an exceptional president. Ronald Reagan was that sort of person. It remains to be determined whether Barack Obama will rise to the same stature. Even if he does, the United States alone should not have to support aggregate demand in the world economy, run trade deficits that generate foreign exchange reserves for its trading partners, and shoulder the burden of IMF lending. Other economies must also carry their share. The United States can do much, but it cannot be expected to deliver the world back on track alone.

Conclusion

The immediate effects of the Great Crisis are clear: fearful creditors, cautious consumers, increased household savings, decimated financial sectors, and dampened global growth prospects. U.S. policy measures are the key for getting the world economy back on track. These should center first and foremost on cleaning up the financial system; but after that, Federal Reserve policy must be dedicated to arresting economic euphoria when next it blossoms. Wisely deployed, these measures need not come at the expense of growth, and they certainly should not reverse the process of globalization.

International understandings are also required. Washington and Beijing need to settle scores on currency questions and imbalances that undermine the bilateral relationship. China needs to consume more and the United States needs to consume less. While global financial governance is still an oxymoron, tools do exist for managing a confederation of global financial players. These include cooperative networks backed up by a policeman and an insurance agency. The G system can coordinate, and the International Monetary Fund, with emerging regional funds, can police and insure. The dollar can be used as the reserve currency into the next decade and perhaps beyond, but alternative means need to be devised for ensuring global liquidity over a longer horizon. In short, limits to globalization need to be erased, but policies that buttress globalization also must be put in place.

There are powerful motivations for the fixes. In an influential paper in 1983, then academic Ben Bernanke argued that Depression-era damage to the financial system impeded its ability to lend to households for purchasing durable goods and to firms for production and trade. Similar patterns are now gathering.[51]

There is a big difference between governing global finance and governing international trade. Finance changes fast, uncertainties lurk behind every corner, and flexible decisions by the main players are of the essence; trade is about locking in commercial practices and leveling the playing field among 150-plus members, and gradually achieving deeper liberalization. Finance is an obstacle course run by individual nations; trade is a marathon run by a team. What happens when there are weak links among the runners? This is where we turn next.

7

TRADE IN TROUBLE

The Great Crisis had an immediate and devastating impact on trade. Finance and trade often meet in times of crisis: when credit shuts down, trade takes a hit. Demand sinks, and so do imports; some firms go out of business and can no longer supply exports. Trade finance—money required to move goods across borders—incurs the instantaneous wrath of financial instability. Letters of credit, if available at all, are considerably more expensive, just like every other bank risk. Some 90 percent of the $14 trillion global export trade depends on trade finance; in fact, both exporters and importers need financiers to consummate their deals. Interest rates on trade finance loans shot up by 3 percentage points in the fall of 2008, prompting the World Trade Organization (WTO) to convene a special meeting and the World Bank to create a trade finance fund. But at a meager $1.5 billion, this new facility supplied a tiny fraction of 1 percent of global requirements for trade finance. Not until the G20 summit, held in London in April 2009, did the international community commit to the significant sum of $250 billion, to be disbursed in a revolving fashion over two years, for the trade finance needs of developing countries.

New Protectionism?

More problematic is the long-term impact on trade policies. The crisis dragged the world economy into a deep recession, bringing about a large contraction of trade for the first time in twenty-seven years. In a worst-case scenario, this will be followed by years of subpar expansion. The flagging world economy, not protectionist trade policy, is responsible for nearly all the contraction, but trade policy unfortunately has moved in the wrong direction—new barriers, not fresh liberalization. Trade offers a natural punching bag when jobs disappear; the trade armory offers multiple weapons—tariffs, quotas, nontariff barriers, and subsidies—for rapid deployment.

And so it was that trade armory was put to use. Many countries imposed tariff hikes and defensive measures to raise revenues and to provide relief to ailing domestic industries. India, Ecuador, Russia, Argentina, South Korea, and Indonesia resorted to new barriers, some of them on multiple products.[1] Russia reduced its meat import quotas, tightened its sanitary and phytosanitary (SPS) and quarantine requirements, and imposed a special road toll on trucks from the European Union (EU), Switzerland, and Turkmenistan.[2] Meanwhile, in early March 2009, the European Union levied duties on U.S. biodiesel imports in retaliation for the $1 per gallon export subsidy that Washington pays to U.S. producers. The United States was planning retaliatory tariffs on Italian water and French cheese to punish the EU for restricting imports of U.S. chicken and beef, but eventually dropped cheese off the retaliation list.[3]

Antidumping filings under General Agreement on Tariffs and Trade (GATT) Article 6, a popular substitute for "escape clause" actions under GATT Article 19, are often used to halt import penetration. Because it is easier for an import-competing industry to obtain relief under Article 6 than Article 19, antidumping actions serve as a useful barometer of protectionist sentiments. Total filings grew by 15 percent between 2007 and 2008, and proceedings that led to the imposition of duties grew by 22 percent over 2007 levels. India, often the world's leading user of antidumping measures, was the most active during 2008 as well, accounting for almost a third of total initiations. In December 2008 alone, India opened antidumping investigations involving hot- and cold-rolled stainless steel products that affected nineteen exporting countries. China once again became the country hit with the most new cases. Besides incurring New Delhi's wrath, China saw its screws and bolts and shoes barred from the EU market, while Washington levied antidumping duties on Chinese mattress springs and graphite electrodes. In a widely debated measure interpreted in many quarters as shameless pandering to American unions, in the fall of 2009, the Obama administration, on the basis of an International Trade Commission analysis, imposed antidumping duties on $1.8 billion worth of tires from China. This inspired another round of "anti-antidumping" cases: China thought the tire duties were unfair and, as a matter of self-help, launched a formal inquiry into imports of chicken feet and chicken wings from America.

The fiscal stimulus packages enacted in response to the financial crisis—implemented or announced at least by the European Union, the United States, Japan, Argentina, Chile, China, Indonesia, Malaysia, Mexico, and Thailand—created two further issues of concern for global trade.

First, the packages contained industrial subsidies that can distort the patterns of global commerce and trigger WTO disputes over "illegal state aids." Besides mass bailouts for the ailing banks, fat lifelines were thrown to the automotive industry. The United States, Canada, Sweden, France, Germany, Australia, Argentina, Korea, and China all extended special packages to support their auto manufacturers in the face of the crisis. Since December 2008, the U.S. government has provided an estimated $162 billion of loans and equity to prop up its automakers.[4] Chrysler got $65 billion and General Motors received $55 billion. European countries rescued their auto firms at the rate of about $31 billion.

Despite some posturing, however, none of the Western auto producers is likely to challenge another country for subsidizing its own auto industry. China is another story. In late 2009, soon after the United States imposed high antidumping duties on $2 billion of Chinese steel, China launched a trade investigation into subsidies received by General Motors, Ford, and Chrysler. While auto firms were the biggest recipients of government rescue money, other industries were also getting emergency cash. In a move criticized by Australia and New Zealand, in late January 2009, the European Commission reintroduced export subsidies for butter, cheese, and whole and skim milk powder. China had done its part, in November 2008, by increasing the value added tax (VAT) rebates on its exports of some textiles and clothing and bamboo products, plastics, and furniture. Tax rebates on exports of about 3,770 items went into effect on December 1, 2008; starting February 1, 2009, import tariffs and VAT on 1,730 items are refunded when these items are bound for reexport.

With the bigger players leading the way, support mechanisms became respectable around the world, risking both a cycle of government intervention and spread of policies to pick winners by supporting losers—a very bad idea. Extending favorable treatment for one sector can easily transmit favoritism fever to other sectors. Moreover, such measures are likely to inspire emulation, if not retaliation, abroad—as illustrated by the European March 2009 tariffs on U.S. biodiesel in response to U.S. renewable-energy stimulus measures. This is possibly a small installment on what lies ahead, given the magnitude of subsidies and border barriers embedded in U.S. and EU climate-change legislation. In some cases, support measures flout multilateral rules.[5] In other cases, the measures are consistent with the rules, but they still amount to new protection.[6] And support measures enacted by the bigger states certainly did elicit the wrath of smaller developing countries, which did not have rich troves of foreign exchange to buttress their own national champions. What do they have instead? Tariff protection at the border.

The second concern raised by stimulus packages centers on the exclusion of foreign suppliers. The "Buy American" provisions in the U.S. economic stimulus plan—aimed at the campaign promises of keeping jobs at home—as passed by the House of Representatives at $819 billion on January 28, 2009, would have required only American iron and steel in stimulus-backed projects. The bill sparked instant and strong protests about protectionism from U.S. trading partners, as well as probusiness think tanks and associations such as the U.S. Chamber of Commerce. However, the Senate's $787 billion version passed on February 13, 2009, included much the same provision, now extended to all manufactures, but stipulated that it be applied consistent with U.S. international obligations. Whether the administrative machinations are, in fact, consistent with international obligations is a matter of legal dispute; both Canada and Japan have criticized the law, while Brazil has threatened to bring a challenge in the WTO.

Following the furor, Paul Krugman argued in his *New York Times* blog that government spending with a "Buy American" flavor might be a good thing, because it would enlist domestic constituencies around the world to welcome Keynesian spending.[7] Perhaps, but in a rapid-response document, Gary Hufbauer and Jeffrey Schott argued that foreign emulation of "Buy American" provisions could end up costing American jobs.[8]

In short, while the crisis did not spark a tidal wave of protection, neither can the damage be ignored. Tallies at different stages are revealing. According to a World Bank analysis released in early March 2009, since the beginning of the crisis, officials had proposed or implemented roughly seventy-eight adverse measures.[9] Of these, sixty-six involved trade restrictions, and forty-seven trade-restricting measures eventually took effect. While many of the measures were rather minor and targeted, the press release item was that no fewer than seventeen of the G20 economies were violators, breaching their November 15, 2008, summit standstill against new trade barriers. Subsequently, in late March 2009, the World Trade Organization published its own list of offenders, and came up with some eighty-seven verifiable adverse measures by leading trade powers, such as the United States, the European Union, China, and India.[10]

By September 2009, the picture had soured. The independent Global Trade Alert calculated that G20 members, after their November 2008 pledge against protectionism, had implemented 121 "blatantly discriminatory measures" and another 48 that directly harmed foreign commercial interests, and another 134 were in the pipeline.[11] The measures affected most categories of traded goods and the vast majority of the world's countries. Instead of tariffs, governments generally promoted "buy local" programs and imposed new sanitary or certification-based restrictions. One piece of good news for the global trade regime was that the worst offender was Russia, not a member of the WTO, with forty-eight measures. Unsurprisingly, the megaexporter China was the major target of protectionist measures by the other G20 powers, followed by the United States and Germany.

Why Has Doha Stalled?

Protectionist maneuvering illustrates a grand global paradox: while shared distress underscores the importance of free trade as a countercyclical force to revive the world economy, the crisis itself invites a global bout of nationalism. Governments want to boost exports and curtail imports, thereby boosting jobs at home. Of course, this approach cannot claim success at a global level.

Two forces that stopped governments from dipping even more freely into the trade policy armory were fear of retaliation and respect for WTO rules. Yet the resilience of these insurance policies came into question even before the crisis reached gale strength. The multilateral trading system reached an inflection point in July 2008, as progress in concluding the Doha Development Round, launched in November 2001, ground to a halt by discord among the power brokers—the United States, the European Union, China, India, and Brazil.

Labeling the talks a "Development Round" was expedient in 2001, but created two misleading expectations: first, that trade liberalization by itself, without complementary policies, could spark economic growth in emerging countries; and second, that Organization for Economic Cooperation and Development (OECD) nations would let *all* developing countries get away without lowering their own barriers. To compound the misleading title, agricultural liberalization was put at the center of the agenda. The implication was that if agricultural barriers could not be slashed, then barriers to manufactured goods and services would remain intact. Ambitions were further scaled back when three of the so-called Singapore Issues, all part of the original Doha agenda—competition policy, government procurement, and investment regulations—were abandoned at Cancun in August 2004, and talks on the fourth topic, trade facilitation, were watered down.

Despite the obstacles, by the summer of 2008, WTO members made enough progress to see the outlines of a package deal with something for every member. But India objected. The root of discord was not *realpolitik* or mercantilism, but old-fashioned protectionism. India's predominantly rural population of small farmers constitutes a massive, well-organized lobby against agricultural liberalization. The issue was not about pushing actual tariffs down—India has already done that—but bringing down the bound tariffs at the WTO to the level of the current applied tariffs. In India's case, this would mean lowering bound agricultural tariffs that average 114 percent to the applied average of 34 percent. This, the country's rural lobby contends, would tie the nation's future ability to hike tariffs in response to damaging import competition.

The Paradox of Unilateralism

The Indian problem is part of a great success story in world trade, unilateral liberalization. Within the WTO framework, countries bind their tariffs to a certain level, never to be raised without paying a penalty to their trading partners. Outside the WTO, the same countries have implemented deep unilateral tariff cuts in their own best interests, and the lower tariffs have effectively become their applied rates. The World Bank's annual report, *Global Economic Prospects 2005*, estimates that two-thirds of tariff cutting in 1983–2003 can be attributed to unilateral trade reform—a quarter to multilateral trade reform and the rest to preferences under free trade agreements.

That is the good news. But unilateral opening has now created a multilateral dilemma. The "water"—or the gap between applied and bound rates—is a source of much haggling in global trade negotiations. Countries with plenty of water are loath to give it up: they want to preserve "policy space" in order to raise their applied tariffs in times of distress—and still comply with the bound rates committed in their WTO schedules.

The water affords a mighty trump card in WTO negotiations: a country that is comfortable with its applied levels can offer a substantial cut in its bound rates to other nations, yet stick to the existing protective barriers. This happens because the same applied rates will continue in force even after much of the water is removed. No actual opening occurs.

While some countries have drained most of their water—the average gap for China is below 2 percentage points, much as it is for the United States, Japan, and the European Union—others hold onto it tooth and nail. The gap often exceeds 50 percentage points for such countries as India, Mexico, Brazil, Argentina, South Africa, and Indonesia; it is largest among agricultural goods. Deep water hides peak applied tariffs that generously protect certain products. To cite some of the most glaring cases, India's average gap in the sensitive cereals sector is 88 percent—119 percent bound tariff average *versus* 31 percent applied tariff average—and the peak applied tariff is 80 percent.[12] South Africa's average gap is 40 percent—50 percent bound tariff to 10 percent applied tariff. Its applied peak tariff is 99 percent (and the bound peak rate is an amazing 597 percent!). To preserve these peaks, many developing countries insist on exceptions from across-the-board cuts in their bound tariffs.

The fact of tariff peaks—in fact, both bound and applied peaks—implies considerable "tariff dispersion," meaning a wide range between the lowest and highest rates, and thus between the least-protected and most-protected goods. Only a few countries, like Chile, have a flat tariff; in many developing countries, the dispersion is spectacular. Large dispersion reflects the prior rounds of industry lobbying and encourages the next. Dispersion also engenders corruption in the customs service, since a small change in a product's tariff classification can mean an enormous change in duty owed. It is, after all, cheaper to bribe the customs official to change the tariff classification than to pay the high duty.

Today's gap between bound and applied tariffs is an overhang from "special and differential treatment" (known as S&D), a policy innovation of the 1970s that exempted developing countries from meaningful trade obligations.[13] The idea was that by allowing countries such as India and Brazil to retain barriers, while the United States and Europe opened their markets, the developing nations could nurture their infant industries and eventually compete on the global field. Owing to S&D, by the late 1980s, developing countries had agreed to bind less than a third of their tariffs.

Alas, shielded from global competition, developing countries often nurtured their least-efficient industries and crops, hampering their competitiveness in global markets. Wedded to an array of protective barriers, they became lesser actors in the world trading system, as they had little to offer in the mercantilist give-and-take of trade talks. An unfortunate consequence was that OECD countries were slow to liberalize their own barriers in sectors of export interest to developing countries, such as apparel, footwear, hand tools, sugar, and peanuts.

But while they held fast to high bound tariffs, and often to no bindings at all, most developing countries unilaterally cut their applied tariffs in order to deliver cheap components to their industrial firms and cheap fertilizer and implements to their farmers.

The specter of tariff hikes by the Indias of the world to their current bound levels is surely annoying and possibly even terrifying. Small wonder that the European Union and the United States have called for substantial bound tariff cuts by successful emerging countries—exemplified by Brazil and India—that retain a substantial gap between their bound and applied rates.

But some unilateral reformers believe they have not been thanked enough for their "selfless" tariff cuts. They argue that proposals to squeeze water from bound rates are but punishment for voluntary reform. They demand that their unilateral liberalization should be matched with concrete concessions by the European Union and the United States.

The coupling of unilateral reform with a reluctance to surrender "policy space" has left little room for fresh liberalization in the Doha Round. The best negotiated outcome now would narrow the gap between bound and applied rates. While this might not boost trade much, it would create a better insurance policy against protection when the world economy next drops. Trade economist Patrick Messerlin observes that a "standstill" would provide valuable assurance to global companies with supply chains in the emerging markets, as they would be insulated from upward hikes in industrial tariffs above the current applied rates.[14] One potential compromise is for the developed countries to agree on a lower "injury" threshold for "escape clause" proceedings (GATT Article 19).[15] This would make it easier for all countries to invoke tariff relief when domestic industries are arguably harmed by imports, but would require a public hearing before the new and lower bound tariff is raised.

Rounding the Round?

In July 2008, trade ministers met in Geneva to map out the endgame of the Doha Round. Instead, the talks bogged down over an arcane issue, the "special safeguard mechanism" (SSM). This new provision would allow developing countries to raise their tariffs on agricultural imports when the import flows reached a certain percentage of domestic production or prices dropped. India's proposed "triggers" for invoking the SSM were viewed as too relaxed by other WTO members, particularly such agricultural exporters as Brazil and the United States.[16] Of course, the Doha Round faltered over more basic disputes than the technicalities of the SSM—notably the absence of any progress on liberalizing services, the tepid cuts in applied tariffs on industrial imports, and severe grievances harbored by Brazil and India over EU and U.S. agricultural subsidies.

There is much justification to complaints over subsidies. Washington doles out plenty of money to American farmers, albeit less than what is permitted under the Uruguay Round rules. Even after agreeing to a lower subsidy ceiling in the Doha Round, the United States could still pay out the same sums as in the past—not unlike the do-nothing attitude of countries that bind their tariffs above applied rates. For its part, the European Union unilaterally locks in its agricultural support funds over ten-year horizons and insists that the figures cannot be changed until the end of the period. This preemption tactic is just what European farmers want, but it clearly discourages the EU's trading partners from making ambitious liberalization offers.

A renewed push for Doha was supposed to be made in December 2008, but little had changed in the negotiating dynamics since July. The financial debacle was not enough to inspire a collective drive for finishing the round. The team of George W. Bush left for Texas and Team Obama had more urgent matters than a difficult trade negotiation. The European Union had its own change in leadership, with trade commissioner Peter Mandelson moving to the British cabinet, to be replaced in Brussels by Baroness Catherine Ashton.

The next window of opportunity was the G20 summit in April 2009 in London. But while the summit communiqué was very strong on calling for a standstill on new protection and providing trade finance to developing countries (the $250 billion revolved over two years), it did not set a deadline for concluding the Doha Round.

India's election, held in May 2009, sparked another flicker of hope, as it should have freed the government from the populist trade politicking of erstwhile Commerce Minister Kamal Nath. The incumbent Congress Party swept the elections, and Nath was moved to the post of transport minister, heralding the possibility of greater flexibility in India's trade policy. So far, however, potential flexibility has not been translated into concrete proposals.

In light of this perpetual "stop and no go," the Doha ministerial starting November 30, 2009, may have been the best news for world trade since the crisis started—even though a deal is still elusive.

The No-Doha Option

What would be the payoff from a spectacularly successful round, by comparison to a Doha-lite agreement that just stumbles over the finish line—or to a complete flop?

According to studies by the Peterson Institute and the World Bank, the potential annual gains from achievable trade liberalization range upwards of $300 billion annually by 2015.[17] The gains would be greater for rich countries in dollar terms, but larger for poor countries as a percentage of GDP. Up to 440 million people could be lifted out of absolute poverty by a highly successful round.

Quite interestingly, half the gains to developing countries would come from liberalization *between* developing countries themselves. Upon reflection, this is not surprising, since developing countries sport the highest tariffs. Paradoxically, the developing countries themselves could make the Doha "Development Round" a stunning success. By sticking to their guns and defending their "policy space"—something that sounds glamorous but buys nothing in reciprocal concessions—key developing countries have succeeded in sucking the lifeblood from the talks.[18]

The main bang would come from cutting agricultural tariffs and service barriers, where protection is far higher than it is in manufactures, and where bound rates (or their nontariff equivalents) exceed applied rates by wide margins. According to the World Bank, most of the agricultural benefits could be captured by capping maximum tariffs at modest levels, and subjecting at least some of the "sensitive products" to tariff cuts. Indeed, the crown jewels of liberalization are a handful of "tariff lines" that are now heavily protected: exempting even 2 percent of them from cuts could eviscerate the payoff. A recent paper by Batshur Gootiiz and Aaditya Mattoo tells pretty much the same story in services.[19]

The World Bank's study of agricultural trade is but one of some twenty computable general equilibrium (CGE) calculations that have been carried out since the round was first contemplated at the end of the 1990s. The outcomes vary immensely. Changing the assumptions about the depth of liberalization and the structure of the world economy—how large are monopoly markups? how great are economies of scale? what will happen to industrial productivity?—dramatically changes the results. The figures computed on the basis of the modest July 2008 draft texts in agriculture and nonagricultural market access yield lower gains, under $100 billion annually. Even at the low end, the outcome could lift 100 million people out of absolute poverty—still a worthy achievement.

But as the size of the Doha package has been whittled down, so has the interest of key players. China, India, and Brazil are in this select group. Simon Evenett, a leading expert, has scaled their short-term gains (based on World Bank calculations) against normal growth in these fast-growing economies.[20] For China, the prospective gains are less than five days of growth; for India, about twenty days; and for Brazil, about sixty days. National leaders can be understood when they place other priorities ahead of the push necessary to achieve such modest payoffs.

But such numbers tell a small part of the story. Even a modest Doha package would create a gateway to globalization gains not captured by the World Bank calculations. The Bank's CGE calculations, like most others, focus on *tariff barriers* to *merchandise trade* in a world of *perfect competition*—because the data and models are readily suited to measure these effects. Other important features—facilitating trade, liberalizing services, and compressing monopoly markups—are usually not measured. Consequently, standard calculations ignore the benefits of a *comprehensive* package—for example, the huge synergies between foreign direct investment, merchandise trade, and service flows, if all are liberalized together, and if accompanied by a competent customs service, fast-turnaround ports, and meaningful antimonopoly policies.[21]

In fact, most quantitative studies fail to capture dynamic gains. Over time, the enhanced productivity of labor, capital, and resources (in technical terms, rising "total factor productivity," or TFP) furnishes the key to economic growth. Trade openness contributes to TFP through several channels. It brings new technology, forces inefficient firms to improve or die, brings just the right components and equipment, and enables the best firms to enjoy economies of scale by selling abroad.[22] According to some estimates, dynamic gains more than double the standard calculations.

If Doha flops, we can forget about the potential benefits projected by CGE models. But there are alternative scenarios, some good, others bad. One extreme is a burst of unilateral liberalization (very good); another extreme is a wave of national decisions to hike tariffs and nontariff barriers toward bound levels (very bad). In between, and more likely, is the proliferation and deepening of preferential trade agreements (a few customs unions, but mostly bilateral and regional free trade agreements). While the preferential trade agreement (PTA) prospect seems better than a frozen *status quo*, no one claims it is the best scenario. Much depends on the depth of liberalization between members and the extent of discrimination against nonmembers, which fortunately so far has been remarkably limited owing to the advances in multilateral and unilateral liberalization.

The consequences of a Doha flop hinge critically on the post-Doha scenario. Economists Antoine Bouët and David Laborde calculate that in a scenario where all tariffs are jacked up to their bound levels, world trade would shrink by $1.8 trillion, and world GDP by $450 billion.[23] In a somewhat less-fanciful scenario, where most tariffs are raised to their applied levels at the end of the Uruguay Round in 1994 (the exceptions are tariff preferences covered by PTAs and tariffs capped by Uruguay Round bindings), trade would drop by $730 billion and world GDP by $170 billion. The tariff hikes would particularly hurt Nigeria (4 percent of the country's GDP) and Pakistan, India, China, and Mexico (all around 2 percent of GDP). In another of their scenarios, a mammoth free trade agreement between all the OECD countries (an illustrative if far-fetched outcome) would augment trade by $92 billion and GDP by $9 billion. By contrast, a modest Doha success would deliver trade gains of $336 billion and welfare gains of $79 billion annually.

Quantitative studies cannot account for the blow that a Doha collapse could deal to the legitimacy of the multilateral trading system and the quality of global cooperation. Core rules and institutions like national treatment, MFN treatment, and the dispute settlement mechanism would all be called into question. Gains in investment, productivity, and growth might be foregone. Pathways out of poverty might be obstructed for the poorest nations of Africa, Asia, and Latin America. The political fallout could be severe, right at a time when cooperation is essential to climb out of the economic chasm and address global imperatives such as climate change and the misery of the bottom billion.

To be sure, Doha is not perfect. Services are probably the most important missing element in negotiations to date. While accounting for two-thirds of global economic output, services as measured in official statistics make up only a fifth of world trade. This is a major understatement, since it does not cover services provided by such firms as Carrefour, HSBC, or IBM when they operate outside their home territories. Thanks to rapid air travel and the Internet, technological barriers to services trade are melting away, but policy barriers are still formidable. Another "mode" of services, movement of labor, has yet to be addressed; even temporary work visas are hard to obtain. Further, foreign direct investment in many service sectors is severely limited.

According to Gooltiiz and Mattoo (2009), bound levels of restrictions in services are nearly twice as severe as applied levels, and calculations of the tariff equivalent of applied levels often suggest rates in the range of 20 to 80 percent *ad valorem*.[24] A couple of studies have attempted to estimate the potential gains from liberalizing services trade. Decreux and Fontagné (2006), for example, calculate that a conservative 10 percent opening from the status quo would yield a further $30 billion in world income.[25]

The business community argues that meaningful trade facilitation would deliver very substantial gains. According to the World Bank, each additional day a product is tied up in customs procedures or port delays reduces trade by more than 1 percent, the equivalent of moving a country a further 70 kilometers from its trading partners.[26] Yet, after years of talk, the Doha trade facilitation agenda is timid.

Despite its many shortcomings, Doha could work wonders to halt the worrisome backsliding, revive world trade, and rally financial markets. It could safeguard the rules-based system that WTO members have painstakingly constructed since 1947. But at the end of the day, politics trumps economics. Free traders can make arguments about national benefits long into the night, but trade agreements are made or broken by interest groups cutting deals in private rooms. If the political stars are not aligned for a modest Doha package in 2010, a decade could pass before a new generation of leaders again tries to scale the mountain. While we wait, countries will not lose their enthusiasm for advancing in smaller groups. The global trading system faces the prospect of splintering into a multitude of preferential arrangements.

Backdoor to Global Free Trade?

Of the three buttons to push for getting to global free trade, the multilateral and unilateral buttons have been out of order for some time, but the preferential button still works just fine. As we discuss in chapter 3, PTAs have skyrocketed. Even some reluctant multilateralists are pursuing PTAs. India, while so far offering limited concessions, has launched talks with the European Union, Korea, and the Association of South-East Asian Nations (ASEAN), and is trying to join the Asia-Pacific Economic Cooperation forum (APEC).

Equally important to the number of PTAs is their scope, which will likely shoot up in the aftermath of Doha, even if the round is a success, but certainly if it is a flop. Will the PTA button ultimately get us to world-wide free trade—or will it be a counterproductive diversion to a beggar-thy-neighbor system of discriminatory arrangements?

Earlier, we contend that most PTAs are now trade-creating, boosting trade both among the member countries and between them and the rest of the world. The worldwide reduction in MFN bound tariffs and unilaterally applied tariffs has decidedly reduced the discriminatory edge of PTAs, rendering them distant and benign cousins of insulated trade blocs that were the bane of the 1930s. But even as PTAs advance the cause of open markets and provide insurance against a WTO breakdown, they are not a substitute for multilateral liberalization. They are second best.

As beneficial as PTAs can be, today's concern is that their proliferation has spawned a hugely complex "spaghetti bowl" of trade rules. The PTA spaghetti raises transaction costs for companies that operate global supply chains across multiple fronts. Studies by the Inter-American and Asian Development Banks indicate that some 60 to 80 percent of large companies in diverse countries such as Peru, Singapore, Thailand, and Mexico would much prefer a world with a single agreement, or at least regional mega-agreements, rather than today's world where they have to comply with multiple and overlapping PTAs.[27]

The PTA spaghetti bowl is also an enormous headache for customs officials in countries with multiple agreements, such as Chile, Mexico, Singapore, Thailand, the United States, and Vietnam. Officials need to verify the origin of goods according to each different PTA because the agreements define "origin" under different rules. Only the European Union network of PTAs has nearly 100 percent identical rules.[28]

At their worst, PTAs could disintegrate the global trading system into miniblocs and disrupt efficient supply chains. The best way to untangle the spaghetti is simply to break the bowl. How? It can be done by reducing all industrial tariffs unilaterally or multilaterally to zero, so that the PTA preferences no longer matter. Customs officers could then devote their time to other matters, such as enforcing phytosanitary standards and searching for weapons and illegal drugs. But, the world of zero tariffs remains a distant dream.

It is hardly surprising, then, that trade ministers are exploring ways to "converge" PTAs or harmonize their rules across larger areas. Pursuing the gastronomic analogy, convergence would transform the spaghetti bowl of PTAs into regional or even continental lasagna plates. The transformation would facilitate regional production and trade, harness scale economies, and undermine protectionist interests.

The foremost example of such continental convergence is the EU's Pan-European system of "cumulation," devised in the 1990s. Under the EU "cumulation system," goods that fulfill the rules of origin of one agreement automatically qualify in other agreements within the system. The convergence process entailed the harmonization of the EU's origin protocols with the European Free Trade Association (EFTA) in the early 1970s, and later among PTAs forged in the early 1990s through European Union agreements with Bulgaria, the Czech Republic, Estonia, Hungary, Latvia, Lithuania, Poland, Slovakia, and Romania.[29]

Other parts of the world have seen the light and followed suit. In January 2007, a group of eleven countries on the Pacific side of Latin America—including Chile, Colombia, Costa Rica, Ecuador, El Salvador, Guatemala, Honduras, Mexico, Nicaragua, Panama, and Peru—formed a work agenda to study, among other things, trade convergence and integration.

Not incidental, most of them have agreements with each other and also with the United States and Canada. In September 2008, a group of ten of them (all but Ecuador) plus Canada and the United States announced another initiative to further the convergence of their common trade deals.

The most significant bang from convergence could come from the Asia-Pacific region, home to some 50 percent of world trade and 60 percent of world GDP. The twenty-one-country APEC itself has as yet accomplished very little liberalization. Member countries, however, have pursued roughly three dozen bilateral and small plurilateral trade deals with each other. Now they are thinking of ways to use their PTA web—called a "noodle bowl" in Asia—to move toward a coherent integration scheme encompassing the twenty-one economies. This, in turn, could offer a path toward a Free Trade Area of the Asia-Pacific (FTAAP). The question of the day is whether "convergence" can best be attained by stitching all of the various deals together or instead by "docking" regional countries to an existing agreement, such as the plurilateral Trans-Pacific Partnership arrangement among APEC members Singapore, New Zealand, Chile, and Brunei that is now joined by new members.

Convergence efforts are made for a reason. Belonging to a larger free trade zone can yield major economic gains, particularly for small countries. Patricia Augier, Michael Gasiorek, and Charles Lai-Tong use the Paneuro system as a natural experiment, finding that cumulation increased trade between the Eastern European spokes by between 7 and 22 percent, and that the increase was between 14 and 72 percent for affected sectors.[30]

Convergent zones should find a natural lobby in multinational companies (MNCs). Given the trend toward fragmentation of production—unbundling and offshoring manufacturing stages across borders—MNCs should be delighted with having access to similar rules across their trade and production theaters and for opportunities to pool production across various jurisdictions, all without the costly irritation of disparate trade rules.

As this discussion illustrates, the PTA universe is complex. Some commentators argue that new PTAs should now be forbidden, before they turn the world trading system into discriminatory silos. This is ivory-tower talk, since the horse has left the barn. Other commentators contend that PTAs could offer the best path toward multilateral free trade and serve as an incubator for multilateral trade rules. "Multilateralization," a term coined by Richard Baldwin, has become the latest focal point of policy proposals.[31] To illustrate by stretching the gastronomical metaphor: if convergence is about making lasagna from PTA spaghetti, multilateralization is about making pizza from the spaghetti and lasagna.[32]

Multilateralization is targeted first and foremost at tariffs, where PTAs are the principal point of departure from MFN treatment and discrimination results from rules of origin. To a small extent, multilateralization may be occurring by default: for example, PTA provisions on competition policy tend to be multilateralized through nondiscrimination clauses. The challenge is to persuade countries to adopt regulations that are blind to the nationality of producers and suppliers. Another area where many PTAs are inviting multilateralization is services, since the rules of origin for services trade are generally quite loose and seldom discriminate against outsiders.[33] In most cases, third-country service providers can free ride on the preferences provided by the PTA by establishing an investment presence in one of the partner countries.[34] This sort of free riding is healthy cholesterol for global commerce.

Gradual bottom-up multilateralization will probably work better than top-down review of PTA credentials through WTO oversight, although both mechanisms can help. GATT Article 24 vaguely requires that PTAs liberalize "substantially all trade" among the partners, eradicate "restrictive regulations on commerce" within a "reasonable length of time," and not raise new barriers to the trade of nonmembers.[35] These phrases obviously allow massive leeway, and few countries want it any other way. The WTO has created a transparency mechanism to review PTAs as they come online, but the short-staffed world body lacks the political cache to shame countries into accepting more-liberal PTA provisions. What it can do is suggest useful pathways from the most vexing and discriminatory PTA clauses.

The likeliest road to multilateralization is the enlightened practice of freer trade when countries design or enlarge their PTAs. Hold your breath, wait and see—or reboot the global system.

How to Mend the WTO System?

With all the good it can potentially deliver, even a well-designed system of PTAs is second best, both from the point of view of companies looking at transaction costs and economists calculating global welfare. How do we get from second best to the best world?

We need a grand Doha bargain on agriculture and services trade between India, Brazil, and China on the one hand, and the European Union and the United States on the other. The United States and Europe should cap distorting subsidies at the level of current payouts (and spend more on nondistorting "Green Box" subsidies that do not affect output) in exchange for India's letting go of a quick trigger of safeguard measures against agricultural imports. India, Brazil, and China should all agree to significant liberalization of services and free trade in selected manufacturing sectors, such as environmental goods, chemicals, and information technology. Europe, the United States, and other industrial countries should commit to zero tariffs on all manufactured imports in ten years. Much hangs in the balance—freer trade in manufactures, more rational world agricultural production, opening the new frontier of services trade, and the very survival of a rules-based world trading system.

Hot and Crowded

Doha's troubles reflect not only deep, substantive differences; they are exaggerated by cumbersome negotiating processes adopted after the Uruguay Round. Besides creating an institution that houses both negotiation and dispute settlement under the WTO umbrella, another innovation was to replace the ad hoc scheduling of GATT ministerial gatherings with biennial WTO ministerial meetings. These guaranteed a forum for a multitude of medium-sized and small nations, such as the UN General Assembly. The voice of smaller players was further amplified by the principles of a "single undertaking" and "consensus": nothing would be agreed in future rounds until everything was agreed, and by *all* WTO members.

Those principles are not ironclad, but whereas success in prior GATT rounds depended on a consensus among just four players—the United States, the European Union, Japan, and Canada—today, China, India, and Brazil each holds enough sway to block any deal. The same is true of any ad hoc coalition of twenty or thirty small players. And whereas prior rounds could accommodate discrete deals on specific issues among smaller groups that wanted to advance further than the mass membership, these deals are no longer possible. Now, the single-undertaking principle—seen as an incentive for horse-trading and deal cutting *across* issue areas—means that even low-hanging fruit cannot be picked until the toughest issues are agreed.

Traditionally, GATT business was done through the Green Room process, a series of *de facto* meetings among the four leading powers. Today, for all intents and purposes, the old Green Room has been replaced by the G7 (Australia, Brazil, China, the European Union, India, Japan, and the United States), which in turn must secure the consent of a new Green Room of 30 main trading powers. When the 30 Green Room members reach a consensus, the proposals move to the rest of the 152 WTO members.

Thus, the Green Room is not what it used to be. To paraphrase Tom Friedman, today it is "hot, flat and crowded." This is not only because there are more heavyweights around the table but also because the issues are both more numerous and more contentious. After all, in the GATT era, trade technicians harvested the easy deals by draining water from Depression-era tariff schedules. Now politicos must wrestle with sensitive questions like lowering agricultural barriers and letting foreign firms operate electric power plants.

Changes in the WTO era—more WTO members, new power players, more difficult issues—put enormous pressure on the consensus and the single-undertaking principles. The single undertaking would not have been a problem in first GATT rounds, when only tariffs were at stake. But the number of discrete issues now addressed under the multilateral umbrella have shot up to more than a dozen, including nontariff barriers, intellectual property rights, trade facilitation, environment, and others. While the first rounds—Geneva, Annecy, and Torquay—centered on tariff liberalization, the Kennedy Round (1964–1967) opened a road beyond tariffs, delivering the Antidumping Agreement and a section on development issues, including the troublesome concept of "special and differential treatment."[36]

Blissfully free to pursue piecemeal deals, the Tokyo Round (1973–1979) negotiators created several "codes" to regulate subsidies and countervailing measures, standards, government procurement, customs valuation, antidumping, and other sectoral subjects. Unlike in today's single-undertaking paradigm, agreement on any of the codes did not have to await agreement on the others. Also, the consensus principle was not in play. Rather, each code was accepted by a subset of GATT members and only applied to relations between the signatories.

It was the Uruguay Round (1986–1994) that installed the consensus principle and enshrined the single undertaking. Perhaps not incidentally, the round was also the longest one to date, with many trips to the brink of collapse. But at the end, Uruguay generalized all but four of the Tokyo Round codes, with the exceptions being trade in civil aircraft, government procurement, dairy products, and bovine meat. The other codes were applied to all GATT members. The Uruguay Round also added services and intellectual property to its subject coverage, and created the WTO to help manage the negotiation, implementation, and arbitration of global trade matters. The conclusion of the Uruguay Round at Marrakech in 1994 was the crowning glory of the multilateral trading system.

The pressing question now is whether the WTO's institutional troubles—consensus, single undertaking, and even a vaguely defined "democratic deficit"—when combined with unilateral tariff cutting herald the end of multilateral reciprocity in international trade talks. Multilateral reciprocity is about give-and-take across a vast range of subjects and players. But if the offers fail to mesh, as they have during the Doha Round, a winning package, let alone a deep and truly meaningful outcome, cannot be assembled under the WTO's umbrella. Looking ahead, what are the alternatives to this failing institution?

Reset Button

Completing a robust Doha Round, not merely a Doha-lite, is the very best means to halt the backsliding on open markets and to revive world trade. But slippage is the hallmark of the day. Protectionist impulses produced by the soaring unemployment rates are translating into hard actions that interrupt commerce around the world. And even with Doha succeeding, the WTO is splitting at the seams. Membership numbers have mushroomed, issues are mounting, and civility is fraying. Crowding on the global agenda are trade rules that mesh with efforts to combat climate change; cargo security measures that are costly to implement; export controls that curtail supply chains; the dropped list of Singapore issues; and the perennial question of labor rights.

Going forward, institutional reengineering is sorely needed to accommodate the burgeoning membership and lengthening trade agenda. The Doha Round will not be the place for accommodation. Doha needs to digest the plate of issues in front of it, not reach for new helpings. But thinking needs to start on the new agenda.

This is not the first trial by fire for the world trading system. In 1957, the original GATT members or "contracting parties" put together a panel of experts to examine problems with world trade, especially sharp fluctuations in commodity prices, persistent agricultural protection, and development gaps in the world economies—issues still with us. The resulting Haberler Report, named after the panel's chairman, Harvard economist Gottfried Haberler, established three committees, respectively, to convene a further tariff negotiating conference, to review the agricultural policies of member governments, and to examine the trade problems facing developing countries.

In the early 1980s, when the world economy turned sour in the wake of the U.S. recession and the Latin American debt crises, GATT director-general Arthur Dunkel asked seven eminent persons to report on problems facing the international trading system. The resulting 115 recommendations propelled and shaped the negotiations leading to the launch of the Uruguay Round in 1986.

The next wave surfaced twenty years later, this time centered on the institutional problems in the WTO. During the tenth anniversary of the WTO's founding in January 2005, the organization issued its high-level panel report on *The Future of the WTO*, led by Peter Sutherland, former director-general of the GATT/WTO. This so-called Sutherland Report calls for "efficient-size sub-group" talks, and serves as the benchmark for recommendations to carry the WTO into the twenty-first century.[37]

Back to Plurilaterals

Today, the toughest reform issues are structural, centered on the consensus principle and the single-undertaking rule. Players with an intense interest in a particular issue naturally want to be in the Green Room, and by disagreeing on a discreet issue can hold up a global bargain. Given the sevenfold increase in members since the GATT was first launched, this demand ensures more confusion than coordination.

The requirement of a single undertaking has the effect of delaying the complete package—the same problem as a convoy of freighters in submarine-infested water—whereas a single-issue approach would enable faster conclusion of easier deals. Concluding bargains on one issue at a time could be practical and fast, especially if full unanimity would not have to be reached.

So why not go back to plurilateralism in world trade? Here, only a coalition of the willing would accede to an agreement, receiving all the rights and accepting all the obligations. The benefit of plurilateralism over multilateralism is speed, as those who do not want to accede are left out and do not constrain the talks. Plurilaterals also would be simple: you either join or you do not; you are free to join when you want, but if you do not join, many years will pass before you can claim the benefits. An added beauty of plurilaterals is that members self-select into the deals; as such, compliance will be easier. Furthermore, given the experience that 152 members in the Doha Round already have agreed on tough issues like cutting tariffs on manufactures and trade facilitation, it is far from certain that plurilaterals would be narrow-based. The incentives are substantial: accession to any one deal, while requiring policy adjustments at home, would also mean more hospitable practices by as many as 151 trading partners abroad.

One example is the Information Technology Agreement (ITA), which brought tariffs of IT goods to zero. It was initially negotiated in 1996 by only fourteen WTO members (the then fifteen-member EU counted as one member). Under the ITA's talk-and-sign model, only the interested members genuinely committed to signing the ultimate deal took part in the negotiations. This approach was nimble and allowed a committed coalition of the willing to move forward. The ITA now claims seventy of the largest WTO members, such as the United States, the EU, Japan, and China.

The downside of the talk-and-sign approach is that possible new members are presented with a *fait accompli*, inevitably leading to resentment ("we didn't write these rules"). This approach in today's world could create a sense of exclusion that would alienate many WTO members. A potentially better plurilateral modality would be optional participation. All WTO members could participate in the negotiations, but then each could decide whether to sign the resulting agreement. Once countries become enthused about a certain plurilateral, they would be free to join and enjoy the rights and meet the obligations required. Such a "talk–don't sign" model would give everyone a place at the table, not unlike the process leading up to the General Agreement on Trade in Services (GATS) during the Uruguay Round.

How do we keep the entire WTO system together if our proposal leads to numerous plurilaterals? Harvard professor Robert Lawrence has called for the WTO to become a "club-of-clubs," with many voluntary associations (plurilaterals), but with all clubs ultimately subsumed in the club-of-clubs that is the WTO.[38] The WTO would coordinate the various clubs and boost dialogue among them, particularly on cross-cutting issues such as environmental protection affecting trade. The WTO's research director, Patrick Low, has proposed something similar, envisioning the WTO as a system of "soft law" with rules that countries could gradually adopt (as was done with the ITA) while the mother ship institution acts as the grand coordinator of the global trade chessboard.[39]

Conclusion

Open trade regimes cannot be taken for granted. The experience of the past two hundred years is that isolationist sentiments and economic hard landings can interrupt liberalization and spawn outright worldwide protection. The global trade agenda was already in trouble before the Great Crisis, with trade ministers dropping the ball on Doha. Once the crisis started to roll, countries from the United States to India to Russia and China broke their pledge not to raise new trade barriers. The G20's pledges against protection and for the conclusion of Doha talks are to be commended. The open question, at this writing, is whether fine words will be put into daily practice. The most remarkable show of resolve to ensure progress in global trade lies in the future, post-Doha: meaningful reduction in the bound tariff rates of emerging nations in order to add certainty to the plans of companies operating on a global scale; and cuts in services trade barriers in order to unleash this potential gusher of world trade. The biggest beneficiaries of advances in these areas would be the developing nations themselves.

The good news is that the intellectual backing for free trade is strong; leaders have learned from the disaster of beggar-thy-neighbor policies of the 1930s; and the multilateral system still commands the respect of member states. But to deliver global trade liberalization, the WTO system will have to be refashioned to meet the twenty-first-century challenges: an array of issues best dealt with globally, but in a complex, multipolar world economy.

8

ANXIOUS WORKERS

While India's protectionism belongs to a class of its own, worrisome trends are found in the United States and Europe, both of which have experienced a decade of "blue-collar blues" in traditional industries.[1] Low-income workers blame outsourcing and import competition for their hardships. Well-paid blue-collar workers in manufacturing industries harbor the same complaints. Affluent professionals in some service sectors, such as software designers and medical technicians, are alarmed by offshoring. Blue-collar blues have become white-collar worries.

Poll after poll in the five years leading to the Great Crisis evinced these concerns.[2] In a 2007 Pew Foundation poll, 59 percent of Americans still endorsed free trade, but the level of support dropped markedly from the 78 percent figure recorded in 2002. A nearly unprecedented 31 percent of Republicans viewed trade in a negative light. In a March–April 2008 *New York Times*-CBS News poll, 68 percent favored trade restrictions to protect domestic industries instead of allowing unrestrained trade, up from 55 percent in 1996. Only 24 percent agreed that "free trade must be allowed, even if domestic industries are hurt by foreign competition," down from 36 percent in 1996.[3] In Europe, where voters are torn between their favorable view of the European Union (EU) and their reticence to embrace free trade with poor countries, the level of support was higher and the drop in trade ratings was less severe. In the Pew poll, some 85 percent of Germans and 78 percent of British respondents were in favor of trade in 2007, as opposed to 91 percent and 87 percent, respectively, in 2002.[4]

In the United States, popular hostility has translated into diminishing congressional votes in favor of trade pacts. From the 1970s up until the implementation of NAFTA in 1994, trade deals usually garnered support from more than three-quarters of congressmen in both political parties. The Tokyo Round package was passed in the U.S. House of Representatives by 395 votes to 7 in 1979, the Uruguay Round by 288 to 148 in 1994, and even the controversial NAFTA pact got a 34-vote majority in 1993. But support, particularly from Democrats, has dwindled since then.[5] While free trade agreements (FTAs) have been passed—and some of them, as with Peru, Oman, or Singapore, with comfortable margins—the renewal of Trade Promotion Authority (TPA), which limits Congress to a no-amendments, up-or-down vote on trade agreements submitted by the president, only passed by one vote, 215 to 214, in the House of Representatives in 2002. The U.S. free trade agreement with Central America and the Dominican Republic (known as CAFTA-DR) squeaked through the House by 217 to 215 in 2005.

To be sure, some of the tough votes reflect years of intense partisanship on the part of Democrats in a Congress narrowly controlled by the Republicans. But in the 2006 and 2008 fall elections, many Democrats who were decidedly unexcited about trade and openness won congressional seats, and now constitute a majority. The 2008 Democratic presidential primary campaign candidates—including Barack Obama—called for a pause on FTAs, floated the idea of renegotiating NAFTA, and showed no interest in the Doha Round. Congressional resistance put the brakes on approval of FTAs negotiated by the Bush administration with Korea, Colombia, and Panama.

Insult to Injury

The Great Crisis seriously aggravated the blue-collar blues and white-collar worries. Millions lost their jobs and unemployment shot up to twenty-year highs in advanced countries. By March 2009, almost half of Americans said they feared for their jobs, as opposed to 28 percent a year prior.[6] Mass demonstrations that called for keeping jobs at home spread across Europe; tens of thousands of Americans jammed the phones and e-mails of their congressional representatives with bouts of anger and pleas for help. Trade became a favorite punching bag, and a stiff breeze of anti-openness swept through Washington and Brussels. The new Team Obama decided not to send the pending FTAs for congressional approval and froze negotiations with Malaysia, allowed Congress to terminate a trucking agreement with Mexico (in flat violation of NAFTA), and accepted a "Buy American" provision in the giant stimulus bill (but promised on paper that the provision would not trample U.S. obligations in the World Trade Organization or bilateral FTAs).[7]

The crisis has tarnished open trade regimes, but at this juncture, one wishes that was the only damage. More telling, the crisis has dealt a severe blow to public confidence; discredited capitalism; disillusioned believers in fair play, job security, and flexible labor markets; downgraded expectations of young adults about their future; and devastated the financial nest eggs of millions of households. People around the world are angry and embittered, and are calling on politicians to shut down the economic roller coaster that is ruining their lives.

This reality could herald a paradigm shift. Regulations and subsidies are in; free markets and self-reliance are out. In past recessions, public assistance was a way of building bridges to freer trade. This time around, open markets may not be found on the other side of the river. This is a problem of grand scale. Open trade and investment regimes are required to deliver the world from its doldrums and pave the way for poor countries to become rich nations.

How can governments cope? Should they provide not only trade adjustment assistance but also, more broadly, globalization adjustment assistance topped off by capitalism adjustment assistance? Is self-reliance a fad of the past?

That depends on the objective. If the aim is equality of outcomes, then capitalism is on the chopping block and much more is needed than adjustment programs; hugely ambitious tax and spending programs must be rolled out. But if the aim is to change the political economy equation—to buy space for globalization—then two answers are possible.

First, a growing sense of precariousness among workers need not automatically spell rising protection. Other forces are at work. Intellectual support for free trade has strengthened since the age of Adam Smith. The foreign policy establishment reliably champions the cause, as exemplified by a remark attributed to Cordell Hull: "When trade doesn't cross borders, armies will." Globalization boosts the influence of lobbies with a vested interest in open trade: export industries, of course, but also port workers, retail employees, and repair personnel. Instructive was the U.S. decision in December 2003 to lift "emergency" tariffs on steel products imposed in March 2002. The tariffs aggravated not only foreign suppliers but also a range of U.S. industries that rely on imported steel products, from oil drilling to autos to heavy machinery. Finally, the militancy of labor lobbies waxes and wanes. When a president like Clinton or Obama occupies the White House, labor opposition is less strident than under a Bush administration. Taking all these forces into account, adjustment programs should seemingly be enough, in normal economic times, to pave the way for future free trade initiatives.

The second answer is grimmer. These are not normal times, one might surmise, and the link between the sense of precariousness and antiglobalization sentiment could become more formidable than at any time since the 1930s. It does not matter that trade accounts for only a modest slice of job losses, or that new technologies and competition between domestic firms create most of the job churn even in good times. World history has memorable instances when domestic distress generated protectionist waves, some in the tsunami class. Everyone recalls the awful Smoot-Hawley Tariff of 1930,[8] but how many remember that, after a series of crises, the last decades of the nineteenth century were capped by the McKinley tariff of 1890? More recently, the economic downturn of the 1980s, when U.S. unemployment exceeded 10 percent, hurried in a heyday of "hidden protectionism," both in the United States and Europe. Washington created its "Super 301" provision to combat unfair foreign trade practices; even supposedly free trader Ronald Reagan fostered "voluntary export restraints" to protect American semiconductors, autos, and steel; and European countries devised ingenious behind-the-border barriers. Antidumping actions skyrocketed on both sides of the Atlantic. In the Great Crisis, America's unemployment figures again climbed to the levels seen in the 1980s, and could well be stuck above 8 percent through 2012. A jobless recovery will only reinforce the fed-up mood that has crept into the psyche of blue-collar and white-collar workers alike since the turn of the century. This is not good news for trade policy.

The point here is that trade is a dark force in popular perceptions, and perceptions drive the debate. The political theater of this era may make trade deals much tougher to pull off, even when coupled with generous adjustment assistance. If a new policy tool kit is needed, where is the place to begin?

Addressing the Angst

Trade has always been responsible for some polarization. For decades, there were two knee-jerk reactions: first, implant "trade remedies" in trade legislation—countervailing duties (against subsidized imports), antidumping duties (against imports sold at "too low" prices), and safeguard measures (against fairly traded but still "injurious" imports)—and second, opening the public coffers for people hurt by trade. National trade remedy measures are largely framed within the strictures of the General Agreement on Tariffs and Trade (GATT) and the World Trade Organization (WTO), and are broadly similar among the major trading powers. Unfortunately, the assured existence of trade remedies to ward off both unfair trade and fair trade that injures domestic firms no longer suffices to carry the battle flag of liberalization. Adjustment assistance has been brought to the front as an additional standard carrier particularly in the developed economies. It has quite distinct expressions on the two sides of the Atlantic.

Beefed-Up Trade Adjustment Assistance

In the United States, the broad instrument for dealing with the negative effects of globalization—apart from the targeted suite of trade remedies—has been the Trade Adjustment Assistance (TAA) program. Originally launched in 1962 to provide assistance to manufacturing workers adversely affected by negotiated tariff liberalization, the program had been rather modest in scale, with strict eligibility requirements and funding that ran well under $1 billion annually, until it was about doubled by President Obama's 2009 stimulus package.

The TAA has inched toward a more generous and encompassing model. The latest TAA bill, arduously championed by congressional Democrats for two years and finally passed in February 2009, represented the biggest overhaul to date. It declared the Democrats winners in their prolonged battle to expand TAA coverage from blue-collar to white-collar workers, both in manufacturing and services. It expanded coverage to workers whose jobs are shifted to countries that do not have reciprocal trade agreements with the United States, such as China or India. And it addressed secondary effects, providing benefits to workers who supply component parts to firms that are hurt by trade. In a spectacle of Washington's efforts to cushion workers in the ailing economy of early 2009, the new TAA law also assists public-sector workers who staff such nontradable services as transportation, hospital care, and state and local benefit offices.

Republicans also scored a victory, securing a 160 percent increase of funding for job training, to $575 million a year. They managed to squash Democratic effort to move from firm-by-firm certification to industrywide certification, namely TAA benefits for any industry when three petitions from firms in that industry are certified within a six-month period.[9]

The expansion legislated in 2009 is expected to vastly increase the pool of workers certified for eligibility. Over the period 2002 to 2006, TAA petitions covered some 235,000 workers annually, 175,000 of whom were certified; and of those certified, 54,000 actually received assistance money.[10] The expansion is expected to double the number of those actually assisted to some 100,000 annually. What is the bill to be footed by taxpayers? Not much compared to bank bailouts, but still around $2 billion per year.

END OF *QUID PRO QUO* TAA politics became a feature of Washington life in 2007, when the 2002 Trade Act was expiring. Democrats made a number of arguments for revising and expanding TAA: evidence from public opinion surveys that Americans would support trade liberalization *if* the government assisted affected workers, firms, and communities; the fact that other industrialized countries devote far more resources to labor-market adjustment programs; and the fact that, despite the many changes in the U.S. economy, including the growth in job churn and global exposure, efforts to assist workers displaced by larger imports or outsourcing have remained modest.

The mighty American Federation of Labor and Congress of Industrial Organizations (AFL-CIO) has mixed feelings about the TAA. Of course, the union movement wants the best deal possible for displaced workers.

But privately, labor leaders tend to fear that a successful program will facilitate the transition to nonunionized jobs, relax public opposition to globalization, and in the end undercut the power of unions. Publicly, they deride the program as "burial insurance." Liberal Democrats often buy these arguments.

Republicans, in the meantime, are trapped between a rock and a hard place. The rock is fear of a vast expansion of fiscal outlays that will give the U.S. social safety net a European flavor. This fear is not baseless: some Democrats do see expanded TAA as a model for retraining programs in the twenty-first century, at far larger expense per worker than traditional unemployment insurance. Republicans argue that, as such programs expand, they "buy" long-term unemployment, not adjustment. Witness France, where structural unemployment (amply compensated with an array of benefits) is stuck above 9 percent.

The hard place is the accusation of Republican insensitivity. Republican leaders also read the polls, which report that a majority of Americans (including Republicans for the first time in sixty years) believe that free trade should be pursued only if laid-off workers are given a helping hand by the government. In the summer of 2008, alarmed by the negative attitudes toward trade liberalization on Capitol Hill and the campaign trail—and obviously buying into the political economy argument for cushioning workers against shocks—a group of twenty-six Republican-leaning trade associations and firms, including Citibank, IBM, and General Motors, lobbied for increased federal help for workers roughed up by globalization.[11]

The TAA got stuck in 2008 in the Senate Finance Committee, with Democrat and Republican staffers locking horns. The main sticking point was a proposed *quid pro quo*: in exchange for the TAA, Republicans wanted to secure Democratic support for free trade agreements with Colombia, Panama, and Korea. But Democrats, in the majority and under growing pressure to reverse globalization and protect American workers, refused to deal.

Now that Team Obama has wrapped TAA in its giant stimulus package, Republican instincts seem to have proven right. There is TAA, but there are no FTAs or Trade Promotion Authority (previously known as "fast track"). The political economy of *quid pro quo* has broken down. This alone says quite a lot about the public mood.

IMPLEMENTATION GAPS The results of the TAA expansion have yet to come in. As far as past experience goes, TAA is a program of good intentions and mediocre results. The real issue going forward is implementation.

On the bright side, the Department of Labor process for enrolling trade-affected workers in the TAA program is swift—on average, 32 days, a huge improvement over the 107 days reported in 2002. Another positive aspect is information and advice. In a 2006 study of five U.S. locations, some three-quarters of surveyed workers received reemployment assistance through a one-stop center, and most often one-on-one services such as job search assistance.[12] Depending on the site, between 36 and 78 percent were reemployed within six months; in cases where the reemployment rate was lower, worker training was more extensive.[13]

But the program has not worked to perfection. First, TAA recipients often experience salary loss when reemployed. In the five-site study, workers who were reemployed earned less than they had made previously, or 79 to 94 percent of their prior wages.

Second, while the 2002 TAA bill was expanded to provide health insurance assistance and wage insurance for older workers (the so-called Alternative TAA, or ATAA), uptake has been meager. Fewer than 5 percent of TAA participants received wage insurance in 2006,[14] and wage insurance benefits totaled only $17 million, far less than the 2002 Congressional Budget Office forecast of $50 million per annum.

Participation in the health coverage benefit is also low. Fewer than seven thousand workers enrolled for the first time in the advance health coverage benefit in 2006. In the five-site study, no more than 12 percent of workers at any location received the health insurance benefit, and fewer than half the workers were even aware of it. High out-of-pocket cost was one explanation. Just 20 percent of older workers received the wage insurance benefit, and many were unaware of it. Only 7 percent of the workers that were eligible for the extended income support took advantage of the advance income tax credit.

These low uptake figures mainly reflect lack of awareness about the health-care and wage insurance benefits. The complexities of a federal program executed by states largely explain why information and implementation falls through the cracks.

The third misgiving over TAA is that execution has not been accompanied by solid performance measures. There are a slew of problems. Data used by the Labor Department to calculate program outcomes, such as reemployment and retention rates, does not pretend to cover all participants. Half of the states did not report on all the individuals who stopped receiving benefits or services. Performance data is thereby skewed toward individuals who stick with the program, and fails to capture success (employment prior to conclusion of program) and plain giving up. Other such problems could be listed at length.

There is a budgetary mismatch between demand and supply. The money that states receive at the beginning of the fiscal year does not reflect projected demand for training services. Instead, large amounts are distributed on the last day of the fiscal year, even to states that have spent less than 1 percent of their training allocation. States have relegated TAA programs to the back burner because they have received no funds from the federal government for the costs of case management.

Overall, the usefulness and execution of TAA has improved, especially since the 2002 Reform Act, but much remains to be done, even with the new law rolled out. Any of the expansions presents challenges—to service workers, to industry-wide certifications, to those affected by trade from non-FTA partners. Better coordination between the Department of Labor and state administrators is high on the list. States should have more leeway in providing services to workers, including counseling to help workers decide whether they need training and which training would be most appropriate. The new law appropriated $86 million of new federal money to compensate states for administering the program.

If and when the federal and state governments prove that they can deliver a successful TAA program, it might be time to expand its scope to cover a wide swath of workers dislocated by economic change, whether or not associated with trade, outsourcing, or foreign investment.

"Flexicurity" and Other European Answers

On the European side of the Atlantic, workers have fretted about globalization for years, but the consequences to them have been less acute than for their American counterparts. Europeans, after all, have a tradition of generous welfare and unemployment regimes. While America wrestled over the expansion of TAA, Europeans have held fast, some countries tooth and nail, to generous unemployment and social benefits. The programs in some countries are so lavish that from a financial standpoint, staying home pays better than going to work.

While the U.S. and UK unemployment insurance programs provide six months of support, according to 2004 data, southern European countries provide benefits for an average of sixteen months, the French thirty months, and Nordic countries for thirty-six months, or three years![15] Unlike the United States and Britain where a laid-off person would initially receive some 54 percent of his salary, in most European countries, the starting point is well above 60 percent, and continues high for a good many years.[16] The spending levels as a share of the GDP on unemployment insurance also tend to be higher in Europe than in the United States—and support for trade follows a similar pattern (figure 8.1), except for the stalwart British, who might actually remember the teachings of David Ricardo.

Labor laws, meanwhile, favor workers over employers, with job rights and long severance pay—provisions that discourage firing, but also hiring. No wonder the benefit lobby musters political clout. Even France's conservative president, Nicolas Sarkozy, doesn't have the political stomach for making welfare recipients go to work.

Several smaller European countries such as Austria, Belgium, Ireland, Sweden, Finland, and the Netherlands also operate consensual labor-employer-government systems in an effort to preempt social friction. Peter Katzenstein has famously linked corporatist practices to small economies: these countries must remain open to trade or perish, but to ensure political acceptance, adjustment costs are distributed among the three partners—labor, capital, and government—through managed bargains.[17] This model aims at dividing productivity gains in a "fair" manner while restraining wage hikes, both in periods of recession and inflation. In other words, capital concedes on guarantees for employment and labor concedes on pay—stability, *über alles*.

Chapter 3 shows that the United States tends to have the greatest income gaps between the top and bottom wage earners among advanced nations. The top 10th percentile of U.S. wage earners made on average five times more in wages than the bottom 10th percentile in 2005. The ratio in

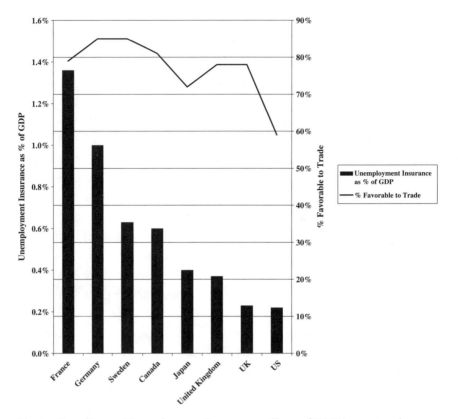

Fig. 8.1 Spending on Unemployment Programs as Share of GDP in 2006 and Attitudes toward Trade in 2007, Select OECD Economies. *Sources*: Organization for Economic Cooperation and Development; BBC.

Europe and Japan, the top 10th makes three times as much as the bottom 10th percentile. Transatlantic differences in wage and salary outcomes are associated with different degrees of labor flexibility. When Americans (and Brits) lose their jobs, they are quicker to get new ones, even at less pay; Europeans are slower to get new jobs but, thanks to the safety net, they can afford to wait around for work with similar pay.[18]

While the welfare state and rigid labor laws may serve to narrow income inequalities, they also undercut Europe's economic dynamism. For this reason, the package started to unravel in the 1990s, in part owing to Margaret Thatcher's stern reforms, in part due to the consolidation of the single European market, and in good part because of the euro. When exchange rates can no longer be adjusted at the national level, flexible labor markets are essential for absorbing external shocks. More recently, escalating public expenditures to pay for the retirement of baby boomers have stretched budgets across Europe and led to questions of solvency unless benefits are curbed—and hurried a new wave of purse-strings conservatives like Angela Merkel in Germany and Nicholas Sarkozy in France.

The collective reckoning discovered a new consensus: European youth need to move from cafes to work. The European Commission threw its weight behind flexible labor markets. The Old Continent began to look somewhat more like the Wild West. A mosaic of experiments emerged.[19] Belgium, France, Germany, Ireland, Italy, and the Netherlands relaxed regulations for part-time work; France and Belgium shortened weekly work hours; in Germany, collective agreements allowed certain firms to use a range of flexibility clauses. Spain, France, Ireland, the Netherlands, Austria, and Portugal cut payroll taxes; Finland, France, Portugal, and Spain changed the rules of the game for collective bargaining.

The real champion has been the "flexicurity" model, first implemented by Denmark's social democratic prime minister, Poul Nyrup Rasmussen, in the 1990s. Flexicurity combines flexible labor markets with security in the event of unemployment—easy hiring and firing (flexibility for employers) and high benefits for the unemployed (security for the employees).

In a widely cited article, journalist Robert Kuttner celebrated Denmark's success.[20] The country is competitive, devoted to free trade, unfettered by industrial policies, and enjoys one of the world's lowest unemployment rates and most equal income distributions. On the other side of the coin are strong trade unions, public spending that amounts to 50 percent of GDP, and the second-highest tax rate in the world after Sweden. With this combo, the Danes buy generous child-care and family-leave arrangements, unemployment compensation that covers some 95 percent of lost wages, free higher education, secure pensions in old age, and the world's most creative system of worker retraining. Similar stories are found throughout the Nordic countries; Ireland and Britain offer variants of flexicurity, high on the flexibility axis.

Flexicurity has performed well, particularly in contrast to Italy, which has Europe's most rigid labor laws, and as a result, the highest unemployment rate. Italy also has a dual economy, with a flexible informal system operating alongside the rigid formal one. The core flexicurity countries, meanwhile, saw unemployment rates plunge from the low teens to around 5 to 7 percent before the Great Crisis. To be sure, flexicurity was just part of the picture: it happened to be adopted by governments with records of good macroeconomic management.

Seeing a marketable concept, the European Commission has hailed flexicurity for employers and employees alike, as a way to meet the global challenge. But trade worriers urge further action because they doubt that the generous but costly welfare state can last. The European Commission jumped on the issue in 2005 by publishing a report titled "European Values in a Globalized World," which cherishes market liberalization but also calls for greater assistance in finding new jobs for workers whose jobs disappear. The report was followed by the establishment of a European Globalization Adjustment Fund (EGF), a cushion against trade and all other ills of globalization.[21]

The EGF's armory is colorful. It provides job search assistance and occupational guidance, tailor-made training including information technology (IT) skills, certification of acquired experience, outplacement assistance, aid for entrepreneurs and self-employment, job search and mobility allowances, and encouragement for disadvantaged or older workers to remain in the job market. But at €500 million a year, the EGF is decidedly smaller than the TAA, yet aimed at a larger audience. But it is good public relations for the European Commission that it can free ride on the second layer of cushioning provided by member states. The EGF does not cover "passive" social-protection measures, such as retirement pensions or unemployment benefits, because the commission deems these the responsibility of the member states. Instead, the EGF is an "active" complement to "passive" national support systems. Member states, not individual firms, bear the burden of sending petitions for EGF aid—this typically happens when they foresee "large-scale redundancies" caused by globalization stalking their national economies.[22]

After the EU organs churned away, the EGF started operations in 2007. The track record is too short to judge. The EGF has already been visited by France on behalf of its automaker Peugeot and Renault suppliers for €3.8 million and Portugal for various car and car part companies, totaling €2.4 million to cushion the blow to 1,549 redundant workers. Italy has requested aid on behalf of textile producers in the regions of Piedmonte, Lombardia, and Sardegna for as much as €43 million, and Lithuania for Alytaus Tekstile for as little as €0.3 million. Spain, Malta, and Finland have also requested assistance.[23]

More Morphine?

The TAA and EGF were fine as instruments for pacifying protesters and allaying workers in the years before the Great Crisis. But events since 2007 make them look like feeble, absentminded nibbling around the edges of distress that requires broader and sturdier attention.

Even in a good economy, job churn is a perennial issue. As much as a quarter of the workforce changes jobs every year; in the Great Crisis, many have lost their jobs forever. Most of this distress has nothing to do with foreign trade, but many of the woes are blamed on globalization. Forces at play in the political economy equation can deliver a very poor economic result. Something will have to give, and it will likely be bigger than an annual appropriations program to address consequences of factories moving to China.

Five-Point Plan

The European cushions are fluffy enough; what is needed rather than security is more labor market flexibility. The best means to encourage hiring of full-time employees is to enable expeditious and low-cost firing. European employers for too long have had the short end of the stick.

In the United States, the story is different. Here, a new policy paradigm is needed for attacking the source of the problem. The real problem is not China or India or computers, it is stickiness of labor to a city or town when an external shock of any sort occurs. The new system should marry security with labor mobility. We propose an action plan on five legs.

HEALTH CARE First, portable and resilient health insurance would wipe out one of the main sources of fears over losing a job, namely losing health insurance as well. America's employer-sponsored insurance system is unique among major economies. By default not by design, it represents the path-dependent consequence of wage controls imposed during the Second World War. Wage controls in an overheated war economy gave employers the incentive to offer, and employees every reason to accept, uncontrolled and untaxed fringe benefits.[24] Sixty years later, this system is completely unsuited to a world of massive job churn, part-time employment, and the considerable disparity between firms in their financial ability to pay the health costs of their employees and retirees. In recognition of today's labor market, health insurance should be made portable, or "citizen-based" rather than employer-based, through a combination of taxes and personal mandates.[25] However, whether this will truly be the outcome of the new health-care law will remain to be seen. Congress and Team Obama have enlarged the scope of health subsidies for low-income households and limited the ability of insurance companies to cancel existing coverage or deny new coverage. The legislative dust has just settled, but it is a safe prediction that health-care costs will continue to escalate faster than GDP, and that many American families will still be dissatisfied with their health coverage.

In Europe, universal, government-sponsored health care is pretty much in place. But the common way of controlling costs is to ration care, sometimes very severely, such as hip replacements and end-of-life operations. While we claim no expertise in health care, it is clear that the United States must not end up with a health-care system where the chronically ill queue for months to receive care, where overworked doctors have every incentive to regard patients as cattle, and where medical companies have no financial reason to push for better drugs and equipment. Such outcomes are a sad reality in many welfare states. On the other hand, if the United States replicates the lavish systems found in a few countries, such as France, the arithmetic dictates either a big increase in taxes or a hefty debt burden passed to future generations.

In America, access cannot come at the expense of quality. Whatever government comes up with that combination will be voted into the wilderness. But the system must have floor: any American child or adult who simply cannot pay should still have access to preventive and basic health care. Pertinent for this chapter, the system should guarantee that workers would not need to forgo job offers to keep their existing health insurance, and employees should not lose their insurance as a consequence of being laid off.

Curbing the responsibility of employers for health care would take a massive burden off the shoulders of American companies: a good 10 percent of the price of a Ford Mustang is health insurance. At the national level, this change would sharply improve the competitive standing of firms that today are responsible for the health not only of their employees but also of numerous retirees.

Portability is not untested in America. There is an existing citizen-based health insurance program, Medicaid. But details make the deal. Among other experts, Stuart Butler has drawn the picture.[26] First, create large, stable insurance pools for all workers in order to spread insurance risks widely. This is particularly important for small- and medium-sized firms. Second, organize coverage that is portable between jobs. This only can be done if the insurance is effectively owned by the worker. Employers can help by deducting premiums from the paycheck and contributing to the health plan, but ownership should rest with the employee. Unfortunately, these two ideas have been lost in the current U.S. health debate. The third idea is to make the $200 billion in federal and state tax breaks for health care more uniform between employees, whatever their salary, in order to increase the share of working families able to afford coverage. A small version of this idea may be enacted in the form of a new tax on "Cadillac" health-care plans.

HOUSING A second agent of worker immobility is the housing market. About 12 percent of U.S. home-owning households move within a typical two-year period, according to the American Housing Survey. Getting stuck with a house in a dead market, with not enough income to double up on mortgage and rent, stops many workers from looking for a job beyond a two-hour driving distance. The plunge in house values in the Great Crisis has turned a local problem into a national problem. According to one recent study, having negative equity reduces the two-year mobility rate by 5.6 percentage points, thus cutting the baseline mobility rate of 12 percent by almost half.[27] A $1,000 higher real annual mortgage interest cost is estimated to reduce mobility by 2.8 percentage points, or about one-quarter of the baseline.

An improved ability to bridge the process of selling and buying (or renting) a home might complement portable health insurance in terms of labor mobility. But the implications of a meaningful solution are not clear. Public money might produce only marginal benefits. It seems to us that this is an area calling for narrowly targeted experiments to determine whether a better bridge can be designed.

UNEMPLOYMENT INSURANCE Third, unemployment insurance should possibly be configured to resemble its generous TAA cousin. The current unemployment insurance (UI) system is rightly criticized for providing too few benefits (an average of about $281 a week, not enough to pay a mortgage and feed a family) for too short a time (twenty-six weeks). This is not much, and in the Great Crisis meant that millions of workers feared their UI checks would run out prior to landing a new job. However, as usually happens, Congress extended the UI benefit period when it became clear that economic recovery was not delivering new jobs. However, the UI system lets millions of workers fall through the cracks: those who are employed part-time, those who voluntarily leave one job to take another, and those who are unemployed for long periods. As a consequence, the average "recipiency rate"—the percent of unemployed individuals receiving UI over the past twenty-seven years—has been a meager 37 percent.[28]

The lowest common denominator of proposals is this: establish a uniform duration at a minimum of twenty-six weeks in all state programs, and standardize UI benefit levels to at least 50 percent of lost earnings (the coverage since the 1980s has been about 36 percent of lost earnings) up to a maximum of $10,000 a year for at least two years. The time frame would thus be roughly the same as for the TAA program, which provides seventy-eight weeks of income maintenance payments in addition to an initial twenty-six weeks of UI, as long as the job hunter is enrolled in training. The support for lost earnings would match the TAA benefits for some workers above fifty years old who are earning less than their prior salaries. All together, a rather modest UI "top-up" along these lines is estimated to cost around $3 to $4 billion per year. This estimate includes the cost of a tax credit that eligible displaced workers could use to purchase health insurance. Compared to bailout money in the Great Crisis, this seems like pocket change.

A more ambitious program would substantially raise unemployment benefits (though not all the way to the TAA level) and launch widespread adult retraining programs. This change would answer the charge that it is unfair that workers who lose their jobs to imports are far more handsomely compensated than those who lose their jobs to a computer. Programs for all displaced workers—regardless of why and where the job disappears—are obviously more equitable than programs targeted at a single source of job loss, like trade.

Head of the TAA Coalition Howard Rosen calls for a more tailor-made approach: standardization across states, but customization by the worker's wage history, local labor market conditions, and the reason for separation.[29] Workers living in regions with poor labor market conditions might receive a higher level of assistance, assistance for longer periods, or both. The idea, in short, is to standardize benefits nationally and customize them individually.

Assuming that the budget burden of more-generous UI benefits can be met, a balance still needs to be struck so as not to encourage slouching and form new pools of welfare beneficiaries. Programs like the Earned Income Tax Credit, the TAA's wage insurance program, or the UK Working Families Tax Credit (a targeted wage subsidy paid to employers) are far superior to unemployment benefits with no link to new jobs.

Public policy expert Robert J. LaLonde of the University of Chicago makes an excellent argument in this direction. He posits that rather than higher UI spending, the right approach to encourage work is using the UI trust funds to bridge the wage gap between earnings on pre- and postdisplacement jobs.[30] But LaLonde would not strive to match the workers' prior salaries fully, arguing that such a full recovery of one's wages upon assuming a new job would lead to moral hazard and undermine incentives for searching while on the job for better paying positions, a feature that adds to America's productivity. LaLonde would, however, extend the eligibility period for the displaced workers up to four years, particularly for middle-aged workers who lose their jobs and have trouble getting back to the same earning bracket.

EDUCATION The fourth leg of the action plan is well known in globalization debates: the quality of formal education and lifelong training. The United States compensates somewhat for its lackluster performance in primary and secondary schooling with superb universities and high rates of college attendance. The current, soaring tuition costs of universities and draining of financial aid now in the face of the Great Crisis do, however, risk drops in college attendance. And while lifelong training opportunities are improving, they have some distance to go.

Europe does quite well on the primary and secondary education legs, but falls behind America at the university level, both in terms of quality and attendance rates. This has prompted the European Commission to initiate a competitiveness agenda, including a "European MIT." Stateside, successive administrations have sought to rectify U.S. educational gaps through the secondary school level, but union pressures and state responsibility for schooling have stifled federal efforts. In a world where the main source of job churn is technology, and where technology jumps in giant leaps, the basics of math, science, and language will have to be vastly improved in order for American workers to compete. Perhaps federal efforts should concentrate on the lifelong training part of the equation, making adult education more accessible and affordable through the Internet and in group settings for a wider range of skills.

ENTREPRENEURS The final leg of the economic mobility agenda is entrepreneurship. According to the Kauffman Foundation, a major incubator of entrepreneurship, in 2007 an average of 0.3 percent of the adult population in America started a new business *each month*. In other words, approximately 450,000 new businesses were created monthly during the year.[31] In some regions, like Phoenix or Washington, D.C., the rate is around 0.5 percent.

Small firms, when successful, are the backbone of U.S. economy and the main source of jobs in the nation. The rationale of tax breaks and subsidies for start-ups can be contested on the grounds of equity as well as economic efficiency.[32] But a fresh case can be made that starting one's own business can be viewed not as a luxury, but as a safety valve for workers across the economy.

Entrepreneurship, even if at the margins of the formal sector, has been precisely this safety valve for millions in the crisis-stricken developing economies. The pattern is now taking hold also in America's ailing economy. Workers exhausted by futile job searches have launched ventures from coast to coast. Starting a business should always be an option, especially when the economy turns bad and other options are depleted. Of course, companies started out of necessity may not be as vibrant as those started out of opportunity. But who knows? Some of the greatest U.S. companies like Hewlett-Packard, General Electric, Microsoft, Sports Illustrated, and Trader Joe's have been launched in the depths of recessions.

Conclusion

The story of workers in the global economy has been recounted many times. Few mysteries remain. We know what the trouble is—the sense of precariousness driven by many factors, with trade and globalization too often seen as the most important. We know the longer-term consequence—a powerful political backlash against globalization. We also know what should be done to reduce precariousness—higher health-care and benefit floors for dislocated workers, and better education and training for everyone. And we know the troubles in getting there, including union opposition, fiscal limitations, and administrative hurdles.

The real and most-effective remedy, both short-term and long-term, is pure and simple economic growth. If jobs are plenty and pocketbooks grow, concerns about a hit through trade will diminish. This should be our aspiration. Safeguarding free markets to deliver the economy both from the immediate crisis and from sluggish growth is the challenge of our time. A supplementary answer, of some importance for the United States, is to pursue macroeconomic policies that ensure roughly balanced trade in goods and services, not structural trade deficits that exceed 4 percent of GDP year after year and hurt America's trade agenda. Cutting the massive fiscal deficit is essential for getting that done.

The Great Crisis has dealt a devastating blow to wallets, life prospects, and the worldview of workers who were already skeptical of trade and globalization. This is paradoxical, because open trade and free markets offer the keys to recovery and another golden era. Even before the crisis, each move toward openness seemed more painstaking than the prior move; the climb will get more difficult unless the bad equilibrium between economics and politics is put right.

New floors and fresh incentives are required to reduce the precariousness of workers that leads to other ills, not only to resistance to open markets but also to reduced risk taking and pure bitterness. Getting more mobility and opportunity in the system is far from un-American. These features are about equipping the workforce to take a chance when it arises and to take a blow when it hits. And they are about fueling the country's economic engines, which need to run at full steam to get prosperity back.

A general effort also can reduce the catch-22 created by the very labels "trade adjustment" and "globalization fund." Though potentially useful in overcoming political resistance to particular trade deals, these terms are hugely counterproductive in the long run. They cement the public perception that trade and globalization threaten our way of life. Our proposals are not targeted at adjustment *per se*, or at particular trade deals, but rather at furthering flexibility and mobility of workers in the new technology economy.

These ideas are hardly new. The policy consensus in Washington has in the past few years moved toward comprehensive remedies to the precariousness syndrome. Whether better health-care coverage or unemployment insurance will bring Americans around to cherish globalization is a tall question. These things would certainly not hurt and probably would help. They would have to be accompanied by a building of awareness about the benefits of trade and the expanded social safety net.

What will not work is steeply progressive taxation. The Organization for Economic Cooperation and Development (OECD) secretary general Angel Gurria has correctly argued that: "[A]lthough the role of the tax and benefit system in redistributing incomes and in curbing poverty remains important in many OECD countries, our data confirms that its effectiveness has gone down in the past ten years. Trying to patch the gaps in income distribution solely through more social spending is like treating the symptoms instead of the disease. Increasing employment is the best way of reducing poverty."[33]

What should work is improved mobility and opportunity. Health care and houses should not be a reason for people to stay in dead-end jobs and communities. Wage insurance for a broad class of dislocated workers might be in order; an even better approach is stronger incentives to search for well-paying jobs. Continued, lifelong access to quality education and training are as good for mobility as they are for minds, mind-sets, and morality. The tough design issues are to avoid disincentives to work, to get implementation right, and to customize the package to the worker— and to do it within our means.

9

NEW FRICTIONS

Globalization has been jammed before. It slowed in the late nineteenth century, as European powers raised their protective tariffs. After the First World War, the United States, the United Kingdom, France, and others raised their tariff walls against a feared avalanche of German merchandise. In the wake of Black Friday, the United States enacted the Smoot-Hawley Tariff, and countries from Canada to France, Italy, Spain, and Switzerland followed suit. In the 1980s, oil shocks, recession, and inflation spurred a wave of "voluntary" export restraints and antidumping petitions. But globalization was revived every time by technological advances, political pressure by globalized firms, eventual policy leadership by the United States, and concerted multilateral action.

The situation created by the Great Crisis is not all that different: a Wall Street shock, deep recession, and sprouts of protection. The lead players convened the G20 to reiterate their commitment to open markets and to clear rules of the game. Public intellectuals have flooded blogs and air time to remind politicians about the dangers of protectionism.

Looming behind more traditional barriers are many new and subtle threats to world trade and finance that have thus far escaped multilateral management. One such threat is climate change; another is national security.

Climate policies can lead to rules that are justified as a means to limit greenhouse gas (GHG) emissions, yet end up imposing unnecessary barriers to trade; national security can be cited as a reason to block foreign investment and hoard energy supplies. Both are tough to deal with because of overriding reasons to stop pollution, terrorism, and rogue nations. Can the world learn to walk and chew gum at the same time—to address the dangers, yet harvest the payoff from future globalization?

Preserving the Climate—for Trade?

The potential for climate measures to become trade barriers is cut-and-dried: countries may enact rules that both limit GHG-intensive imports and badger reluctant countries (notably, India and China) to slow their GHG trajectories. Under the worthy umbrella of safeguarding the environment, climate change can quickly be turned into an argument for protecting domestic industries.[1]

There are two main reasons why governments want to include trade-related measures in their climate programs.[2] First, there is a concern that emissions reductions done at home would go for naught if production and emissions migrated to other countries with lax regulations. This is the "polluter haven" problem, a.k.a. "leakage" or "carbon laundering."

Second, there is an adverse competitiveness impact if a country reduces its own emissions while its trading partners do not. This prospect gives rise to demands for a "level playing field"—that countries should shoulder the burdens of climate change rules together rather than taking advantage, in the trade and investment realm, of nations that are better world citizens. Governments may thus impose trade penalties as sanctions against free riders.

Complicating the legislative dynamics around the world are the various interests playing the climate-change game. Environmentalists want tough rules everywhere—behind the border and at the border. Developed country firms that worry about erosion of their competitiveness vis-à-vis the BRICKs (Brazil, Russia, India, China, and Korea) would like to see meaningful border controls. China, despite its newfound commitment to a national cleanup, provokes particular concern. U.S. and European Union (EU) companies argue that China's growing emissions and weak controls give Chinese producers an unfair advantage, and ought to be answered with tough border adjustments. Such measures, they argue, would compel China and other climate-unfriendly nations to curb their GHG emissions.

Labor unions are another lobby in the environmental mix. They fear that domestic firms will depart for countries with relaxed controls to escape costly GHG regulations at home. The "leakage" argument is potent in Europe and the United States, particularly now that politicians are called to keep jobs at home.[3] Offshoring could be preempted, unions say, by tough at-the-border barriers on GHG-heavy goods made abroad.[4]

Indeed, various policy measures have been proposed, and several have been deployed, at least on a modest scale, to curb GHG emissions around the planet. These include carbon taxes, cap-and-trade systems, comparability measures, performance standards, and, of course, declarations of improved carbon efficiency.

But countries differ sharply in the details and toughness of their measures. The European Union has moved furthest in the direction of trading carbon permits, but several teeth were pulled from the EU Phase III agreement, announced in December 2008, due to strong opposition from industry lobbies already recoiling in the economic downturn.[5] Special exemptions were made for high-polluting industries such as cement, autos, steel, and aluminum. Some coal-fired electric power plants were granted free allowances for a significant period. To its credit, in Phase III, the European Commission deferred the consideration of trade restrictions on imports until 2013.

In the United States, the Lieberman-Warner-Boxer Bill, among the most ambitious U.S. efforts at climate legislation, was temporarily defeated in 2008, mainly due to fierce lobbying by energy-intensive industries, but also because of its implications for trade relations. Among other features, the bill would have required foreign suppliers that had not taken "comparable action" to the U.S. control measures to purchase GHG allowances before their exports would be allowed entry into the U.S. market. This provision, along with several others, would set the table for trade disputes with China, India, and other emerging industrial powers.[6]

A blended version of House and Senate legislation could be enacted during the Obama administration. A 600-page draft House bill—the American Clean Energy and Security Act, sponsored by Congressmen Henry Waxman and Edward Markey—was approved by a 219 to 212 margin in the House in June 2009. This bill establishes a cap-and-trade system and calls for a cut of 17 percent from 2005 levels by 2020, slightly more aggressive than President Obama's goal of a 14 percent cut by 2020. In the realm of international trade, the bill seeks to prevent leakage of energy-intensive industries to countries without the same climate standards by providing free allowances and even cash rebates to energy-intensive industries. If that does not do the trick, the bill has an insurance clause, or a requirement for importers of energy-intensive goods from countries that do not have similar GHG goals to purchase emission permits—not right away, but after 2017. In September 2009, Senate Democrats rolled out an even more ambitious version: 20 percent reduction from 2005 levels by 2020 and an 83 percent reduction by 2050.

There may be other climate troubles ahead, besides whatever trade provisions are nested in the final version of U.S. climate legislation and whatever measures the European Union may enact. Brazil has argued that a 54 cent-per-gallon import tax on its ethanol exports to the United States is World Trade Organization (WTO) illegal and should be dropped. In February 2008, Canada warned the United States against an overly broad interpretation of the Energy Independence and Security Act of December 2007, which prohibits the Pentagon from purchasing "dirty oil"— essentially meaning oil extracted from Alberta's sands in the McKenzie Delta.[7] For its part, the U.S. government has complained that the EU plan to cover aviation in its Emissions Trading Scheme (ETS) breaches a bilateral agreement that precludes the imposition of charges on carriers from the other country.[8] Similar concerns relate to maritime trade. The European Commission has thus far steered clear from souring transatlantic ties with Washington, and has postponed a decision on applying the ETS system to imported merchandise or aviation until 2013.

Battle of the Rules

It is hard to wiggle out of the trade effects of climate-change legislation. As long as countries apply differing standards and enforcement, costly action at home will cry out for barriers at the border. Yet such barriers can be literally taxing. World Bank simulations suggest that the potential impact of EU trade measures could reduce U.S. exports to Europe by 7 percent; the most energy-intensive industries, such as steel and cement, could suffer losses of up to 30 percent.[9] Of course, if the United States and other major trading nations implement their own GHG trade restrictions, the cumulative trade losses could be greater.

The real problem surrounding the climate-trade clash is simple—and fixable. Clear multilateral rules do not yet exist to guide countries toward controls that are both effective against GHG and trade friendly, nor do rules clearly define appropriate responses to excessive and trade-distorting standards.

The 1992 United Nations Framework Convention on Climate Change (UNFCCC) established global guidelines aimed at clamping down on emissions. This was a watershed convention, but before and after the UNFCCC, each country has been cooking its own dish of subsidies, border adjustments, and other GHG controls in response to environmental lobbies, industries, and unions—and to nurture both national champions and declining sectors.[10] The United States is well along this path with its ethanol, wind and solar subsidies, and chatter about "green jobs." European leaders warm to the same approach.

WTO director general Pascal Lamy has warned against unilateralism in climate change policies, arguing that "the notion of go-it-alone is clearly a distant second-best to an international solution, which sets a level playing field."[11] We agree.[12]

But multilateralism at the juncture of climate and commerce has a long way to go. Article 3.5 of the UNFCCC states: "Measures taken to combat climate change, including unilateral ones, should not constitute a means of arbitrary or unjustifiable discrimination or a disguised restriction on international trade," sentiments echoed in the Kyoto Protocol.[13] UNFCCC representatives participate in meetings of the WTO Committee on Trade and Environment, while the WTO Secretariat attends UNFCCC Conference of Parties meetings. This is all well and good—but far short of the concrete detail needed to define "unjustifiable discrimination" or avert "disguised restrictions."

Border adjustment measures are only one sort of hazard potentially created by GHG controls. Other rules can end up violating any one of GATT Articles 1, 3, and 9 (on Most Favored Nation Treatment, National Treatment, and General Elimination of Quantitative Restrictions, respectively), the Agreement on Subsidies and Countervailing Measures, or the Agreement on Technical Barriers to Trade. For instance, the Energy Independence and Security Act, signed by President George W. Bush in December 2007, may violate the Agreement on Technical Barriers to Trade, while the renewable fuel standards in the bill may violate national treatment clauses.[14]

To be sure, there is a great deal of wiggle room in the GATT: the system allows a waiver of sorts through Article 20 (General Exceptions), which permits otherwise inconsistent trade restrictions if they are "necessary" to protect human, animal, or plant life or health, or if they conserve exhaustible natural resources—language that covers GHG emissions. However, the application of Article 20 is limited by its own *chapeau*, which precludes "arbitrary or unjustifiable discrimination between countries where the same conditions prevail, or a disguised restriction on international trade." Not surprisingly, this limitation reads much the same as in the UNFCCC, since the United Nations borrowed its language from the GATT. Again, the sentiments are fine, but the devil is in the details, and the only way details will be discovered—given the ambiguity of today's trade rules—is through prolonged litigation in the WTO, possibly in the wake of tit-for-tat retaliation.

The most worrisome initiatives from the trade perspective are national cap-and-trade systems, such as the ones envisioned in American bills and already in effect in Europe. Traded emissions permits created by cap-and-trade systems—sometimes auctioned, sometimes given away free—may or may not be a subsidy or a tax; with these ambiguities, they could fall through the cracks in the WTO rules. While cap-and-trade systems are not necessarily incompatible with the WTO in their own right, they often are accompanied by standards and regulations, eco-labeling, and other measures that are more likely to be incompatible with current WTO rules.

Finding Middle Ground

A trade-friendly approach that would please both environmentalists and import-competing industries and be less distorting would entail carbon taxes collected at the border. The best tax would be uniform across industries as well as across countries. But carbon taxes find little political support; political energy everywhere is directed toward cap-and-trade systems with various exemptions and free allowances. Meshing the trade dimension of differing cap-and-trade systems will be a challenge of the first order.

The outcome of the meshing exercise remains to be determined, but if extensive trade barriers are enacted, the atmosphere for commerce will worsen. At the same time, it is questionable whether trade restrictions will do much to save the planet from drought and flood, since power generation (especially coal-fired plants), transportation (trucks and autos), and agriculture (slash-and-burn clearing and methane-belching livestock) are largely responsible for GHG emissions.[15]

It is no stretch to argue that a casualty of climate-related trade battles could be fatigue in fighting climate change. To minimize trade battles, climate legislation that includes trade restrictive measures should reflect the core disciplines of the existing WTO system. If and when WTO members negotiate a new code on trade rules with respect to GHG emissions, these core disciplines should become the reference point.

A good solution, advocated by Hufbauer, Charnovitz, and Kim (2009), would entail a new Climate Code that enumerates both permitted and proscribed trade measures in the name of climate control.[16] The key for the code would be to enlist a critical mass of countries. It could start out as a plurilateral agreement, whereby a subset of WTO members commits to a set of rules that is binding among them and that can be enforced in a WTO dispute settlement system. Although such a code would require a consensus of all WTO members to be formally added to the WTO agreement, that consent might be politically acceptable because it would not require that all WTO members agree to the disciplines of the code.

If such a code could prevent disputes coming to the WTO between the United States, the European Union, Canada, Japan, and a few other Organization for Economic Cooperation and Development (OECD) countries, it would certainly have achieved much. If it could head off disputes involving China and India as well, it would be a splendid accomplishment. Shared leadership by the United States, the European Union, and China is the key for climate change and trade talks alike.

Another option is to initiate sectoral WTO agreements on climate that would restrict international trade in a particular commodity (for example, steel) to countries with qualifying GHG emission limits. The use of trade-restrictive sectoral agreements (for example, textiles and apparel) has a long and doubtful history in the multilateral trading system, and one of the achievements of the Uruguay Round was the phaseout of those agreements.[17] It is a step backward to contemplate a new round of sectoral accords, but that may turn out to be the least-damaging means of reconciling climate imperatives with the trading system.

Climate rules might offer an opportunity to get the Doha talks moving. For example, to encourage WTO negotiating efforts and discourage potential acrimony about climate, the climate legislation fashioned in Washington and other world capitals could contain a moratorium on the application of border measures or other extraterritorial controls to imported products—say, through 2013. This breathing spell would enable industries to get over the tough economic hump and reduce the political pressures against retaliatory climate rules.

To be sure, the WTO is not the only forum for rule making. If negotiating the Climate Code as a WTO plurilateral agreement proves politically impossible, a group of like-minded WTO member governments could negotiate a compact outside the WTO. While the WTO dispute settlement would not be available for enforcement of such a deal, the compact members could devise their own dispute settlement mechanism. Also within the compact, the international environmental forums could establish nonbinding principles for the use of trade measures for climate change. But this is a stretch: many countries would object to trying to write policies that might conflict with existing WTO rules.

Efforts to fashion meaningful multilateral trade rules related to climate change face a political catch-22. While all countries would like to discipline climate measures that might restrict *their* access to foreign markets, few have an interest in limiting their *own* maneuvering room. Political incentives are in place to tackle climate change at the WTO, but the vast array of nested issues—involving tariffs, nontariff barriers, subsidies, domestic standards, labeling, and more—almost certainly spells long months of negotiation. A WTO Climate Code thus appears as distant as it is urgent, but the further countries progress in devising their own national systems for regulating climate change, the harder it will become to agree on a global body of rules. Better later than never, but better sooner than later.

Freeing Pollution-Lites

Fortunately, the coin of trade-related climate policies has two sides. The promising side is trade in environmental goods and services (EGS). Here the issue is not blocking pollution-generating goods, but rather liberalizing pollution-reduction goods. The political economy, however, is not all that different.

The EGS idea was planted on the multilateral agenda by the Clinton administration during the ill-fated WTO Seattle Ministerial held in Seattle in 1999. EGS was subsequently carried over to the Doha agenda. The underlying notions are three: (1) trade is an important channel for diffusing goods and services that can reduce GHG emissions (and other pollutants); (2) lowering trade barriers brings down the price of such goods and services; which (3) makes them more affordable to industry and households and cuts the cost of climate mitigation efforts.

One corollary of this reasoning is that trade liberalization would boost the incentives for countries to produce and export low-carbon goods and energy-efficient technologies. Another corollary is that trade liberalization can give developing countries rapid access to advanced technologies. The coverage of both goods and services reflects the fact that environmental goods are inherently bundled with services. For example, solar panels for building require consulting, design, and construction services.

The WTO has hailed EGS as "win-win-win" for climate, trade, and development. In fact, the WTO finds that countries that are more open to trade adopt clean technologies more quickly.[18] The World Bank has thrown its weight behind the idea. A 2007 World Bank study, *International Trade and Climate Change*, finds that removing tariffs on four basic clean energy technologies (wind, solar, clean coal, and efficient lighting) in eighteen developing countries would boost trade up to 7 percent; if nontariff barriers were also eliminated, trade would go up by 13 percent.

The United States and the European Union have diligently pushed the EGS agenda. In the fall of 2007, they developed a two-tiered joint proposal for a WTO environmental goods and services agreement (EGSA). The first tier aims at eliminating tariffs and nontariff barriers on goods directly linked to mitigating climate change, and removing barriers on air pollution and climate control services, technical testing and analysis, and services for the design and construction of carbon dioxide (CO_2)–efficient plants and buildings.

The second tier centers on eliminating tariffs and nontariff barriers (NTBs) on a detailed list of more than 150 goods, ranging from air vacuums and pumps to filtering and purifying machinery and wind-powered electric generators—all items that indirectly reduce GHG emissions.[19] The list was the joint work of a group that styled itself as Friends of Environmental Goods—the United States, the European Union, and also Canada, Japan, Korea, New Zealand, Norway, Taiwan, and Switzerland. For services, the second tier would start by binding present levels of market access and then further liberalize an array of environmental and climate-related services.[20]

Overall, global trade in environmental goods (not counting services) covered by the proposal is a meaningful $610 billion plus per year, growing at 15 percent annually. But when push for an initiative comes from the United States and Europe, push back often comes from developing countries more bent on building domestic capacity than opening their markets. Where EGS friends want permanent liberalization on a predetermined list of products, less-enthusiastic countries such as Brazil seek case-by-case negotiation on the basis of bilateral or plurilateral requests. Variants offered by India and Argentina would temporarily liberalize barriers for "designated projects," while several countries propose differentiated treatment among WTO members, with commitments staged to the level of development.

Trade proposals for CO_2-lite items are just the reverse of proposals for CO_2-heavy goods. Developing countries want no restrictions on CO_2-heavy goods, but want to keep existing barriers on CO_2-lite goods; advanced countries want new restrictions on CO_2-heavy goods, and new opening on CO_2-lites. These conflicting positions echo postures in other arenas of the WTO negotiations. But in important respects, they are out of kilter with national export capabilities. Brazil, for example, leads in the production of biofuels; China and India are players in the wind power market; and India has multiplied its capacity for manufacturing quality solar panels.

Even if paved with the best of intentions, the road to open EGS trade is rocky, simply due to measurement problems. It is difficult to assess the net climate impact of a product throughout its life cycle, starting with pollution from making inputs, to the assembly, transportation, and installation of the final widget. Given the measurement hurdles, it is also tough to argue that some goods are ultimately better for the environment than the *status quo*. When, for example does the coal-heavy construction and oil-dependent transportation of solar panels pay itself back in terms of coal and conventional fuels saved?[21]

Protecting Trees, Not Trade

How do we best address the complex intersection of trade and climate change? For EGS, making policy headway will require two immediate steps: reaching an agreed definition of environmental goods and services, and then classifying such goods in international tariff schedules for customs purposes, a prerequisite to selective liberalization.

A good way to start is through a forum other than the WTO, which already has enough worries as it struggles with the Doha Round. One option is Asia-Pacific Economic Cooperation (APEC), the arena for nearly a half of world trade, where the twenty-one member economies have already made a push to free EGS trade. The United States has also worked with Australia, China, Japan, and Korea, as well as with India, in the context of the Asia-Pacific Partnership on Clean Development and Climate. Free trade in climate-friendly goods is akin to free trade in information technology products, which also started in APEC and translated into a global success story—the Information Technology Agreement (ITA) within the WTO that freed the bulk of world trade on IT products. As with the ITA, countries collectively representing a threshold percentage of trade in climate-friendly products would get the ball rolling. Acceptance by other developing countries in a broader WTO bargain might be facilitated by the aid-for-trade philosophy, namely combining the liberalization package with financial and technical assistance to boost domestic industries for making environmental goods.[22]

Removal of barriers on EGS trade is not enough, however. Also hampering clean technologies are national requirements that discourage inward direct investment: joint ownership rules, restrictions on work visas for engineers, differing equipment and safety standards, and weak protection of intellectual property rights. All these domestic policies should be made EGS-compatible and foreign investors should be welcomed, not turned away.

Of War and Commerce

Trading with the enemy has been controversial throughout world history. Commerce remains a favorite tool of statecraft, whether in the form of import, export, or financial sanctions.[23] But the larger front where globalization and security intersect today is foreign investment. Economic sanctions are typically directed at nations of the second and third rank, and inflict costs of under $40 billion annually on all target countries. By contrast, foreign direct investment (FDI) crisscrosses the globe and all major countries are both home and hosts for multinational enterprises. As seen in chapter 4, the global stock of foreign direct investment now exceeds $15 trillion. Portfolio investment—characteristically of a passive nature—likewise flows in every direction, and the global stock of cross-border capital flows of all kinds now totals more than $90 trillion.[24]

While policy debates are often centered on emerging markets, the bulk of foreign direct investment takes place between the advanced nations. The United States, notably, is the world's largest exporter as well as importer of FDI, absorbing some 15 percent of global flows and as much as inflows to India, China, and Latin America *combined*. The United States is also the destination of a quarter of the world's portfolio financial flows, and home to no less than a staggering 85 percent of the world's official financial flows, particularly from Japan, China, and the Middle East, countries where booming exports have earned massive reserves that are then invested abroad—mostly in the United States.

Investment Protectionism

The current crisis has induced some governments to turn toward financial or investment protectionism, for instance, by nudging financial institutions based in their countries to invest in companies within their borders.

As evinced by the "Buy American" legislation tagged on the U.S. stimulus bill, governments sport a populist penchant for rewarding domestic companies with whatever goodies are served up by the national legislature.

Unfair incentives are deployed to attract or retain investments and jobs that might otherwise evaporate. French president Nicolas Sarkozy's announcement in early 2009 that he would like PSA Peugeot Citroen and Renault SA to shift production from low-wage nations back to France in return for €7 billion in soft loans raised a firestorm of adverse comments and was ultimately blocked by the European Commission. But the proposal resonated in the minds of many national leaders faced with protesters who want jobs kept at home. Smaller countries, hungry for foreign money and new jobs, may resort to local content and export performance rules to suck the most out of incoming multinationals.

Thus far we have been spared from beggar-thy-neighbor investment policy warfare.[25] While alarmism is not yet in order, worries are certainly justified. Frictions to unfettered flow of capital were on a troubling ascent well before economies around the world started to crumble. Post-9/11 security fears, coupled with a massive buildup of foreign exchange reserves by the BRICKs, heightened the scrutiny on incoming investment. Money seems particularly suspicious when it arrives from countries that have not been confidants in the game of global politics; in the United States and Europe, "strangers" include China and the Middle East.

The takeover of IBM's personal computer operations by the Chinese firm Lenovo in 2005 sparked a great deal of controversy. But it was the bid by the state-owned China National Offshore Oil Corporation (CNOOC) to buy the U.S. oil firm Unocal the same year that set off a political firestorm. CNOOC withdrew its offer after the House of Representatives overwhelmingly approved a provision that would significantly delay the acquisition.

Another political volcano erupted when Dubai Ports World, based in the United Arab Emirates, made a bid in 2006 to purchase the U.S. port operations of the UK-based Peninsular and Oriental Steam Navigation Company. The deal was approved by the Committee on Foreign Investment in the United States (CFIUS), an interagency body led by the Treasury Department and charged with monitoring foreign investment in the United States. But the deal was ultimately shot down by a bipartisan group of House lawmakers. Even Republicans expressed outrage that a Middle Eastern firm, owned by the state of Dubai, could control port facilities in the United States. In making their charges, congressmen conveniently downplayed two facts: Dubai is a military ally of the United States, and the ports in question, along with JFK Airport in New York, are already operated by foreign firms. Dubai Ports World ultimately agreed to sell its interest in the U.S. ports to U.S. operators.

A 2006 Pew Foundation poll found that an astonishing 41 percent of Americans followed the Dubai Ports World issue, just 2 percentage points less than those who followed the war in Iraq. Some 58 percent of Americans who knew about the issue believed Congress acted appropriately in opposing the Dubai Ports World deal, and only 24 percent stated that lawmakers made too much of the situation.[26]

Compounding the concerns about FDI has been the rise of state-owned sovereign wealth funds (SWFs) as major sources of portfolio investments. As we catalog in chapter 3, these forty or so government-owned investment institutions already manage $3 trillion of global assets, and are projected to reach $10–12 trillion by 2015.[27] Unlike central banks, they do not confine their holdings to Treasury bills and government-guaranteed debt. Instead, they invest in shares, corporate debt, and sometimes whole companies.

Sovereign wealth funds can provide stability and liquidity in financial markets since they are generally interested in long-run results rather than quarterly outcomes. And they are not all from emerging markets—witness Norway's giant fund. Moreover, by stretching the definition, the term SWF could include huge pension funds run by U.S. states, such as Calpers serving California's retired public-sector workers, and even the U.S. Social Security Trust Fund, which conceivably could diversify into investments other than Treasury bills and bonds.

But SWFs from the Middle East and China in particular have elicited hand-wringing in some quarters, since they are seen as instruments to advance political goals, not mere investment returns. Perhaps, the critics suggest, they are established to gain control of strategic assets in areas such as telecommunications, energy, and finance, and perhaps, in scenarios worthy of Michael Crichton thrillers, to destabilize financial markets in times of crisis.[28] Hardly helping the SWF cause is the fact that nine of the ten largest traditional SWFs are from countries that are not liberal democracies, let alone that many SWFs have a poor record of transparency.

In 2007, the Chinese sovereign wealth fund CIC made investments totaling $8 billion in investment bank Morgan Stanley and the renowned U.S. private equity firm Blackstone. This was followed in 2008 by a $2 billion investment by China's State Administration of Foreign Exchange (SAFE) in U.S. private equity firm TPG. Middle Eastern money also got in the game: the Abu Dhabi Investment Authority purchased a small stake in Apollo Management in July 2007, and Dubai's Mubadala Development Company bought a 7.5 percent interest in the Carlyle Group in September 2007. These transactions prompted hostile comment that crown jewels of the U.S. financial services industry would be gobbled up by foreign SWFs. The financial collapse in the second half of 2008 inflicted huge losses on the foreign SWFs, but there was no acknowledgment by erstwhile critics that maybe the investments weren't so bad for the United States after all.

A Global Pattern

These controversies might be brushed aside as isolated incidents provoked by China's amazing rise and seemingly endless U.S. wars in the Middle East. But events in the United States are emblematic of a broader global trend to block high-profile transactions.

Go back a few years. In 2006, Germany stopped Russian Sistema from acquiring a stake in Deutsche Telekom, while Italy blocked Spanish firm Abertis's intentions to acquire the Italian motorway toll operator Autostrade. In early 2007, the Italian company Olimpia began negotiations with AT&T and Mexican operator America Movil to sell Olimpia's stake in Telecom Italia; the deal folded owing to political pressures to bar foreign investment in a firm that was once Italy's national monopoly telecom.

India-based Mittal Steel's eventual takeover of the European conglomerate Arcelor in 2006–2007 was difficult in its own right due to labor union opposition, but it also triggered a battle between Mittal and Russia's Severstal, a firm backed by the Kremlin and viewed with suspicion by Europeans. Russia's Gazprom, a giant state-controlled company with soaring ambitions, also sparked concerns across the European Union—especially since Gazprom was used by the Kremlin to browbeat the Ukraine by shutting off gas supplies. (In late 2008 and early 2009, Gazprom was brought to its knees by plunging oil and gas prices; just retribution in the eyes of many Europeans.) In the wake of the rogue trader scandal at Societe Generale in January 2008, French prime minister Francois Fillon preempted any foreign investors from scooping up the weakened firm by stating that "Societe Generale is a great French bank and will remain a great French bank."

Cases abound outside Europe, as well. Canada recently prevented Alliant Techsystems, a firm based in the United States, from buying the space technology division of MacDonald-Dettwiler that specializes in satellites and space robotics. Japan rejected expanded investment by the British Children's Investment Fund in a Japanese power producer on the grounds of a potential disruption of "public order." New Zealand prevented the Canada Pension Plan from buying a substantial stake in the Auckland Airport because the investment failed to meet the test of bringing a "benefit to New Zealand."

In an unexpected spat against foreign investment, in March 2009, Chinese regulators cited new antitrust rules in rejecting Coca-Cola Company's $2.3 billion bid for China Huiyuan Juice Group Ltd., China's largest juice company. The move surprised many analysts, as it can boomerang against China: not only does it discourage other large corporations from pursuing mergers in China but also it will pave the way for Western countries to block Chinese companies from acquiring overseas targets. Indeed, two weeks later, Australia, citing national security, stopped the purchase of OZ Minerals, a mining company, by state-owned China Minmetals Corporation, one of several acquisitions China is seeking in Australia's natural resources sector.

Old Menace, New Vengeance

Fears of foreign influence are nothing new. A quick survey of American history tells the story; similar accounts could be traced for Europe, Japan, and nearly all developing countries.

American ire was provoked in the 1910s by English investment, because Britain was then regarded as the main military rival owing to its dominance of the high seas. During the First World War, the U.S. Congress adopted restrictions on foreign investments in shipping, air services, and broadcasting sectors (many remain in force to this day) and passed the Trading with the Enemy Act, which was used to seize both German and

British assets. In the 1970s, apprehension swept America over Middle Eastern takeovers ("the Arabs are coming"), in the wake of the first oil spike. The 1980s were days of a Japan scare, and Congress passed the Exon-Florio Amendment in 1988, which authorized the president to suspend or prohibit foreign acquisitions of U.S. companies, and conferred statutory authority on reviews by the CFIUS.[29]

Foreign investment is supposedly liberalized by more than two thousand bilateral investment treaties (BITs) crisscrossing the world, but nearly all of these agreements contain national security and public safety exceptions. More recent BITs also stress that foreign money is not to undermine the host country's health and environmental standards, core labor rights, cultural diversity, or prudential measures that safeguard financial services. In short, the network of BITs does nothing to deter investment restrictions in "sensitive" areas.

The ongoing global push back on investment is a turnabout from the 1990s, when policy increasingly favored FDI, particularly to facilitate the privatization frenzy that was then sweeping across emerging markets. According to a UN report, in 2000, out of 150 regulatory changes, only 3 were restricted and the rest liberalized FDI; but in 2005, some 41 of the 203 policy measures were restrictive; in 2006, the figure was 25 out of 177; and in 2007, some 24 of 98. The trend is clear.

More than half of OECD members have lists of sectors closed to foreign investment, many with vague connections to national security.[30] Consider the following laundry list.

In August 2007, Japan revised its rules on inward investment flows to meet the "changed security environment surrounding Japan and trends in international investment activity." The new rules require prenotification to the government of investments on making dual-use items, defense products, and a poorly defined list of "technology infrastructure."

In September 2007, the European Commission put forward a proposal to establish a European energy policy that would prohibit non-EU companies from acquiring control of an EU energy transmission system or transmission system operator, unless the deal was specifically permitted by an agreement between the European Union and the foreign company.[31] The EU's stated goal is to promote competition, but the proposal would often block foreign companies (especially state-owned enterprises like Russia's Gazprom) from acquiring energy assets in the European Union—or from jeopardizing reliable energy flows.[32]

In December 2007, the Canadian government expanded its examination of acquisitions by foreign state-owned enterprises to consider their adherence to Canadian corporate governance standards. The new rules do more: they call for Canada to assess the impact of the acquisition on exports, the location of its manufacturing and R&D facilities, and whether the acquirer will provide "the appropriate level of capital expenditures to maintain the Canadian business in a globally competitive position."

In December 2007, Greece proposed new hurdles on private investments exceeding 20 percent in companies of "strategic importance"—despite the European Commission's warning that the law would be inconsistent with the EU rules requiring the free flow of capital. Warnings are just warnings: in 2005, France ignored commission warnings by issuing a decree that requires ministerial authorization for foreign investments in eleven sectors that may affect the "national interest," not only dual-use technologies and other security-related industries but also gambling.

In February 2008, Australia announced six principles that will govern the Foreign Investment Review Board when examining investments by sovereign wealth funds and other government-linked entities. Satisfying the principles will require the investor to observe common standards of business behavior, not harm "the operations and directions" of an Australian business, nor undermine competition, cut into government revenue, or erode other policies, including "but not limited to" national security.

In April 2008, the German government, facing persistent political pressure against foreign private equity investments, unveiled new legislation to authorize the Ministry of Economics and Technology to review certain foreign deals, particularly those coming from state-owned entities. The legislation also has a test for "public order," as well as for national security.

Russia has played a tough hand. Only days before stepping down as president in May 2008, Vladimir Putin signed a law restricting foreign investment in forty-two sectors, ranging from oil and gas to fishing and publishing. Foreign private investors must get government approval to buy majority stakes in companies in these sectors and foreign state-run companies must get approval to acquire stakes exceeding 25 percent. The rules proved highly popular: 68 percent of Russians, in a May 2008 poll, said government should prohibit foreign companies from buying big Russian firms.[33] Former Soviet republics echoed this sentiment—ranging from 40 percent of the populace against takeovers in Moldova to 63 percent against takeovers in Kazakhstan.

China is in a league of its own, triggering anxiety not only as a roving investor but also as a protected target. For a long time, China has walled off sectors considered crucial to national security, such as news agencies, broadcasting and programming, press and audiovisual products, certain mining operations, and, of course, arms production. In December 2006, China's State-Owned Assets Supervision and Administration Commission (SASAC) expanded the foreign investment reviews to cover acquisitions that might impact national *economic* security. SASAC listed a host of "critical economic sectors" where China ought to maintain strong state control and restrict foreign participation, including automotive, chemical, construction, electronic information, equipment manufacturing, iron and steel, nonferrous metal, science and technology, and survey and design.

China's Foreign Investment Catalogue, issued in November 2007, indicates a move toward greater selectivity in allowing foreign investment by actively courting attractive sectors, such as high-technology research and development, advanced manufacturing, and energy efficiency, rather than basic manufacturing. In August 2008, China published a new antimonopoly law, which allows regulators further discretion in interpreting competition rules in order to favor state-owned companies that are "relied upon by the national economy and national security."[34] The U.S. Trade Representative's 2009 *National Trade Estimate Report on Foreign Trade Barriers* notes that China's restrictions are often "accompanied by other problematic industrial policies, such as the increased use of subsidies and the development of China-specific standards." Many of these policies appear to represent protectionist tools designed to shield inefficient or monopolistic enterprises from competition.[35]

Scrubbing Intentions

In the United States, some two dozen bills were introduced in Congress after the Dubai Ports World fracas to tighten the prior Exon-

Florio legislation and to beef up the CFIUS process, all with a view to more-rigorous screening of foreign investment in the United States.[36] The tougher proposals that circulated on Capitol Hill would have made the secretary of defense, rather than the secretary of the Treasury, the CFIUS chair; mandated filings of all foreign acquisitions; and empowered Congress to overturn CFIUS rulings. None of this happened.

But scrutiny seemed to tighten. A total of 1,593 notifications was made to the CFIUS between 1988 and 2005; of these, only 25 investigations were initiated, 13 resulted in withdrawals, and only in one case—China National Aero Tech's bid for MAMCO Manufacturing Inc. in 1990—was the deal formally blocked by the White House.[37] By contrast to 25 investigations and 13 withdrawals in the 18 previous years, in the span of three years between 2005 and 2007, there were 14 investigations and 11 of them resulted in withdrawals.[38] In addition, there were also 35 mitigation agreements— deals that were approved conditionally by the executive branch—during that period.

In July 2007, Congress passed the Foreign Investment and National Security Act (FINSA), which tightened scrutiny of acquisitions by government-owned companies, and also called for additional reporting to Congress (although not allowing Congress to override the executive branch's decisions).[39]

On the basis of FINSA, the Treasury developed new rules on CFIUS reviews issued in November 2008. These are reasonable. Notification of proposed acquisitions to CFIUS remains voluntary (but competent lawyers will invariably recommend that their foreign clients submit a notification), and CFIUS will conduct thirty-day reviews, followed by forty-five-day evaluations for exceptional cases. At the end of an extended review, CFIUS reports to the president, who has fifteen days to announce whether he approves the investment. The rules also clarify the process for determining whether the buyer is gaining "control" of a U.S. company or asset.[40] And they amplify the extent of CFIUS reports to Congress. Finally, the rules encourage interested investors to seek prenotification reviews before making a formal filing to CFIUS. This enables the Treasury and the concerned agencies to assess sensitive and complex cases "off the clock."

FOREIGN VERSUS SOVEREIGN New investment screens enacted around the world can be helpful when they clarify the investment review processes and answer legitimate fears about foreign control of national assets. But muddying the waters are several other currents. Some countries do not use the term "national security" in their laws, and countries that do use the term seldom define its scope. The range of review in many countries is now much broader than in the United States, extending to any impact on the public order or economic security. Many countries have an opaque enforcement regime.[41] Legislative and regulatory tools are now readily at hand to interrupt a serious amount of international investment, if that is how the political winds blow.

Why the uproar over investment to begin with? At the international level, we see two drivers—new investors and sensitive targets.[42] Investment inroads from nontraditional sources—the Middle East, China, and Russia—create a lot of anxiety. Direct investment in the United States from Russia has increased about five times between 2003 and 2008; from China, six times; and from the Middle East, perhaps thirty times. It is not clear that the new investors are reading the same commercial playbook as Western firms, since much of their investment is tied up with governing circles in the home country. In fact, a quarter of the top one hundred multinational companies (MNCs) in developing countries are government-owned, as opposed to only five of the world's one hundred largest MNCs.

In 2008, the U.S.-China Economic and Security Review Commission (USCC), a congressionally chartered group, argued that Chinese state-controlled funding not only lacks transparency but often makes investments that are "almost guaranteed to lose money," both potential triggers for national security concerns.[43]

The second reason for the controversies about foreign investment is that more FDI has recently gone into "strategic assets," such as telecom, ports, and roads. Beijing's history in seeking foreign acquisitions in car manufacturing, telecommunications, and aerospace is particularly sensitive.

Security and strategic reasons are only part of the explanation. In the globalized world of freely flowing capital and stiffening competition, FDI has become tainted by domestic politics well beyond national security, and investments from friends and allies also have created resistance.

Take the United States. First, during the George W. Bush administration, sour executive-legislative relations were at play. The Dubai Ports World "scandal" was in good part perpetrated by Democrats intent on freezing President Bush's low approval ratings earned from the unpopular Iraq War. Congress also long felt excluded from the CFIUS process. The ordeal pushed the president's approval ratings further along their tailspin and prompted both chambers to move quickly on overhauling the CFIUS process.

Second, many cases have become severely politicized due to hardball played by other American suitors or rivals of the companies to be acquired.[44] In 2002, corporate raider Carl Icahn put pressure on Congress to take issue with Singaporean firm ST Telemedia's proposed acquisition of Global Crossing, a firm that was in Icahn's sights. In 2005, Crest Communications sought to undermine a bid by Indian telecom company Videsh Sanchar Nigam Limited to acquire Crest's rival, Tyco, citing national security concerns about network security. In the Unocal case, Chevron, which had bid for Unocal before CNOOC entered the stage, ended up buying the company for a billion dollars less than CNOOC would have paid. The Dubai Ports World issue was partly sparked by a Miami-based firm that had a long-standing commercial dispute with the to-be-acquired Peninsular and Oriental Steam Navigation Company.

Third, the firms to be acquired can strive to raise the bid by pushing Congress to threaten the suitors with elaborate CFIUS reviews. In 1990, congressional members cited economic and national security concerns in British Tire and Rubber's bid for the Norton Company in Massachusetts. Congressional furor quelled when a French company offered $15 more per share than did the British. Allies and friends have been dealt the national security excuse before. Indiana governor Mitch Daniels brought a political hailstorm over his decision to lease the Indiana Toll Road to a private Spanish-Australian consortium, Macquarie-Cintra, for $3.8 billion.

Fourth, union politics have crept under the umbrella of national security. Democrats in particular have been pressed by unions concerned about job losses resulting from foreign takeovers. In June 2005, the Haier Group, a leading Chinese manufacturer of household appliances, participated in a bid for Maytag, the American appliance icon. Inconveniently coinciding with the more-sensitive Unocal bid, Haier's offer became infused with security concerns. But Haier ultimately dropped its bid following speculation that Chinese ownership would reduce the number of manufacturing jobs in the United States. The U.S. company Whirlpool took over Maytag.

Rule making on investment inflows has become something of a political football between competing agencies. In the United States, the main contests were waged between national security hawks in Congress and business lobbies, and between defense and intelligence agencies on the one hand and the trade and finance agencies on the other. Security agencies—the Homeland Security, Justice, and Defense Departments—would have preferred much tougher rules than what emerged, but they lost out to the proinvestment agencies, Treasury and Commerce.[45] This was in part the result of business lobbyists—representing both foreign and domestic firms—who worked to soften the sharpest edges of various FDI-curbing laws.

The real question, of course, is whether investment reviews matter in practice. The drift to tighten rules and scrutiny certainly has not curtailed global investment flows: before the stock market crash of 2008, mergers and acquisitions (M&A) activity was at all-time highs. FDI restrictions are only part of the calculus of companies eyeing an overseas commitment. Many forces drive M&A transactions, and one more legal obstacle is not an insurmountable hurdle.

But the new regulations have impacted investments in sensitive sectors. And while data do not reveal transactions that have been deterred, the fact that a good number of notices to CFIUS are withdrawn during the review process (the count is 50 out of 358 notices withdrawn in 2007–2009 before or during investigations) suggests some nervousness. Also, realized transactions now take more time to go through. In the United States, many transactions that could have been done in thirty days are sometimes done in six to nine months, even when there are no security issues. Some approved deals are also saddled with conditions. Policy frictions can dampen the appetite for M&A in poor economic times. As in trade, there are strategic considerations to think about: tough scrutiny overseas may be matched by tough scrutiny at home: backtracking on investment liberalization could invite countermeasures and imitation elsewhere in the world.

Extricating Government from Economics

A U.S.-German joint statement issued during the May 2008 Transatlantic Economic Council noted that: "an open investment environment is compatible with policies that address genuine national security concerns." This is perhaps the most emblematic pronouncement of the current state of policy making toward foreign investment.

Regulations and reviews are necessary. Governments have a legitimate stake in ensuring that a foreign power will not squander domestic water reserves or cripple financial firms, or listen in on phone calls. More generally, questionable investments are those with a potential to undermine law enforcement, abet economic espionage, or damage critical infrastructures.

In the United States, the various reforms to laws governing investment inflows seem to have produced a collective sense of completion across the Washington policy community. Indeed, the reforms have been for the better, the worst ideas were dropped, and more tinkering seems unnecessary. While the views of the Obama administration on CFIUS are not clear, several key members of Obama's economic team previously served on CFIUS and are expected to keep the Treasury as the CFIUS chair.

Globally, wholesale protection in the realm of investment seems very unlikely to emerge, either. The founder of British private-equity firm Terra Firma, Guy Hands, has predicted that SWFs, and in particular the Abu Dhabi Investment Authority, have elbow room to "effectively replace Wall Street" as lenders to the private-equity industry as a result of the Great Crisis. But at the moment, it appears that SWFs are retreating to invest in their home economies in an attempt to spark growth amid trying economic times. Meanwhile, Prime Minister Gordon Brown has welcomed fresh credit from state-owned entities in the Middle East to ignite the British economy.[46] Evidently, the suspect features of SWFs fade into oblivion when their cash becomes handy.

But the general deterioration in the global investment climate over the past few years will not necessarily improve if bad economic times persist for another two or three years. Measures to keep domestic firms in and foreigners out are popular in a period of widespread distress. Of course, when countries get desperate for cash and jobs, barriers can come down, as well. So far, in the wake of the Great Crisis, rather few investment protection measures have been enacted. But these are early days. How can leaders ensure an open-door policy for investment globally long after the bruises of the crisis fade?

Clear rules and consistent enforcement should be the policy response. Worse than tough rules are opaque and changing rules, coupled with arbitrary enforcement. This is a general statement about managing globalization: exporters, importers, and investors alike thrive on rules that are clear, precise, and well-implemented with dispatch. Regulatory uncertainty heightens risk, which in turn compels companies to demand a higher return before they venture abroad.

As in the United States, investment reviews should be voluntary. A mandatory process, covering 100 percent of incoming investments, will require a large and cumbersome structure, unnecessary when many small- and medium-size investments are of no concern.

Confidentiality of business transactions should be safeguarded. Exposure, competitor pressures, and potential bad press have deterred many an investment in the past. Investment reviews should be limited to national security and public safety. An economic security test is extremely difficult to define; it can easily generate a tremendous workload; and it invites lobbying by rival firms and unions.

Politics should be kept out of the reviews. CFIUS reviews are carried out in a professional fashion, but congressional posturing on individual cases is another matter. The same goes for Europe. The prospect of political water boarding, if it becomes common, will deter future foreign investment.

Ideally, these core principles would gain global acceptance. But decision making on FDI policies remains a national prerogative. As discussed in chapter 4, efforts to craft global rules on FDI have faded. Even so, it is worth calling for a global "code of conduct" for foreign investment reviews, as propounded by David Marchick and Matthew Slaughter in a Council of Foreign Relations report.[47] The code would apply particularly on investments related to national security and strategic assets, and would enunciate a handful of principles. Besides the principles of clarity and transparency, the code could require countries to focus investment screening on national security. A multilateral code could best be fashioned under the auspices of the OECD, with China, India, and Russia joining the process.

While much can be done on the side of receiving countries to separate politics from economics, state-owned enterprises and SWFs investing abroad need to improve their standards of transparency and disclosure by 1,000 percent. Until that happens, conspiracy theories will continue to flourish.[48] SWFs in particular ought to be clear about their mission and investment strategies, adhere to good governance, and steer clear from political agendas.

Constructive multilateral efforts would improve the transparency of SWF operations. In February 2008, the European Commission adopted a communication endorsed by EU finance ministers that proposed a common EU-wide approach to "increasing the transparency, predictability and accountability of SWFs." This is only in the interest of SWFs. In October 2008, twenty-three countries with SWFs agreed on a set of voluntary "generally accepted principles and practices" (GAPP), developed under the International Monetary Fund (IMF) auspices, to make investments purely on a commercial basis.[49] The challenge now is to put these fine words into practice.

Conclusion

Many seemingly domestic measures shape trade and investment patterns in the global economy. As previewed by the coming battles on climate change, new domestic rules can easily constrain trade or investment—and leave a dark imprint that is hard to clean up. And many a homemade rule, devised for worthy environmental or security purposes, can serve as a screen for protectionist designs.

The thorny issues addressed in this chapter point to a two-pronged test for twenty-first-century rule making. The first test is transparency and evenhanded application. Domestic rules are fine, but opaque rules, arbitrarily applied—whether on climate change, direct investment, or something else—will throw a monkey wrench, deliberately or accidentally, into the wheels of globalization. The second test is an effort to make slow but steady progress toward convergent rules, at least among the great powers. This will require effective global forums and the endless patience of diplomats who will be challenged to reconcile the tensions between politic forces, which are national, and economic forces, which are international.

10

After the Deluge

Prospects for the global economy have brightened since we set out to write this book. U.S. unemployment has reached just over 10 percent but looks like a plateau, global trade is picking up, stock markets have rebounded 50 percent or more, and consumers are feeling better. Overall, it seems that debate on the shape of the recovery—U, V, or W—is eclipsed by expectations for a better tomorrow.

Were there any winners in the past two years of turmoil? John Paulson, the hedge fund primo who raked in $2 billion by short-selling mortgage-backed securities and banks, was a winner, to be sure. Among financial giants, Goldman Sachs and JPMorgan Chase surfed the crisis with skill, emerging far ahead of Citigroup and Bank of America. But as for between countries, in this roulette, no one won, but some were less scathed than others. China came out far better than most. Following the U.S. financial collapse, Chinese banks suddenly found themselves among the largest in the world. Armed with billions in reserves, Beijing has been able to funnel stimulus money into domestic projects. This tack, Beijing hopes, will provide a new lifeline—economic and thus political—while the export-led growth model of the past two decades languishes in the face of sluggish global demand.

Asia as a whole is doing better than other parts of the world, largely for the same reasons as China: solid reserves to cushion adverse shocks, and sound fiscal positions, two things Asian nations like to boast about. The region sounds ever-more intent on building its common defenses as insurance against future turmoil, perhaps in the form of an Asian Monetary Fund. The emerging markets of Asia may indeed be the global growth poles of the coming decade—perhaps best encapsulated by the suggestions making the rounds of New York and Washington to add two new members to the BRICs of yesteryear, adding K for Korea and I for Indonesia, making BRIICKS.

The sense of relief is less palpable in other main markets, notably the United States and Europe. U.S. unemployment rates—at highs not seen since the economic turbulence of the early 1980s—have left working Americans fearful for their jobs, and the long-term unemployed bracing for the day when their government benefits run out. The Treasury's burgeoning deficit has inspired conservatives across the nation to rise up against a further expansion of the public sector, particularly under the guise of government-run health care. Paul Krugman thinks there is no such thing as too much stimulus, but most Americans disagree.

America is America, the cradle of die-hard optimists: shoppers are starting to spend, new cars are being bought (with some initial prodding from the "Cash for Clunkers" program), and consumer optimism continues to rise along with the stock market. A major challenge for the Obama administration will be to deliver a jobs recovery—while not resorting to new bouts of spending or social engineering, which are now viewed, as shown by the bruising health-care battle, with hostility across swaths of the electorate.

Good news seems to be reaching Europe even a little faster. In the Old Continent, unemployment delivers less of a personal blow than in the New World, but being laid off is still demoralizing, and rising unemployment rates are bad news for incumbent governments. Even so, continuity may win out at the end of the day. German chancellor Angela Merkel resoundingly trounced the center-left in the September 2009 elections. The vote signaled a thirst to get the sleepy European giant wound up and rolling. The Eastern European countries that teetered on the brink in the midst of the crisis may see major political changes, presaging less enthusiasm for the European integration project. Prime Minister Gordon Brown got voted out but more because the British public is tired of the Labour Party than because they are tired of labor policies. The Southern European debt crisis will hurt growth in the continent for years and poses a test for European integration.

Elsewhere, there are decent and bad stories. Latin America is not well, but a couple of countries—Brazil and Peru, both with strong macroeconomic fundamentals and financial systems—have weathered the crisis better than their neighbors. Mexico is hurt by its heavy reliance on the anemic U.S. auto market and an eruption of drug violence (another curse of proximity to the United States). India grew an enviable 7 percent in 2009 just a bit below the 8 to 9 percent annual growth clocked previously. Russians would probably change places with Indians any time. Their economy boomed for a decade, but was in 2009 pushed into a deep recession. The opportunity in the crisis might be a realization, dawning on President Dmitri Medvedev, that excessive reliance on commodities and monopoly capitalism imparts a brittle quality to the Russian economy.

Globalization Tomorrow

If countries around the globe have a mixed record as they exit from the Great Crisis, what is the scorecard for globalization?

The big news is that globalization has survived. Trade is still down, but the rebound looks V-shaped. The much discussed deglobalization of finance—retreating to national institutions and imposing strict regulations on international flows—seems more talk than real. Investors with cash (read: China and the Middle East) are eyeing bets in cash-strapped Europe and the United States, where good companies still go for cheap prices. But even with green shoots and bargains for bold investors, the main tenet of this book remains—that better policies are required to harness the full potential of globalization. We are not home free.

Dust has yet to settle on the frenzy to devise new financial regulations. In Washington, reformers have been held back by industry lobbyists, and most significant, by turf wars both among the alphabet soup of regulatory agencies—all the way from the Commodity Futures Trading Commission (CFTC) and the comptroller of the currency to the Securities and Exchange Commission (SEC)—and among their congressional masters in the various oversight committees. Surrendering responsibility for systemic vigilance to the Federal Reserve does not sit well with the other players, or with many members of Congress. In Europe, similar battles are waged among nations, with most countries reluctant to delegate regulatory powers to an EU-wide body, particularly the European Central Bank, and with Frankfurt and Paris vying for position against the City of London.

Efforts to revive and conclude the multilateral Doha Trade Round are questioned across capitals. A few optimists predict that a deal will be struck in 2010; most trade watchers are hoping for action in 2011. The trade effects of revising climate-change rules, including the new U.S. cap-and-trade regime approved by the House in July 2009 and at the time of this writing stuck in the Senate, have yet to be defined. But already, companies are regionalizing their global supply chains, not only to save money on transportation costs but also to hedge themselves against green rules. While the global economy has weathered a hailstorm of protectionism, nearly all the hailstones are tiny, and they are collectively responsible for only a small part of the contraction in world trade.

Policy liberalization—both in trade and investment—has sunk to a low priority. Claude Barfield and Phil Levy have nicely summarized the record of the Obama administration: domestic constraints and a fleeting interest in trade.[1] U.S. bilateral trade deals negotiated by the George W. Bush administration with Colombia, Panama, and Korea got stuck behind the Obama administration's priority on health-care and financial reforms. In Asia, however, trade deals are made and passed, including a recent pact between Korea and India. The European Union, no rabbit in the race, is nevertheless moving faster than the United States, both with Korea and India. In his Asian tour during November 2009, President Obama held out the promise of a new emphasis on regional and global trade agreements; inside the Washington beltway and other capitals, observers are now waiting for Team Obama to walk the walk.

The future roles of core postwar institutions of globalization—the G system, the International Monetary Fund (IMF), and the dollar—are hazy. Each has a few alternatives, but all provoke dissatisfaction. Up to now, the institutions are ignored while policy makers are engrossed by crisis management. The postcrisis phase of policy making will see more emphasis on institutions.

It Never Ends: New Challenges

Besides the challenges we have laid out in this volume, there are now fresh issues directly resulting from the crisis that can either brew into problems or create possibilities for the future of globalization.

U.S. FISCAL MESS The first problem is the growing size of U.S. public debt, which already ballooned to 13.5 percent of gross domestic product (GDP) in 2009, and under even the most optimistic scenario, will be hovering around 5 percent of GDP in 2014.[2] Public debt of this magnitude can provoke punishing tax rates and crowd out private investment. On the bright side, it also could prompt major reforms.

Catherine Mann assesses the sustainability of the U.S. current account deficit—both in terms of America's ability to finance its deficits and the willingness of foreigners to buy U.S. assets—in light of the fiscal deficit.[3] She argues that external deficits generated by a "benign baseline" scenario, in which the budget deficit levels off at 2 percent of GDP by 2030, could be readily financed because that would not require excessive calls on foreign portfolios of wealth. However, under a "fiscal erosion scenario"—the apparent trajectory in the absence of dramatic reform—entailing a deficit of 10 percent of GDP in 2030, the rest of the world would need to devote more than 65 percent of all offshore investments to dollar assets. This would require more than a doubling of the share that foreign holders currently allocate to investments in the United States, something highly implausible.

A scenario of soaring budget deficits would have truly grim effects. For starters, some 7 percent of U.S. GDP would be paid annually to foreigners, representing foregone consumption or investment in the United States. The eventual squeeze to pay down the foreign debt, Mann calculates, could force a reduction in U.S. domestic demand by 13 percent of GDP annually, perhaps twice as great as the maximum impact of the current crisis. This would certainly dampen global economic growth. If the United States is not out and about generating economic expansion, who will?

WHERE IS DEMAND? The second question mark created by the crisis is very much related: the future structure of global demand. The world economy still relies on the U.S. consumer for growth. But Wall

Street players uniformly tell us that America is not where the action will be in the postcrisis years. While many things can happen in America and in the world that defy bleak prognoses, a grand restructuring of world demand seems likely. Perhaps the rise of materialistic Asian middle classes coupled with a young army of frugal American savers will propel a grand correction bottom-up. We have our doubts. In our view, policies are required—a real commitment by China, India, and other well-off Asian nations to channel money into household demand, a burst of infrastructure spending in Africa and other poor developing regions, and a sharp correction of U.S. federal budget deficits will be essential top-down correctives.

The questions facing the top-down script are many. Can Asian leaders in the well-off countries really find the heart to boost consumption? Can the poor countries of Africa, Asia, and Latin America govern themselves so that external money is spent on productive infrastructure rather than unproductive corruption? Can America wean itself from the luxury of budget deficits? And can Germany discover another path to growth besides its familiar export-led paradigm?

CHINESE FINANCES The third potential problem to globalization is China's multibillion-dollar loans issued to buoy domestic demand in response to the crisis.[4] While banks in the United States and Europe kept loans at bay for fears that they would not get their money back, Chinese banks issued a record 7.4 trillion yuan, or $1.1 trillion, in loans during the first six months of 2009. The pace continued in the second half of 2009. Most of the money went into large, state-owned companies and government infrastructure projects. Lending accounted for as much as 90 percent of China's GDP growth during the period. But the problems are twofold—one, the loans did little to tilt the source of growth from investment to consumption, thus creating an unhealthy balance; and two, the quality of the projects funded can be flimsy. Analysts like Morgan Stanley's Asia director Stephen Roach now worry that if the returns do not realize and loans go bad on a large scale, China's quick fix can wreak a lot of damage across Asia and the world. The danger is hard to detect and assess, much like it was during the Asian financial crisis driven by some of the similar dynamics of fishy lending practices and excessive leverage.

New Opportunities for Globalization

All crises create opportunities, and for globalization there are now at least three: foreign exchange reserves, proglobalization policies, and fixing corporate governance.

FOREIGN EXCHANGE RESERVES The first is a solution for the vexing issue of creating adequate foreign exchange reserves to fuel global commerce in a world of multiple national currencies. As we catalog in chapter 6, just to keep up with global import growth—which, at least in the previous years, was almost 10 percent annually—official global reserves should grow by another $13 trillion. The question is how those extra reserves will be created without a continuation of outsized U.S. external deficits, driven by irresponsible fiscal policies.[5] The reserve gap we estimated—$8.5 trillion, after allowing for a responsible creation of $4.5 trillion of new dollar reserves over the next decade—will have to be covered by other means. Yet, in a world where currency is almost as precious as the flag, arriving at sensible alternatives will take a great deal of political commitment.

PROGLOBALIZATION POLICIES A second opportunity arising from the Great Crisis is the real possibility that economic policies conducive to globalization will be revived. It is our hunch that the November 2009 Doha Ministerial might never have taken place had the crisis not brought the G20 leaders together and kept them sufficiently anxious to show real progress in global trade talks. Cooperation in curbing climate change will be all the stronger in the wake of the crisis. Indeed, G20 summitry itself might still be only a glimmer on the horizon but for the crisis. In the United States, fresh polls can be interpreted as saying that Americans believe cooperation and trade with other economic hubs will assist a U.S. rebound. Even on Main Street, where the outsourcing bogeyman continues to lurk, there is an aversion to blatant protectionism. National leaders now have a golden opportunity to ride the wave, ascend the bully pulpit, and preach the payoffs from global cooperation in politics and economics.

FIXING CORPORATE GOVERNANCE The third opportunity offered by the Great Crisis is a dramatic improvement in corporate governance, especially in the financial sector. The record of the past decade, from En-ron to WorldCom to AIG, is not pretty and has dramatically eroded pub-lic trust in major companies. Corporate leaders are getting the message, and fresh MBAs are now pledging lifetime integrity as they climb the ca-reer ladder. Still, once growth picks up and offers fresh ways to make big money, it will be incentive structures that matter most. The great oppor-tunity and challenge for regulatory authorities is to mold rules in ways that encourage innovative risk taking, but which ensure a measure of per-sonal responsibility for bad outcomes. That, along with reinvigorated glo-balization, we hope, will be a legacy of the Great Crisis.

NOTES

Chapter 1: Introduction

1. The U.S. response to the crisis owes much to the learning of Ben S. Bernanke, chairman of the Federal Reserve and acclaimed author of *Essays on the Great Depression* (Princeton, NJ: Princeton University Press, 2000).

2. See Horst Siebert, *Rules for the Global Economy* (Princeton, NJ: Princeton University Press, 2009). Siebert emphasizes the organic growth of international rules and institutions, each step forward answering the interests of leading players in the world economy.

3. Rodrigo de Rato, "Capital Flows in an Interconnected World" (Speech at the South East Asian Central Banks (SEACEN) Research and Training Centre Governors Conference, Bangkok, Thailand, July 28, 2007), available at http://www.imf.org/external/np/speeches/2007/072807.htm.

4. Ronald Findlay and Kevin H. O'Rourke, *Power and Plenty: Trade, War, and the World Economy in the Second Millennium* (Princeton, NJ: Princeton University Press, 2007).

5. United Nations Conference on Trade and Development (UNCTAD), *World Investment Report 2008* (Geneva: UNCTAD, 2008).

6. Money market mutual funds, for example, emerged in the 1970s, when inflation drove market interest rates far above the regulated rates that banks could pay their depositors.

7. Intra-European holdings grew from 13.5 percent to 17.8 percent of the world's total assets and liabilities in 1999–2006; external euro area holdings grew from 21.5 percent to 24.5 percent.

8. Scott L. Baier and Jeffrey H. Bergstrand, "The Growth of World Trade: Tariffs, Transport Costs, and Income Similarity," *Journal of International Economics* 53, no. 1 (February 2001): 1–27.

9. Gary Clyde Hufbauer and Matthew Adler, "Policy Liberalization and U.S. Merchandise Trade Growth, 1980–2006" (Draft, Peterson Institute for International Economics, 2009), available at http://www.iie.com/publications/papers/adler-hufbauer0409.pdf.

10. For an excellent exposé on the insides of the multilateral trading system, see Paul Blustein, *Misadventures of the Most Favored Nations: Clashing Egos, Inflated Ambitions, and the Great Shambles of the World Trade System* (New York: Public Affairs, 2009).

11. Tax treaties also may have some effect on trade flows, as firms adjust their sourcing patterns to minimize their tax liabilities. See Ronald B. Davies, Pehr-Johan Norbäck, and Ayça Tekin-Koru, "The Effect of Tax Treaties on Multinational Firms: New Evidence from Microdata" (Working Paper 0721, Oxford University Centre for Business Taxation, 2007).

12. Gary Clyde Hufbauer and Matthew Adler, "Policy Liberalization and FDI Growth, 1982 to 2006" (Working Paper 08-7, Peterson Institute for International Economics, 2008), available at http://www.iie.com/publications/wp/wp08-7.pdf.

13. Grant D. Aldonas, Robert Z. Lawrence, and Matthew J. Slaughter, "Succeeding in the Global Economy: A New Policy Agenda for the American Worker" (Financial Services Forum Policy Research Paper, June 26, 2007).

14. Harald Badinger, "Growth Effects of Economic Integration: The Case of the EU Member States (1950–2000)" (Institute for Fiscal Studies (Instituto de Estudios Fiscales, IEF) Working Paper No. 40, Research Institute for European Affairs, December 2001). See also Georgios Karras, "Trade and Growth in Europe, Evidence from a Panel of 18 Countries," *Icfai University Journal of Applied Economics* 2 (March 2004): 19–30. Karras arrives at similar magnitudes, arguing that doubling the share of trade in GDP increases an average European country's GDP per capita growth by 4 to 6 percent.

15. Carmen Fillat Castejón, Joseph Francois, and Julia Woerz, "Cross-Border Trade and FDI in Services" (Center for Economic and Policy Research Discussion Paper 7074, December 2008).

16. See Anusha Chari and Peter Blair Henry, "Risk Sharing and Asset Prices: Evidence from a Natural Experiment," *Journal of Finance* 59 (June 2004): 1295–1324, and Todd Mitton, "Stock Market Liberalization and Operating Performance at the Firm Level," *Journal of Financial Economics* 81 (September 2006): 625–647.

17. See Roberto Chang, Linda Kaltani, and Norman Loayza, "Openness Can Be Good for Growth: The Role of Policy Complementarities" (DEGIT Conference Papers c010_021, Dynamics, Economic Growth, and International Trade, 2005). The authors examine a host of complementary policies—including educational investment, financial depth, public infrastructure, governance, labor market rigidity, and ease of firm entry—and find the most significant effects come from labor and business regulation.

18. J. Bradford Jensen and Lori G. Kletzer, "'Fear' and Offshoring: The Scope and Potential Impact of Imports and Exports of Services" (Policy Brief 08-1, Peterson

Institute for International Economics, January 2008), available at http://www.iie.com/publications/pb/pb08-1.pdf.

19. The trade barrier scenario would also raise the long-run real interest rate by ninety basis points in the industrial countries, and reduce the amount of capital per worker. See Hans Fehr, Sabine Jokisch, and Laurence J. Kotlikoff, "Dynamic Globalization and Its Potentially Alarming Prospects for Low-Wage Workers" (National Bureau of Economic Research (NBER) Working Paper No. 14527, December 2008).

20. Michael P. Devereux, "Developments in the Taxation of Corporate Profit in the OECD since 1965: Rates, Bases and Revenues" (Oxford University Centre for Business Taxation Working Paper No. 704, December 2006).

21. Matthew Adler and Gary Hufbauer, "The Outward Migration of U.S. Firms: Are We Losing Our Best and Are We Forcing Them Out?" (Manuscript, Peterson Institute for International Economics, June 30, 2009).

22. Institute of International Finance (IIF): "Capital Flows to Emerging Market Economies," January 26, 2010; and IIF, "2009 to see sharp declines in capital flows to emerging markets, says IIF" (Press Release, January 27, 2009), available at http://www.iif.com/press/press+90.php. Examples of retrenchment in 2008: private investors pulled $45 billion from Korea, $6 billion from South Africa, and $16 billion from India.

23. World Trade Organization: "WTO sees 9 percent global trade decline in 2009 as recession strike" (Press Release, March 23, 2009), available at http://www.wto.org/english/news_e/pres09_e/pr554_e.htm#fntext1.

24. See United Nations Conference on Trade and Development (UNCTAD) Foreign Direct Investment database, available at http://www.unctad.org/Templates/Page.asp?intItemID=1923&lang=1.

25. UNCTAD, "Global and Regional FDI Trends in 2009," *Global Investment Trends Monitor,* no. 2, 19 January 2010, available at http://www.unctad.org/en/docs/webdiaeia20101_en.pdf.

26. CDO is an investment-grade security backed by a pool of bonds, loans, and other assets. CPDO is a type of credit derivative sold to investors looking for long-term exposure to credit risk on a highly rated note.

27. See Simon J. Evenett, "Broken Promises: A G20 Summit Report by Global Trade Alert," Global Trade Alert and Center for Economic and Policy Research, September 2009.

28. See *New York Times*-CBS News Poll, March–April 2008, available at http://www.graphics8.nytimes.com/packages/pdf/politics/20080403_POLL.pdf.

29. World Bank, *International Trade and Climate Change: Economic, Legal, and Institutional Perspectives* (Washington, DC: World Bank, 2007).

30. Gary Hufbauer, Steve Charnovitz, and Jisun Kim, *Global Warming and the World Trading System* (Washington, DC: Peterson Institute for International Economics, 2009).

31. See World Trade Organization, "Report to the TPRB [Trade Policy Review Body] from the Director-General on the Financial and Economic Crisis and Trade

Related Developments" (JOB(09)/30, March 26, 2009); Elisa Gamberoni and Richard Newfarmer, "Trade Protection: Incipient but Worrisome Trends," World Bank, March 26, 2009; Gary Hufbauer and Sherry Stephenson, "Trade Policy in a Time of Crisis: Suggestions for Developing Countries" (Center for Economic Policy Research (CEPR) Policy Insight No. 33, May 2009), available at http://www.cepr.org/pubs/policyinsights/PolicyInsight33.pdf.

32. David M. Marchick and Matthew J. Slaughter, *Global FDI Policy: Correcting a Protectionist Drift* (New York: Council of Foreign Relations, June 2008), available at http://www.cfr.org/content/publications/attachments/FDl_CSR34.pdf.

Chapter 2: Booming Finance

1. Rodrigo de Rato, "Capital Flows in an Interconnected World" (Speech at the South East Asian Central Banks (SEACEN) Research and Training Centre Governors Conference, Bangkok, Thailand, July 28, 2007), available at http://www.imf.org/external/np/speeches/2007/072807.htm.

2. McKinsey Global Institute, *Mapping the Global Capital Markets: Fourth Annual Report*, January 2008.

3. Institute of International Finance (IIF): "2009 to see sharp declines in capital flows to emerging markets, says IIF" (Press Release, January 27, 2009), available at http://www.iif.com/press/press+90.php.

4. Phillip D. Wooldridge, Dietrich Domanski, and Anna Cobau, "Changing Links between Mature and Emerging Financial Markets," *BIS Quarterly Review*, September 2003, available at http://www.bis.org/publ/qtrpdf/r_qt0309e.pdf.

5. McKinsey Global Institute, *Mapping the Global Capital Markets: Fourth Annual Report*, January 2008.

6. McKinsey Global Institute, *Mapping the Global Capital Markets: Fourth Annual Report*, January 2008.

7. ABA Securities Association et al., *EU-U.S. Coalition on Financial Regulation: Mutual Recognition, Exemptive Relief and "Targeted" Rules' Standardisation: The Basis for Regulatory Modernisation*, Futures and Options Association (FOA), March 2008, available at http://www.foa.co.uk/publications/eu-us%20report-%20mar08.pdf.

8. Peter Blair Henry and Peter Lombard Lorentzen, "Domestic Capital Market Reform and Access to Global Finance: Making Markets Work" (Center on Democracy, Development, and the Rule of Law, 2007), available at http://www.iis-db.stanford.edu/pubs/21505/No_78_Domestic_Capital_Reform.pdf.

9. Henry and Lorentzen, "Domestic Capital."

10. Wooldridge, Domanski, and Cobau, *Changing Links*.

11. U.S. Department of Treasury, "Major Foreign Holders of Treasury Securities," available at http://www.treas.gov/tic/mfh.txt.

12. In 2006, China accounted for 13.2 percent of global capital exports, Japan 12.2 percent, and Russia, Saudi Arabia, and Germany some 9 percent each.

13. Peterson Institute for International Economics, "U.S. Current Account Deficit," available at http://www.iie.com/research/topics/hottopic.cfm?HotTopicID=9.

14. Philip R. Lane and Gian Maria Milesi-Ferretti, "The Drivers of Financial Globalization" (Discussion Paper No. 238, Institute for International Integration Studies, January 2008), available at http://www.ecb.int/events/pdf/conferences/ecbcfs_cmfi2/Philip_Lane_paper.pdf?397f060a275b897cb229619c49b9793d.

15. Michael D. Bordo, Barry Eichengreen, and Douglas A. Irwin, "Is Globalization Today Really Different than Globalization a Hundred Years Ago?" (Conference Paper, Brookings Trade Policy Forum on "Governing in a Global Economy," Washington, DC, April 15–16, 1999), available at http://www.econ.berkeley.edu/~eichengr/research/brooking.pdf).

16. Between 1870 and 1914, the world turned on the gold standard, a global fixed exchange rate that linked currencies to gold. The gold standard allowed for unfettered movement of capital and stable world currencies—but only if countries were willing to endure deflation and depression to defend the currency peg. As time went on, countries became less willing to take this medicine, especially during the Great Depression. The global fix returned after the Second World War, but pretty well ran its course by 1971. Attempts to move back to a global peg were abandoned once and for all in 1985.

The downside of fixing is that it precludes a country from devaluing its currency as a means of adjustment. Consequently a country with a severe trade deficit has only one tool in its arsenal: raise interest rates to attract sufficient foreign capital to finance the deficit in the short term and to compress imports and boost exports in the medium term. The interest rate medicine in turn leads to economic contraction and more unemployment.

Economic historians like Berkeley's Barry Eichengreen have argued that the fixation on fixing hobbled government efforts to fight the 1929–1931 recession helped turn the depression into the Great Depression (see Barry J. Eichengreen, *Golden Fetters: The Gold Standard and the Great Depression, 1919–1939* (New York: Oxford University Press, 1992). In fact, countries that were not on the gold standard in 1929, or that quickly left the standard, managed to escape the worst of the Great Depression. Countries that held to the gold standard through 1933, such as the United States, or until 1936, such as France, were hit very hard. This story repeated itself in Mexico in 1994 and in Argentina in 2000, when the fix was to the U.S. dollar, not gold.

17. Gabriel Moser, Wolfgang Pointner, and Johann Scharler, "Financial Globalization, Capital Account Liberalization and International Consumption Risk-Sharing" (Focus1/05, Oesterreichische Nationalbank (2005), 98-106), available at http://www.oenb.at/en/img/feei_05_1_financial_glob_tcm16-29797.pdf.

18. One of the drivers was a revolt of sorts against the European Monetary System (EMS) founded in 1979, which sought continental monetary stability by mandating that a downward pressure on a member country's currency be offset with intervention from other currencies. Germany and the Netherlands saw the EMS as a burden on responsible members of the European Communities (like themselves) and argued that free movement of capital was a better way to deepen European integration; effectively, they put an end to the EMS in 1982.

19. See Menzie D. Chinn and Hiro Ito, "A New Measure of Financial Openness," *Journal of Comparative Policy Analysis* 10(3) (September 2008): 307–320. Chinn and Ito devise a "KAOPEN" index that measures the extent of openness in capital account transactions as well as capital controls. The index is based on information from the IMF's Annual Report on Exchange Arrangements and Exchange Restrictions. The openness indicator has four components: the presence of multiple exchange rates; restrictions on current account transactions; restrictions on capital account transactions; and a requirement to surrender export proceeds.

20. Gradual, indirect *ex ante* controls, aimed at reducing instability of short-term flows, were implemented by Brazil (1993–1997), Chile (1991–1998), Colombia (1993–1998), Malaysia (1994), and Thailand (1995–1997); direct and extensive controls have been enforced by China and India since 1990; limited *ex post* controls on capital outflows were imposed during banking or currency crises in Malaysia (1998–2001), Spain (1992), and Thailand (1997–1998); and extensive *ex post* controls entailing currency restrictions on current and capital account transactions were imposed by Romania (1996–1997), Russia (1998–2001), and Venezuela (1994–1996). See Jorge Desormeaux, Karol Fernández, and Pablo García, "Financial Implications of Capital Outflows in Chile: 1998–2008," *BIS Papers* 44 (December 2008): 121–142.

21. Money market mutual funds, for example, emerged in the 1970s, when inflation drove market interest rates far above the regulated rates that banks could pay their depositors.

22. In late 1986, Japanese banks held more than $1 trillion in international assets, a third of total cross-border assets, compared to a fifth held by U.S. banks.

23. See Ricardo Correa and Gustavo A. Suarez, "Firm Volatility and Banks: Evidence from U.S. Banking Deregulation" (Paper presented at the Fourth Workshop of the Latin Finance Network, Bogotá, Colombia, October 3, 2007). Correa and Suarez put forward the thesis that deregulation can lead to real appreciation, external borrowing, and business cycle moderation (domestically and abroad).

24. Lane and Milesi-Ferretti, "The Drivers of Financial Globalization."

25. Intra-European holdings grew from 13.5 percent to 17.8 percent of world total assets and liabilities in 1999–2006; external euro area holdings grew from 21.5 percent to 24.5 percent.

26. Joseph Stiglitz, *Globalization and Its Discontents* (New York: W. W. Norton, 2002).

27. See, for example, Ross Levine and Sara Zervos, "Stock Markets, Banks, and Economic Growth" (World Bank Policy Research Working Paper 1690, December 1996).

28. See, for instance, Philippe Martin and Hélène Rey, "Globalization and Emerging Markets: With or Without Crash?" *American Economic Review* 96, no. 5 (December 2006): 1631–1651.

29. See, for instance, Stanley Fischer, "Capital Account Liberalization and the Role of the IMF," *Princeton Essays in International Finance* 207 (May 1998): 1–10; and Law-

rence H. Summers, "International Financial Crises: Causes, Prevention, and Cures," *American Economic Review* 90, no. 2 (2000): 1–16.

30. See, for instance, Joseph Stiglitz, "Capital Market Liberalization, Economic Growth, and Instability," *World Development* 28, no. 6 (June 2000): 1075–1086; and Dani Rodrik, "Who Needs Capital-Account Convertibility?" *Essays in International Finance* 207 (February 1998).

31. See, for example, Jagdish Bhagwati, "The Capital Myth: The Difference between Trade in Widgets and Dollars," *Foreign Affairs* 77 (May/June 1998): 7–12; and Stiglitz, *Globalization and Its Discontents*.

32. See, for example, Jeffrey Frankel and Andrew Rose, "Currency Crashes in Emerging Markets: An Empirical Treatment," *Journal of International Economics* 41 (November 1996): 351–366.

33. "Thailand Scraps Capital Controls after Stocks Plummet," *International Herald Tribune*, December 19, 2006.

34. Michel Camdessus, "Prospects and Challenges in Our Globalized World Economy," Speech, Wharton School of the University of Pennsylvania, Philadelphia, 4 April 1995, available at http://www.imf.org/external/np/sec/mds/1995/MDS9506.HTM.

35. Charles P. Kindleberger, *Manias, Panics, and Crashes: A History of Financial Crises* (New York: Wiley, 2005).

36. See Morris Goldstein, *The Asian Financial Crisis: Causes, Cures, and Systemic Implications* (Washington, DC: Peterson Institute for International Economics, 1998); and Martin Wolf, *Fixing Global Finance* (Washington, DC: Johns Hopkins University Press, 2008).

37. Carmen Reinhardt and Kenneth S. Rogoff, "Is the 2007 U.S. Subprime Crisis So Different? An International Historical Comparison," *American Economic Review* 98, no. 2 (May 2008): 466–472.

38. Carmen Reinhart and Kenneth Rogoff, "Banking Crises: An Equal Opportunity Menace" (CEPR Discussion Paper No. 7131, Center for Economic and Policy Research, January 2009).

39. Peter Blair Henry and Peter Lombard Lorentzen, "Domestic Capital Market Reform and Access to Global Finance: Making Markets Work" (CDDRL Working Paper No. 78, Center on Democracy, Development and the Rule of Law, January 2007), available at http://www.iis-db.stanford.edu/pubs/21505/No_78_Domestic_Capital_Reform.pdf.

40. Kindleberger, *Manias, Panics*, 20.

41. Bhagwati, *Capital Myth*.

42. Paul Krugman, *The Return of Depression Economics and the Crisis of 2008* (New York: W.W. Norton & Company, 2008).

43. Eswar S. Prasad, Kenneth Rogoff, Shang-Jin Wei, and M. Ayhan Kose, "Effects of Financial Globalization on Developing Countries: Some Empirical Evidence" (IMF Occasional Paper 220, March 2003).

44. Romain Ranciere, Aaron Tornell, and Frank Westermann, "Decomposing the Effects of Financial Liberalization: Crises vs. Growth," *Journal of Banking and Finance*

30, no. 12 (December 2006): 3331–3348. The authors decompose the effect of financial liberalization into direct progrowth effect and an indirect antigrowth effect resulting from higher propensity to crises. They find that the direct effect on growth is plus 1.2 percentage points and the indirect effect is minus 0.25 percentage points.

45. Geert Bekaert, Campbell R. Harvey, and Christian Lundblad, "Does Financial Liberalization Spur Growth? *Journal of Financial Economics* 77, no. 1 (July 2005): 3–55.

46. Peter Blair Henry, "Capital-Account Liberalization, the Cost of Capital, and Economic Growth," *American Economic Review* 93, no. 2 (May 2003): 91–96.

47. Peter Blair Henry and Diego Sasson, "Capital Market Integration and Wages" (NBER Working Paper No. 15204, National Bureau of Economic Research, Cambridge, MA, July 2009).

48. Bekaert, Harvey, and Lundblad, "Does Financial Liberalization Spur Growth?"

49. See Anusha Chari and Peter Blair Henry, "Firm-Specific Information and the Efficiency of Investment," *Journal of Financial Economics* 87, no. 3 (March 2008): 636–655; and Todd Mitton, "Stock Market Liberalization and Operating Performances at the Firm Level," *Journal of Financial Economics* 81 (2006): 625–647.

50. Romain Ranciere, Aaron Tornell, and Frank Westermann, "Systemic Crises and Growth," *Quarterly Journal of Economics* 123, no. 1 (2008): 359–406.

51. It is debatable whether FDI is less volatile than portfolio flows. One study has found that FDI, not portfolio capital, is most responsive to financial liberalization; another found that long-term flows are not necessarily any less volatile than the much-feared short-term flows. See Stijn Claessens, Michael Dooley, and Andrew M. Warner, "Portfolio Capital Flows: Hot or Cold?" *World Bank Economic Review* 9, no. 1 (January 1995): 153–174, available at http://www.ideas.repec.org/a/oup/wbecrv/v9y1995i1p153 -74.html.

52. Aaron Tornell and Frank Westermann, *Boom–Bust Cycles and Financial Liberalization* (Cambridge, MA: MIT Press, 2005).

53. Ranciere, Tornell, and Westermann, "Systemic Crises and Growth."

54. Kristin Forbes, "The Microeconomic Evidence on Capital Controls: No Free Lunch" (NBER Working Paper No. 11372, National Bureau of Economic Research, Cambridge, MA, May 2005), available at http://www.papers.nber.org/papers/w11372.

55. Kristin Forbes, "One Cost of the Chilean Capital Controls: Increased Financial Constraints for Smaller Traded Firms" (NBER Working Paper No. 9777, National Bureau of Economic Research, Cambridge, MA, 2003). Francisco A. Gallego and Leonardo Hernández, "Microeconomic Effects of Capital Controls: The Chilean Experience during the 1990s" (Working Paper No. 203, Central Bank of Chile, 2003).

56. Sebastian Edwards, "Capital Controls, Sudden Stops, and Current Account Reversals" (NBER Working Paper No. 11170, National Bureau of Economic Research, Cambridge, MA, March 2005), available at http://www.nber.org/papers/ w11170.pdf.

57. Eliana Cardoso and Ilan Goldfajn, "Capital Flows to Brazil: The Endogeneity of Capital Controls" (IMF Working Paper No. 97/115, September 1997).

58. See M. Ayhan Kose and Eswar Prasad, "Liberalizing Capital," *IMF Finance & Development* (September 2004), available at http://www.imf.org/external/pubs/ft/fandd/2004/09/pdf/basics.pdf.

59. For a review of financial integration and development, see Maurice Obstfeld, "International Finance and Growth in Developing Countries: What Have We Learned?" (Commission on Growth and Development Working Paper No. 34, World Bank, Washington, DC, 2008), available at http://www.growthcommission.org/storage/cgdev/documents/gcwp034web.pdf.

Chapter 3: Expanding Commerce

1. Ronald Findlay and Kevin H. O'Rourke, *Power and Plenty: Trade, War, and the Global Economy in the Second Millennium* (Princeton, NJ: Princeton University Press, 2007).

2. Findlay and O'Rourke, *Power and Plenty.*

3. See, for example, Gene M. Grossman and Esteban Rossi-Hansberg, "Trading in Tasks: A Simple Theory of Offshoring" (NBER Working Paper No. 12721, National Bureau of Economic Research, Cambridge, MA, December 2006); and J. Bradford Jensen and Lori G. Kletzer, "Tradable Services: Understanding the Scope and Impact of Services Outsourcing" (Working Paper No. 05-9, Peterson Institute for International Economics, Washington, DC, May 2005).

4. World Trade Organization (WTO) data.

5. WTO data.

6. This, however, underestimates the real flows, as services trade is notoriously elusive and international trade statistics do not cover all trade in services as defined by the General Agreement on Trade in Services (GATS).

7. James E. Anderson and Eric van Wincoop, "Gravity with Gravitas: A Solution to the Border Puzzle" (NBER Working Paper No. 8079, National Bureau of Economic Research, Cambridge, MA, 2001).

8. David S. Jacks, Christopher M. Meissner, and Dennis Novy, "Trade Costs, 1870–2000," *American Economic Review* 98, no. 2 (2008): 529–534, available at http://www2.warwick.ac.uk/fac/soc/economics/staff/faculty/novy/tcaea.pdf.

9. Antoni Estevadeordal, Brian Frantz, and Alan M. Taylor, "The Rise and Fall of World Trade, 1870–1939," *Quarterly Journal of Economics* 118, no. 2 (2003): 359–407.

10. Scott L. Baier and Jeffrey H. Bergstrand, "The Growth of World Trade: Tariffs, Transport Costs and Income Similarity," *Journal of International Economics* 53, no. 1 (2001): 1–27.

11. Jacks, Meissner, and Novy, "Trade Costs, 1870–2000."

12. Matthew Adler and Gary Clyde Hufbauer, "Policy Liberalization and U.S. Merchandise Trade Growth, 1980–2006" (Working Paper No. 09-3, Peterson Institute for International Economics, Washington, DC, 2009).

13. David Hummels, Jun Ishii, and Kei-Mu Yi, "The Nature and Growth of Vertical Specialization in World Trade," *Journal of International Economics* 54, no. 1 (2001): 75–96.

14. Matthias Helbe, Ben Sheperd, and John S. Wilson, *Transparency, Trade Costs, and Regional Integration in the Asia Pacific* (Washington, DC: World Bank, 2007).

15. Mauricio Mesquita Moreira, Christian Volpe, and Juan Blyde, *Unclogging the Arteries: The Impact of Transport Costs on Latin American and Caribbean Trade* (Washington, DC: Inter-American Development Bank, 2008).

16. See Marc Levinson, *The Box: How the Shipping Container Made the World Smaller and the World Economy Bigger* (Princeton, NJ: Princeton University Press, 2006).

17. Data from the American Association of Port Authorities.

18. Caroline L. Freund and Diana Weinhold, "The Effect of the Internet on International Trade," *Journal of International Economics* 62, no. 1 (2004): 171–189.
One of the likely reasons why the Internet has enabled commerce to bloom is that it reduces informational gaps on foreign markets and products. There are two main types of gaps. The first is information about a country's products and their quality. This creates a severe entry barrier for firms based in developing countries, as they tend to have weak brands and low national reputations; compare a Swiss brand with a Bulgarian brand. The second informational gap resides at home: domestic firms are unfamiliar with foreign markets. One way to overcome these hurdles is through export promotion offices—sustained campaigns to inform consumers abroad and polish the national image and brand, through efforts by the government, trade associations, or chambers of commerce. The Hong Kong Trade Development Corporation is exemplary, but countries around the world revamped their export promotion institutions in the late 1990s and early 2000s, producing a further spurt in global trade.

19. For a summary, see Antoni Estevadeordal and Kati Suominen, *The Sovereign Remedy: Trade Agreements in the Globalizing World* (Oxford: Oxford University Press, 2009).

20. France signed agreements with Belgium in 1861, the German Zollverein in 1862, Italy in 1863, Switzerland in 1864, Sweden, Norway, Spain, and the Netherlands in 1865, and Austria in 1866. Most favored nation (MFN) treatment enticed other countries to join, with tariff lowering spreading throughout Europe. In 1865, Britain, Belgium, Italy, and other states signed agreements with the Zollverein.

21. See Barry Eichengreen and Douglas A. Irwin, "Trade Blocs, Currency Blocs and the Reorientation of World Trade in the 1930s," *Journal of International Economics* 34 (1995): 1–24; and Charles P. Kindleberger, *Manias, Panics and Crashes: A History of Financial Crises* (New York: Basic Books, 1989). Portugal and France provided tariff preferences to their colonies, and Italy (joined by Austria and Hungary) along with Japan and the Soviet Union created their own defensive trade blocs. In 1930, four Nordic and the three Benelux countries formed the Oslo group to counteract the effects of economic depression through expanded trade and to reduce their dependence on exports to Germany. Meanwhile, the Benelux countries established their own

customs union. In stark contrast to the heyday of the European MFN system and despite resurrection efforts, trade-diverting policies took hold. World trade was regionalized.

22. Findlay and O'Rourke, *Power and Plenty*.

23. See Michael J. Hiscox, "The Magic Bullet? The RTAA, Institutional Reform, and Trade Liberalization," *International Organization* 53, no. 4 (1999): 669–698. Hiscox argues that the Reciprocal Trade Agreements Act (RTAA) did not cause U.S. trade liberalization, but was merely symptomatic of the exogenous changes in party constituencies and social preferences that shaped congressional votes to extend the RTAA authority and liberalize trade after 1945. For the most comprehensive and sweeping study of U.S. trade policy making in the twentieth century, see I. Mac Destler, *American Trade Politics*, 4th edition (Washington, DC: Institute for International Economics, 2005).

24. John H. Jackson, *The World Trading System: Law and Policy of International Economic Relations*, 2nd edition (Cambridge, MA: MIT Press, 1997).

25. The countries that signed the General Agreement on Tariffs and Trade (GATT) were Australia, Belgium, Brazil, Burma, Canada, Ceylon, Chile, China, Cuba, the Czechoslovak Republic, France, India, Lebanon, Luxembourg, the Netherlands, New Zealand, Norway, Pakistan, Southern Rhodesia, Syria, South Africa, the United Kingdom, and the United States.

26. The rounds were Annecy of 1949, Torquay of 1951, Geneva of 1956, Dillon of 1960–1961, Kennedy of 1964–1967, Tokyo of 1973–1979, Uruguay of 1986–1994, and Doha, which has run from 2001 to present.

27. See Findlay and O'Rourke, *Power and Plenty*; and Douglas A. Irwin, "The Rise of U.S. Anti-dumping Activity in Historical Perspective," *World Economy* 28, no. 5 (2005): 651–668.

28. While the first rounds, Annecy and Torquay, centered on tariff liberalization, the Kennedy Round opened a road beyond tariffs, delivering the Anti-Dumping Agreement and a section on development issues. The 1973–1979 Tokyo Round created codes to control nontariff barriers and voluntary export restrictions that had proliferated as a result of the blunting of the tariff instrument and the pessimism over the U.S. economy.

29. See Findlay and O'Rourke, *Power and Plenty*, for construction of data.

30. WTO data.

31. See Estevadeordal and Suominen, *The Sovereign Remedy*. Free trade agreements (FTAs) have surged most notably among the various types of trade agreements in recent years. This in part evinces a drive for more comprehensive and reciprocal liberalization than is achievable in partial-scope agreements, and a push by developed country exporters to open markets in, rather than provide unilateral preferences to, the rapidly growing emerging markets. The rise of FTAs also reflects efforts by developing countries to lock in the preferences of the nonreciprocal schemes via reciprocal agreements, as well as growing questioning in the trade policy world about the effectiveness of nonreciprocal agreements to the intended beneficiaries: lack of reciprocity has come

to be seen as potentially counterproductive since it enables beneficiary countries to postpone tariff liberalization and thus delay efficiency gains.

32. The figure for Mexico excludes partial-scope agreements that cover fewer than 4,100 tariff lines at the 6-digit harmonized system level.

33. To be sure, not all trade among partners of preferential trade agreements (PTAs) enters under PTA rules; some enters under MFN tariffs and other preferences.

34. See Estevadeordal and Suominen, *The Sovereign Remedy*, for an encompassing analysis.

35. These terms were first introduced by Bhagwati. See Jagdish N. Bhagwati, *The World Trading System at Risk* (Princeton, NJ: Princeton University Press, 1991).

36. Jagdish Bhagwati, *Termites in the Trading System* (Oxford: Oxford University Press, 2008).

37. Nuno Limão, "Preferential Trade Agreements as Stumbling Blocks for Multilateral Trade Liberalization: Evidence for the U.S.," *American Economic Review* 96, no. 3 (2006): 896–914; and Nuno Limão and Marcelo Olarreaga, "Trade Preferences to Small Developing Countries and the Welfare Costs of Lost Multilateral Liberalization," *World Bank Economic Review* 20, no. 2 (2006): 217–240. With Marcelo Olarreaga, Limão makes a similar finding in the case of import subsidies afforded to PTA partners by the United States, the European Union, and Japan.

38. Dean A. DeRosa, "The Trade Effects of Preferential Arrangements: New Evidence from the Australia Productivity Commission" (Working Paper No. 07-1, Peterson Institute for International Economics, Washington, DC, 2007).

39. Antoni Estevadeordal, Caroline Freund, and Emanuel Ornelas, "Does Regionalism Affect Trade Liberalization toward Nonmembers?" *Quarterly Journal of Economics* 123, no. 4 (2008): 1531–1575.

40. Richard E. Baldwin, "Multilateralising Regionalism: Spaghetti Bowls as Building Blocs on the Path to Global Free Trade," *World Economy* 29, no. 11 (2006): 1451–1518.

41. Arvind Subramanian and Shang-Jin Wei, "The WTO Promotes Trade Strongly, but Unevenly" (IMF Working Paper WP/03/185, International Monetary Fund, Washington, DC, 2003).

42. See, for example, Michael Tomz, Judith Goldstein, and Douglas Rivers, "Membership Has Its Privileges: The Impact of GATT on International Trade," *American Economic Review* 97, no. 5 (December 2007): 2005–2018.

43. Theo Eicher and Christian Henn, "In Search of WTO Trade Effects: Preferential Trade Agreements Promote Trade Strongly, but Unevenly" (Working Paper, 2008), available at http://www.faculty.washington.edu/te/papers/E_H_WTO.pdf.

44. See Anderson and Neary (2005) and Kee et al. (2006) for an analysis of tariff protection in 2000–2004.

45. Hiscox, "The Magic Bullet?"

46. Helen V. Milner and Keiko Kubota, "Why the Move to Free Trade? Democracy and Trade Policy in the Developing Countries," *International Organization* 59

(Winter 2005): 107–144. See also Stephan Haggard and Robert R. Kaufmann, *The Political Economy of Democratic Transitions* (Princeton, NJ: Princeton University Press, 1995).

47. For a theoretical exposition of the growing strength of export lobbies, see Helen Milner, *Resisting Protectionism: Global Industries and the Politics of International Trade* (Princeton, NJ: Princeton University Press, 1988). For the effects of scale on exports, see Joannes Van Biesebroeck, "Exporting Raises Productivity in Sub-Saharan African Manufacturing Firms," *Journal of International Economics* 67, no. 2 (2005): 373–391.

48. Thus far, the economic heavyweights have an astonishingly good record in complying with the dispute settlement body's verdicts, even when the claimant has been a small country that has no retaliatory power. Philip I. Levy, "China and the WTO: Handle with Care," *Forbes*, April 16, 2007.

49. Kati Suominen, "Rules of Origin in Global Commerce" (PhD Dissertation, University of California, San Diego, CA, 2004).

50. David Dollar and Aart Kraay, "Trade, Growth, and Poverty" (Policy Research Working Paper No. WPS 2615, World Bank, Washington, DC, 2002). Sachs and Warner reached similar conclusions a few years earlier, finding that closed developing countries grew at 0.7 percent annually, while open developing countries sprinted ahead with 4.5 percent average annual growth. They also found that poor open economies grow faster than rich open economies, whereas closed poor economies do not grow as well as closed richer economies. Jeffrey Sachs and Andrew Warner, "Economic Reform and the Process of Global Integration," *Brookings Papers on Economic Activity* 1 (1995): 1–118.

51. Scott C. Bradford, Paul L. E. Grieco, and Gary Clyde Hufbauer, "The Payoff to America from Global Integration," in *The United States and the World Economy: Foreign Economic Policy for the Next Decade*, ed. C. Fred Bergsten and the Institute for International Economics (Washington, DC: Institute for International Economics, 2005).

52. Grant D. Aldonas, Robert Z. Lawrence, and Matthew J. Slaughter, "Succeeding in the Global Economy: A New Policy Agenda for the American Worker," Financial Services Forum Policy Research Report, Washington, DC, 2007.

53. Harald Badinger, "Growth Effects of Economic Integration: The Case of the EU Member States (1950–2000)" (IEF Working Paper No. 40, Research Institute for European Affairs, December 2001). See also Georgios Karras, "Trade and Growth in Europe, Evidence from a Panel of 18 Countries," *Icfai University Journal of Applied Economics* 2 (March 2004): 19–20. Karras arrived at similar magnitudes, arguing that doubling the share of trade in GDP increases an average European country's GDP per capita growth by 4 to 6 percent.

54. See Will Martin and L. Alan Winters, eds., *The Uruguay Round and the Developing Countries* (Cambridge: Cambridge University Press, 1996).

55. Sibylle H. Lehmann and Kevin H. O'Rourke, "The Structure of Protection and Growth in the Late 19th Century" (Institute for International Integration Studies Discussion Paper Series No. 269, Trinity College, Dublin, 2008).

56. Antoni Estevadeordal and Alan M. Taylor, "Is the Washington Consensus Dead? Growth, Openness, and the Great Liberalization, 1970s–2000s" (NBER Working Paper No. 14264, National Bureau of Economic Research, Cambridge, MA, August 2008).

57. Aaditya Mattoo, Randeep Rathindran, and Arvind Subramanian, "Measuring Services Trade Liberalization and Its Impact on Economic Growth: An Illustration," *Journal of Economic Integration* 21, no. 1 (March 2006): 64–98.

58. Francisco Rodriguez and Dani Rodrik, "Trade Policy and Economic Growth: A Skeptic's Guide to Cross-National Evidence" (NBER Working Paper No. 7081, National Bureau of Economic Research, Cambridge, MA, 1999).

59. Jared Bernstein and L. Josh Bivens, "Cheerleaders Gone Wild," April 2007, available at http://www.huffingtonpost.com/jared-bernstein-and-josh-bivens/cheerleaders -gone-wild_b_45405.html.

60. Douglas A. Irwin and Marko Tervio, "Does Trade Raise Income? Evidence from the Twentieth Century," *Journal of International Economics* 58, no. 1 (2002): 1–18. Irwin and Tervio find that the relationship between world trade and world income has changed markedly in the course of history. Trade is not as important a determinant in the year-to-year variation in the growth of income as such factors as business cycles or technological change (think Internet) or education. They find that trade has become extremely responsive to changes in income since the 1980s—quite likely due to the massive change around the world to electronic technologies that propelled growth. Other studies on incomes and growth find similar results: trade affects part of it, but technology, government investment, and policy changes are the key drivers. One implication from this line of analysis is that trade and trade policy do not play a central role in economic downturns or rising inequality.

61. Dani Rodrik, Arvind Subramanian, and Francesco Trebbi, "Institutions Rule: The Primacy of Institutions over Geography and Integration in Economic Development," *Journal of Economic Growth* 9, no. 2 (2004): 131–165.

62. Bineswaree Bolaky and Caroline Freund, "Trade, Regulations, and Growth" (World Bank Working Paper No. 3255, March 2004), available at http://www.wds. worldbank.org/servlet/WDSContentServer/WDSP/IB/2004/04/20/000012009 _20040420160359/Rendered/PDF/WPS3255.pdf.

63. Pinelopi Koujianou Goldberg, Amit Khandelwal, Nina Pavcnik, and Petia To-palova, "Multi-Product Firms and Product Turnover in the Developing World: Evidence from India," *Review of Economics and Statistics*, forthcoming.

64. See Jagdish Bhagwati, "Immiserizing Growth: A Geometrical Note," *Review of Economic Studies* 25 (1958): 201–205; and Harry G. Johnson, "The Possibility of Income Losses from Increased Efficiency or Factor," *Economic Journal* 77, no. 305 (1967): 151–154.

65. Roberto Chang, Linda Kaltani, and Norman Loayza, "Openness Can Be Good for Growth: The Role of Policy Complementarities" (NBER Working Paper No. 11787, National Bureau of Economic Research, Cambridge, MA, 2005). Chang, Kaltani, and Loayza examine a host of complementary policies, including educational investment, financial depth, public infrastructure, governance, labor market rigidity,

and ease of firm entry, and find the most significant effects come from labor and business regulation.

66. Data from the Bureau of Labor Statistics.

67. Howard Rosen, "The Administration's Fiscal 2007 Budget Request for Unemployment Compensation," Testimony before Committee on House Ways and Means, Subcommittee on Human Resources, May 4, 2006, available at http://www.iie.com/publications/papers/rosen0506.pdf.

68. John Haltiwanger, Stefano Scarpetta, and Helena Schweiger, "Assessing Job Flows across Countries: The Role of Industry, Firm Size, and Regulations" (World Bank Policy Research Working Paper No. 4070, November 2006), available at http://www.wds.worldbank.org/external/default/WDSContentServer/IW3P/IB/2006/11/17/000016406_20061117114021/Rendered/PDF/wps4070.pdf.

69. R. Faberman, "Gross Job Flows over the Last Two Business Cycles" (Working Paper No. 372, Bureau of Labor Statistics, 2004).

70. As migration expert Gordon Hanson argues, given the substantial differences in average incomes between countries, "the most striking fact about international migration is that it is so uncommon." Individuals residing outside of their country of birth comprise just 3 percent of the world's population. Moreover, during the last twenty-five years, the stock of international migrants has grown only modestly, rising from 2.2 percent of the world population in 1980 to 2.9 percent in 1990 and to only 3 percent today. Gordon H. Hanson, "The Economic Consequences of the International Migration of Labor" (Draft, University of California, San Diego, October 2008), available at http://www.irps.ucsd.edu/assets/022/8780.pdf.

71. Matthew J. Slaughter, *Insourcing Mergers and Acquisitions* (Washington, DC: Organization for International Investment, 2007).

72. Organization for Economic Cooperation and Development, *OECD Employment Outlook 2005* (Paris: OECD Publishing, 2005).

73. See Mary Amiti and Shang-Jin Wei, "Fear of Service Outsourcing: Is It Justified?" *Economic Policy* 20, no. 42 (2005): 308–347. The authors found a negative effect running from import penetration to jobs in the United States. A study of seven EU countries covering 1995 to 2000 found outsourcing to be associated with substantial employment losses. See also Martin Falk and Yvonne Wolfmayr, "Employment Effects of Outsourcing to Low Wage Countries: Empirical Evidence for EU Countries" (Austrian Institute for Economic Research (WIFO) Working Papers 262, Vienna, Austria, 2005). In another study, a larger wage gap between workers in the parent firms of German and Swedish multinational companies (MNCs) and workers in affiliated firms located in Central and Eastern Europe was linked to employment loss in the parent firms. See Sascha O. Becker, Karolina Ekholm, and Marc-Andreas Muendler, "Offshoring and the Onshore Composition of Occupations, Tasks and Skills" (Working Paper, Ludwig Maximilian University of Munich, Munich, Germany, 2007).

74. See a Bureau of Labor Statistics list of the top thirty fastest-declining jobs in America through 2016, available at http://www.bls.gov/news.release/ecopro.t08.htm.

75. Thus, Christopher Wheeler of the Federal Reserve Bank of St. Louis finds that wage inequalities within industries are strongly linked to education and computer use. Christopher H. Wheeler, "Technology and Industrial Agglomeration: Evidence from Computer Usage" (Working Paper No. 2005-016, Federal Reserve Bank of St. Louis, February 2005).

76. Robert C. Feenstra and Gordon H. Hanson, "The Impact of Outsourcing and High-Technology Capital on Wages: Estimates for the United States, 1979–1990," *Quarterly Journal of Economics* 114 (1999): 907–941.

77. Robert C. Feenstra and Gordon H. Hanson, "Global Production Sharing and Rising Inequality: A Survey of Trade and Wages," NBER Working Paper No. 8372 (July 2001), available at http://www.econ.ucdavis.edu/faculty/fzfeens/pdf/Survey-Feenstra-HansonREV.pdf.

78. See Daniel Drezner, "The Outsourcing Bogeyman," *Foreign Affairs* 83 (2004): 22–34.

79. Alan Blinder, "Offshoring: The Next Industrial Revolution?" *Foreign Affairs* (March/April 2006): 113–128. An OECD analysis of occupational employment data suggests that 15 to 20 percent of total employment in Australia, Canada, the EU-15, and the United States corresponds to service activities that potentially could be subject to international sourcing. See Desiree Van Welsum and Graham Vickery, "Potential Offshoring of ICT-Intensive Using Occupations" (OECD Directorate for Science, Technology and Industry Working Paper DSTI/ICCP/IE (2004) 19/FINAL, Organization for Economic Cooperation and Development, Paris, 2005). The International Labor Organization (2001), using more stringent criteria, estimated that between 1 and 5 percent of service sector jobs were "contestable" by low-wage countries. International Labor Organization, *World Employment Report 2001: Life at Work in the Information Economy* (Geneva: International Labor Organization, 2001). Among available forecasts of services sourcing in the coming years, McCarthy forecasts that a total of 3.4 million white-collar jobs in the United States will move offshore by 2015, while Parker estimates that 1.2 million information technology and service jobs will be outsourced from sixteen European countries over the same time horizon. See John C. McCarthy, *Offshore Outsourcing: The Complete Guide* (Cambridge, MA: Forrester Research, 2004); and Andrew Parker, *Two-Speed Europe: Why 1 Million Jobs Will Move Offshore* (Cambridge, MA: Forrester Research, 2004).

80. See Richard Baldwin's commentary on unbundling and "factory Asia" in Baldwin, "Multilateralising Regionalism."

81. See J. Bradford Jensen and Lori G. Kletzer, "Fear and Offshoring: The Scope and Potential Impact of Imports and Exports of Services" (Policy Brief No. 08-1, Peterson Institute for International Economics, Washington, DC, January 2008), available at http://www.iie.com/publications/interstitial.cfm?ResearchID=880.

82. Robert Z. Lawrence, *Blue-Collar Blues: Is Trade to Blame for Rising U.S. Income Inequality?* (Washington, DC: Peterson Institute for International Economics, 2008); Keith Head and John Ries, "Offshore Production and Skill Upgrading by Japanese Manufacturing Firms," *Journal of International Economics* 58, no. 1 (2002): 81–105; and

Becker, Ekholm, and Muendler, "Offshoring and the Onshore Composition of Occupations, Tasks and Skills." After searching for negative job effects in the United
States from offshoring, following NAFTA's entry into force in 1994, Lawrence found
only a weak relationship. Matthew Slaughter likewise failed to find much evidence of
job destruction, after reviewing the employment experience of U.S. multinationals
between 1977 and 1994. Matthew Slaughter, "Globalization and Employment by US
Multinationals: A Framework and Facts," mimeo, Council of Economic Advisors,
March 2003. Head and Ries showed that the wages of skilled workers in Japanese
MNCs in the period 1965–1990 were positively correlated with the expansion of their
use of labor in low-wage countries. Becker, Ekholm, and Muendler find a slight relationship between offshoring by German multinationals and the compensation of workers in the parent firm, finding that offshoring boosted the wages of home-country
workers with upper secondary education.

83. See Mary Amiti and Shang-Jin Wei, *Service Offshoring, Productivity, and Employment: Evidence from the United States* (IMF Working Paper No. 05/238, International
Monetary Fund, Washington, DC, 2005).

84. Catherine L. Mann, assisted by Jacob Funk Kirkegaard, *Accelerating the Globalization of America: The Role for Information Technology* (Washington, DC: Peterson
Institute, 2006).

85. Organization for Economic Cooperation and Development, *Growing Unequal? Income Distribution and Poverty in OECD Countries* (Paris: OECD, 2008),
available at http://www.sourceoecd.org/upload/810805retemp.pdf. Lawrence (2008)
points out that three different kinds of inequality need to be distinguished: "wage
inequality," namely larger pay differentials for workers with different levels of education, skill, and experience; "super rich inequality," namely an increase in the income
share of the top 1 percent of households whose incomes are strongly related to stock
market and real estate performance; and "class inequality," namely a rising share of
income earned by owners of capital—in particular, corporate profits. Since 1981, all
three types of inequality have increased in the United States, but they have emerged
at very different times, and wage inequality in particular has taken different forms.
Robert Z. Lawrence, *Blue-Collar Blues: Is Trade to Blame for Rising US Income Inequality?* (Washington, DC: Peterson Institute for International Economics, 2008).
The asset market collapse of 2008 and 2009 will sharply reduce the last two types of
inequality.

86. Thomas Harjes, "Globalization and Income Inequality: A European Perspective" (IMF Working Paper No. WP/07/169, International Monetary Fund, Washington, DC, July 2007).

87. Organization for Economic Cooperation and Development, "Globalization,
Jobs and Wages" (OECD Policy Brief, June 2007, available at http://www.oecd.org/
dataoecd/27/1/38796126.pdf).

88. On the role of norms and institutions, see Frank Levy and Peter Temin, "Inequality and Institutions in 20th Century America" (MIT Department of Economics
Working Paper No. 07-17, Massachusetts Institute of Technology, May 2007).

89. A voluminous literature wrestles with the effects of income inequality. Some of the most influential theoretical contributions include: Alberto Alesina and Dani Rodrik, "Distributive Politics and Economic Growth," *Quarterly Journal of Economics* 109, no. 2 (1994): 465–490; Roland Benabou, "Equity and Efficiency in Human Capital Investment: The Local Connection," *Review of Economic Studies* 63, no. 2 (1996): 237–264; Oded Galor and Joseph Zeira, "Income Distribution and Macroeconomics," *Review of Economic Studies* 60, no. 1 (1993): 35–52; Oded Galor and Omer Moav, "From Physical to Human Capital Accumulation: Inequality and the Process of Development," *Review of Economic Studies* 71, no. 4 (2004): 1001–1026; Jeremy Greenwood and Boyan Jovanovic, "Financial Development, Growth, and the Distribution of Income," *Journal of Political Economy* 98, no. 5 (1990): 1076–1107; Michael Kremer and Daniel L. Chen, "Income Distribution Dynamics with Endogenous Fertility," *Journal of Economic Growth* 7, no. 3 (2002): 227–258; and Torsten Persson and Guido Tabellini, "Is Inequality Harmful for Growth?" *American Economic Review* 84, no. 3 (1994): 600–621.

Prominent contributions from the empirical side include: Alberto Alesina and Roberto Perotti, "Income Distribution, Political Instability, and Investment," *European Economic Review* 40, no. 6 (1996): 1203–1228; Robert J. Barro, "Inequality and Growth in a Panel of Countries," *Journal of Economic Growth* 5, no. 1 (2000): 5–32; Kristin Forbes, "A Reassessment of the Relationship between Inequality and Growth," *American Economic Review* 90, no. 4 (2000): 869–887; Jesper Roine and Daniel Waldenstrom, "The Evolution of Top Incomes in an Egalitarian Society: Sweden, 1903–2004," *Journal of Public Economics* 92, nos. 1–2 (2008): 366–387; Thomas Piketty, "Income Inequality in France, 1901–1998," *Journal of Political Economy* 111, no. 5 (2003): 1004–1042; Thomas Piketty and Emmanuel Saez, "Income Inequality in the United States, 1913–1998," *Quarterly Journal of Economics* 118, no. 1 (2003): 1–39; and Kevin Sylwester, "Income Inequality, Education Expenditures, and Growth," *Journal of Development Economics* 63 (2002): 379–398.

90. Lawrence, *Blue-Collar Blues*.

91. Florence Jaumotte, Subir Lall, and Chris Papageorgiou, "Rising Income Inequality: Technology, or Trade and Financial Globalization?" (Working Paper No. WP/08/185, International Monetary Fund, Washington, DC, July 2008).

92. Jose Ernesto López-Córdova, *México: Nota Sectorial Sobre Comercio e Integración* (Washington, DC: Inter-American Development Bank, 2006).

93. See also Nancy Birdsall, M. Nissanke, and E. Thorbecke, "Discussion of Impact of Globalization on the World's Poor" (World Institute for Development Economics Research of the United Nations University (UNU-WIDER) Book Launch, Washington, DC, May 16, 2007).

94. David Card and John E. DiNardo, "Skill-Biased Technological Change and Rising Wage Inequality: Some Problems and Puzzles," *Journal of Labor Economics* 20, no. 4 (2002): 733–783; and Thomas Lemieux, "Increasing Residual Wage Inequality: Composition Effects, Noisy Data, or Rising Demand for Skill?" *American Economic Review* 96, no. 3 (2006): 461–498. Some labor economists are beginning to question

the role of skill-biased technical change (SBTC) in promoting inequality. In particular, Card and DiNardo, after numerous statistical tests, conclude that the connection between the spread of information technology and wage inequality is weak. The timing of increases in wage inequality is hard to reconcile with the timing of SBTC; instead, the authors place more weight on the political failure to raise minimum wages in the early 1980s. Thomas Lemieux similarly finds that "the growth in both residual and between group wage inequality is all concentrated in the 1980s" and he questions the idea of an inequality trend arising from skill-biased technical change.

95. The trade barrier scenario would also raise the long-run real interest rate by ninety basis points in the industrial countries and reduce the amount of capital per worker. See Hans Fehr, Sabine Jokisch, and Laurence J. Kotlikoff, *Dynamic Globalization and Its Potentially Alarming Prospects for Low-Wage Workers* (NBER Working Paper No. 14527, National Bureau of Economic Research, Cambridge, MA, 2008).

Chapter 4: Mighty Multinationals

1. United Nations Conference on Trade and Development (UNCTAD) data.

2. UNCTAD, *World Investment Report 2008* (Geneva: UNCTAD, 2008).

3. UNCTAD, *World Investment Report 2008*. Multinational companies (MNCs) are seeing the rise of other players—notably sovereign wealth funds and private equity firms—as sources of FDI. But less than 1 percent of the total assets of sovereign wealth funds (SWFs) go to FDI, most of it in developed countries.

4. UNCTAD, *World Investment Report 2008*.

5. UNCTAD, *World Investment Report 2008*.

6. UNCTAD, *World Investment Report 2008*.

7. A. B. Bernard, J. B. Jensen, and P. K. Schott, "Importers, Exporters and Multinationals: A Portrait of the Firms in the U.S. that Trade Goods" (NBER Working Paper No. 11404, National Bureau of Economic Research, Cambridge, MA, June 2005).

8. Steven J. Landefeld and Raymond Mataloni, "Offshore Outsourcing and Multinational Companies" (Presentation, Brookings Institution, June 22, 2004), available at http://www.bea.gov/papers/pdf/multinationals.pdf.

9. UNCTAD, *World Investment Report 2008*. Here, we focus largely on manufacturing and services MNCs, rather than on the vast literature on MNCs in extractive industries.

10. UNCTAD data.

11. UNCTAD, *World Investment Report 2008*.

12. See Antoine van Agtmael, *The Emerging Markets Century: How a New Breed of World-Class Companies Is Overtaking the World* (New York: Free Press, 2007).

13. Thierry Mayer and Gianmarco I. P. Ottaviano, "The Happy Few: The Internationalization of European Firms: New Facts Based on Firm-Level Evidence" (Bruegel Blueprint Series, Volume III, Bruegel, 2007).

14. Matthew Adler and Gary Clyde Hufbauer, "Policy Liberalization and FDI Growth, 1982 to 2006" (Working Paper No. 08-7, Peterson Institute for International

Economics, Washington, DC, August 2008), available at http://www.iie.com/publications/wp/wp08-7.pdf.

15. Thomas Horst, "Theoretical and Empirical Analysis of American Exports and Direct Investments" (PhD Dissertation, University of Rochester, Rochester, NY, 1969).

16. Antoni Estevadeordal, José Ernesto López-Córdova, and Kati Suominen, "How Do Rules of Origin Affect Investment Flows? Some Hypotheses and the Case of Mexico" (Institute for the Integration of Latin America and the Caribbean (IN-TAL), Integration and Trade Division (ITD) Working Paper No. 22, 2006).

17. Michael J. Ferrantino and Keith Hall, "The Direct Effects of Trade Liberalization on Foreign Direct Investment: A Partial Equilibrium Analysis" (USITC Office of Economics Working Paper No. 2001-10-B, US International Trade Commission, Washington, DC, October 2001).

18. Bishwanath Goldar and Rashmi Banga, "Impact of Trade Liberalization on Foreign Direct Investment in Indian Industries" (Working Paper No. 35, United Nations Economic and Social Commission for Asia and the Pacific (ESCAP) Asia-Pacific Research and Training Network on Trade, June 2007).

19. Bruce A. Blonigen, "Tariff-Jumping Antidumping Duties," *Journal of International Economics* 57, no. 1 (June 2002): 31–49.

20. Dean DeRosa, "Morocco's Economic Performance under the US-Morocco Free Trade Agreement," in *Capitalizing on the Morocco-US Free Trade Agreement: A Road Map for Success*, ed. Gary Hufbauer and Claire Brunel (Washington, DC: Peterson Institute for International Economics, 2009).

21. Mihir A. Desai, C. Fritz Foley, and James R. Hines Jr., "Do Tax Havens Divert Economic Activity?" *Economics Letters* 90 (2006): 219–224; Mihir A. Desai, C. Fritz Foley, and James R. Hines Jr., "The Demand for Tax Haven Operations," *Journal of Public Economics* 90 (2006): 513–531.

22. Torfinn Harding and Beata Smarzynska Javorcik, "Developing Economies and International Investors: Do Investment Promotion Agencies Bring Them Together?" (World Bank Policy Research Working Paper No. 4339, 2007); and Andrew Charlton and Nicholas Davis, "Does Investment Promotion Work?" *Journal of Economics Analysis & Policy* 7, no. 1 (2007). Harding and Javorcik and Charlton and Davis investigate the impact of investment promotion agencies on inward FDI flows and find a strong positive relationship. However, it is unclear from the empirical studies whether these agencies increase the global volume of FDI or merely shift it around. Harding and Javorcik suggest that agencies in the same region can divert FDI flows from one country to another.

23. UNCTAD data.

24. See, for example, Karl P. Sauvant and Lisa E. Sachs, eds., *The Effect of Treaties on Foreign Direct Investment: Bilateral Investment Treaties, Double Taxation Treaties and Investment Flows* (New York: Oxford University Press, 2009). See also Len J. Trevino, Douglas E. Thomas, and John Cullen, "The Three Pillars of Institutional Theory and FDI in Latin America: An Institutionalization Process," *International Business Review*

118 (2008). In their study, Trevino, Thomas, and Cullen also found bilateral invest-ment treaties (BITs) to be "significant indicators of inward FDI in Latin America."

25. Bruce Blonigen and Ronald Davies, "The Effects of Bilateral Tax Treaties on U.S. FDI Activity," *International Tax and Public Finance* 11 (2004): 601–622.

26. Tax treaties also may have some effect on trade flows, as firms adjust their sourcing patterns to minimize their tax liabilities. See Ronald B. Davies, Pehr-Johan Norbäck, and Ayça Tekin-Koru, "The Effect of Tax Treaties on Multinational Firms: New Evidence from Microdata" (Working Paper No. 0721, Oxford University Centre for Business Taxation, 2007).

27. See Barbara Kotschwar, "Mapping Investment Provisions in Regional Trade Agreements: Towards an International Investment Regime?" in *Regional Rules in the Global Trading System*, ed. Antoni Estevadeordal, Kati Suominen, and Robert Teh (Cambridge: Cambridge University Press, 2009). See also Edward M. Graham, *Fighting the Wrong Enemy: Antiglobal Activists and Multinational Enterprises* (Wash-ington, DC: Peterson Institute for International Economics, 2000).

28. Neil Kong Jr., "Pension Funds Fret as Chevron Faces Ecuador Ruling," *Wall Street Journal*, April 8, 2009, available at http://www.online.wsj.com/article/SB12391486728 4999153.html.

29. *The Economist*, May 23, 2009, 61–63.

30. Giuseppe Nicoletti, Stephen S. Golub, Dana Hajkova, Daniel Mirza, and Kwang-Yeol Yoo, "The Influence of Policies on Trade and Foreign Direct Invest-ment," *OECD Economic Studies* 36 (2003).

31. The calculation is based on the actual realized flows over the period 1980–2000. A 1989 assessment of foreign bank activity in the United States from 1973 to 1986 found that the rise in incoming banking activity could be attributed to the U.S. Inter-national Banking Act of 1978, which leveled the playing field between foreign and U.S.-owned banks in the American market. C. W. Hultman and R. McGee, "Factors Affecting the Foreign Banking Presence in the United States," *Journal of Banking and Finance* 13, no. 3 (July 1989): 383–396.

32. E. Asiedu and D. Lien, Capital Controls and Foreign Direct Investment," *World Development* 32, no. 3 (2004): 479–490.

33. There is systematic empirical evidence to this effect: Davies, for example, finds that FDI increases in the skilled-labor stock of either the sending or the recipient country. See Ronald B. Davies, "Fragmentation of Headquarter Services and FDI," *North American Journal of Economics and Finance* 16, no. 1 (March 2005): 61–79.

34. See United Nations Conference on Trade and Development, "Stability, Skilled Labour and Infrastructure Top Locational Factors for Foreign Affiliates," *UNCTAD Investment Brief* 3 (2007).

35. United Nations Conference on Trade and Development, "Worldwide Survey of Foreign Affiliates" (UNCTAD Occasional Note, November 5, 2007).

36. Multilateral Investment Guarantee Agency, *Foreign Direct Investment Survey* (Washington, DC: World Bank, 2002), available at http://www.miga.org/documents/ FDIsurvey.pdf. Larger companies are less likely to identify labor relations and

unionization as critical location factors, and more likely to focus on labor cost. They also are more likely than smaller companies to select national taxes as a key factor. Smaller companies more often select the ability to hire skilled laborers, technical professionals, and management staff as very important issues. They also are more likely than larger companies to be concerned with the availability of fully serviced land and the reliability and quality of utilities.

37. See Susan George, *The Lugano Report* (London: Pluto Press, 1999).

38. Leftist scholars differentiated further between globe-trotting upper-class elites who would stash their money in tax-haven banks and the truly immobile working stiffs who would end up paying the national tax burden. Analysts from the developing world argued that their governments would now lose "policy space," being at the mercy of MNCs and a giant race to the bottom. The globalization process would make everyone's policies look pretty much the same.

39. For the most encompassing study on regulatory issues related to MNC activity, see Dale D. Murphy, *The Structure of Regulatory Competition: Corporations and Public Policies in a Global Economy* (Oxford: Oxford University Press, 2004).

40. Daniel J. Mitchell, "Why Tax Havens Are a Blessing," *Foreign Policy*, March 18, 2008.

41. Mitchell, "Why Tax Havens Are a Blessing."

42. Michael Devereux, Ben Lockwood, and Michela Redoano, "Is There a 'Race to the Bottom' in Corporate Taxes? An Overview of Recent Research" (Working Paper, Draft, May 2003), available at http://www2.warwick.ac.uk/fac/soc/csgr/research/keytopic/race/Lockwood_Overview_May03.pdf.

43. Michael Devereux, "Developments in the Taxation of Corporate Profit in the OECD since 1965: Rates, Bases and Revenues" (Centre for Business Taxation Working Paper No. 704, Oxford University, 2007).

44. Kimberly Clausing, "Corporate Tax Revenues in OECD Countries," *International Tax and Public Finance* 14, no. 2. (April 2006): 115–134.

45. Larger, more trade-intensive countries also collect more corporate tax, but this may reflect the fact that these countries are more attractive venues for investment. Joel Slemrod, "Are Corporate Tax Rates, or Countries, Converging?" *Journal of Public Economics* 88, no. 6 (June 2004): 1169–1186.

46. Geoffrey Garrett, "Global Markets and National Politics: Collision Course or Virtuous Circle?" *International Organization* 52 (1998): 787–824; Dennis P. Quinn, "The Correlates of Changes in International Financial Regulation," *American Political Science Review* 91 (1997): 531–551; Duane Swank, "Funding the Welfare State," *Political Studies* 46 (1998): 672–692; and Duane Swank, "Global Capital, Democracy and the Welfare State" (Political Economy of European Integration Working Paper 1, No. 66, 1998).

47. Geoffrey Garrett and Deborah Mitchell, "Globalization and the Welfare State" (Draft, Yale University, 1999), available at http://www.yale.edu/leitner/resources/docs/1999-04.pdf). It is often argued that the marginal effective tax rate—the tax

paid on an additional million dollars of corporate income—determines incremental investment by firms already based in a country. The marginal effective rate is often near the statutory tax rate. The decision whether to locate in county A rather than country B is often said to be influenced by the average effective tax rate, which is the ratio of total corporate tax paid to total pretax profit. See Michael Devereux and Rachel Griffith, "Evaluating Tax Policy for Location Decisions," *Asia-Pacific Financial Markets* 10, no. 2 (March 2003): 107–126.

48. Alberto Alesina and Roberto Perotti, "Fiscal Discipline and the Budget Process," *American Economic Review* 86 (1996): 401–407; Geoffrey Garrett, "Shrinking States? Globalisation and National Autonomy in the OECD," *Oxford Development Studies* 26 (1998): 71–97.

49. Richard E. Baldwin and Paul Krugman, "Agglomeration, Integration and Tax Harmonization," *European Economic Review* 48, no. 1 (February 2004): 1–23.

50. Organization for Economic Cooperation and Development, *International Trade and Core Labour Standards* (Paris: OECD, 2000).

51. Steve Charnowitz, "Promoting Higher Labor Standards," in *New Forces in the World Economy*, ed. Brad Roberts (Cambridge and London: MIT Press, 1996), 403–426.

52. See Daniel Drezner, "The Race to the Bottom Hypothesis: An Empirical and Theoretical Review" (The Fletcher School, Tufts University, December 2006), available at http://www.danieldrezner.com/policy/RTBreview.doc.

53. Keith E. Maskus, "Should Core Labor Standards Be Imposed through International Trade Policy?" (World Bank Policy Research Working Paper Series 1817, World Bank, Washington, DC, 1997). See also A. Romero, "Labour Standards and Export Processing Zones: Situation and Pressures for Change," *Development Policy Review* 13, no. 3 (1995). According to Romero, workers in export processing zones (EPZs) also tend to enjoy better working conditions, especially from firms headquartered in an OECD country. Exceptions tend to occur in low-skilled, labor-intensive assembly operations where enforcement is lax, such as garment and gem-cutting firms. Poor working conditions are also likely to prevail in older plants.

54. On standards, see Johannes Moenius, "Three Studies on Trade Barriers and Trade Volumes" (PhD Dissertation, University of California, San Diego, 2000). K. Edmiston, S. Muss, and N. Valev, "Tax Structure and FDI: The Deterrent Effects of Complexity and Uncertainty," *Fiscal Studies* 24 (2003): 341–359. Edmiston, Muss, and Valev find that uncertainty over tax policy is a significant barrier to FDI.

55. Elizabeth DeSombre, *Domestic Sources of International Environmental Policy: Industry, Environmentalists, and U.S. Power* (Cambridge, MA: MIT Press, 2000).

56. See Drezner, "The Race to the Bottom Hypothesis: An Empirical and Theoretical Review."

57. See Diana Farrell, "The Case for Globalization: The Results of McKinsey's Latest Study of the Pros and Cons of Emerging Market Foreign Investment," *International Economy* (Winter 2004).

58. Theodore H. Moran, Edward M. Graham, and Magnus Blomström, eds., *Does Foreign Direct Investment Promote Development?* (Washington, DC: Peterson Institute for International Economics, May 2005).

59. Jagdish Bhagwati, "U.S. Trade Policy: The Infatuation with Free Trade Areas," in *The Dangerous Drift to Preferential Trade Agreements*, ed. Jagdish Bhagwati and Anne O. Krueger (Washington, DC: AEI Press, 1995), 1–18.

60. See Daniel Drezner, "The Race to the Bottom Hypothesis: An Empirical and Theoretical Review," Draft, The Fletcher School, Tufts University, December 2006.

61. See various articles at Corporate Social Responsibility Officer, available at http://www.thecro.com.

62. Corporate Social Responsibility Officer, available at http://www.thecro.com.

63. Corporate Social Responsibility Officer, available at http://www.thecro.com.

64. See David Jonas, "Study: CSR Focus Withstanding Financial Crisis," *Transnational Travel*, February 10, 2009, available at http://www.thetransnational.travel/news.php?cid=ACTE-KDS-CSR.Feb-09.11; and Social Investment Forum, *Report on Responsible Investing Trends in the U.S. 2007* (Washington, DC: Social Investment Forum, 2007).

65. See Chevron, "Working Safely Every Day," available at http://www.chevron.com/globalissues/healthsafety.

66. See Microsoft, "Unlimited Potential," available at http://www.microsoft.com/unlimitedpotential/default.mspx.

67. Evidence suggests that in Ireland, multinationals are more likely to exit the market than indigenous plants, after controlling for industry specific characteristics. See Holger Görg and Eric Strobl, "Footloose Multinationals?" *Manchester School* 71, no. 1 (2003):1–19. See also Neil Hood and Stephen Young, "The United Kingdom," in *Governments, Globalization and International Business*, ed. John Dunning (Oxford: Oxford University Press, 1997). Hood and Young argue that MNCs in the United Kingdom may be more footloose than UK-owned firms due to their shallow roots in the host country.

68. Gary Clyde Hufbauer and Ariel Assa, *U.S. Taxation of Foreign Income* (Washington, DC: Peterson Institute for International Economics, 2007).

69. See Görg and Strobl, "Footloose Multinationals."

70. For an extensive new survey of the effects of FDI on development, see Theodore H. Moran, *Foreign Direct Investment and Development. Launching a Second Generation of Policy Research: Avoiding the Mistakes of the First, Re-Evaluating Policies for Developed and Developing Countries* (Washington, DC: The Peterson Institute for International Economics, 2009).

71. Multinational companies are expected to have "knowledge capital"—large R&D expenditures and a large share of technical workers—and produce technically advanced products.

72. Moran, *Launching a Second Generation of Policy Research*. See also Susan E. Feinberg and Michael P. Keane, "Intrafirm Trade of U.S. MNCs: Findings and Implications for Models and Politics toward Trade and Investment," in *Does Foreign Direct*

Investment Promote Development? ed. Theodore H. Moran, Edward M. Graham, and Magnus Blomstrom (Washington, DC: Center for Global Development and Institute for International Economics, 2005).

73. Barry P. Bosworth and Susan M. Collins, "Capital Flows to Developing Economies: Implications for Saving and Investment," *Brookings Papers on Economic Activity* 1 (1999): 143–169.

74. Anil Kumar, "Does Foreign Direct Investment Help Emerging Economies?" *Federal Reserve Bank of Dallas Economic Letter* 2, no. 1 (January 2007).

75. Carmen Fillat Castejón, Joseph Francois, and Julia Woerz, "Cross-Border Trade and FDI in Services" (CEPR Discussion Paper No. 7074, Center for Economic and Policy Research, December 2008).

76. Ricardo Hausmann, Jason Hwang, and Dani Rodrik, "What You Export Matters" (NBER Working Paper No. 11905, National Bureau of Economic Research, Cambridge, MA, December 2005).

77. See, for example, Brian Aitken, Ann Harrison, and Robert E. Lipsey, "Wages and Foreign Ownership: A Comparative Study of Mexico, Venezuela, and the United States," *Journal of International Economics* 40, nos. 3–4 (May 1996): 345–371.

78. The authors thank Ted Moran for the comment.

79. See Eduardo Fernández-Arias and Ricardo Hausmann, "What's Wrong with International Financial Markets," and "Getting It Right: What to Reform in International Financial Markets," in *Global Finance from a Latin American Viewpoint*, ed. Richardo Hausmann and U. Hiemenz (Washington, DC: Inter-American Development Bank, 2000); Eduardo Borensztein, Jose De Gregorio, and J.-W. Lee, "How Does Foreign Direct Investment Affect Economic Growth?" *Journal of International Economics* 45 (1998): 115–135; Marta Bengoa and Blanca Sanchez-Robles, "Foreign Direct Investment, Economic Freedom and Growth: New Evidence from Latin America," *European Journal of Political Economy* 19 (2003): 529–545; V. N. Balasubramanyam, M. Salisu, and David Sapsford, "Foreign Direct Investment and Growth in EP and IS Countries," *The Economic Journal* 106 (1996): 92-105; Kevin H. Zhang, "Does Foreign Direct Investment Promote Economic Growth? Evidence from East Asia and Latin America," *Contemporary Economic Policy* 19, no. 2 (2001): 175–185. See Fernández-Arias and Hausmann in general, and de Melo (1999) and Borensztein, De Gregorio, and Lee on human capital. Bengoa and Sanchez-Robles and Balasubramanyam et al. (1996) find that FDI has a positive effect on economic growth in host countries that use an export-promoting strategy, but not in countries using an import-substitution strategy. Zhang finds host country conditions such as trade regime and macroeconomic stability to be central.

80. See, for example, Beata Smarzynska Javorcik and Mariana Spatareanu, "Liquidity Constraints and Linkages with Multinationals" (Centre for Institutions and Economic Performance (LICOS) Discussion Paper No. 225/2008, 2008).

81. Keith Head, John Ries, and Deborah Swenson, "Agglomeration Benefits and Location Choice: Evidence from Japanese Manufacturing Investments in the United States," *Journal of International Economics* 38, nos. 3–4 (May 1995): 223–247; S. Feinberg

and S. K. Majumdar, "Technology Spillovers from Foreign Direct Investment in the Indian Pharmaceutical Industry," *Journal of International Business Studies* 32, no. 3 (2001): 421–437; S. Feinberg and A. K. Gupta, "Knowledge Spillovers and the Assignment of R&D Responsibilities to Foreign Subsidiaries," *Strategic Management Journal* 25 (2004): 823–845.

82. Badi H. Baltagi, Peter Egger, and Michael Pfaffermayr, "Estimating Models of Complex FDI: Are There Third-Country Effects?" *Journal of Econometrics* 140, no. 1 (September 2007): 260–281.

83. Canadian Chamber of Commerce, "Finding the Balance: Reducing Border Costs while Strengthening Security" (Report, February 2008), available at http://www.uschamber.com/NR/rdonlyres/ehbod3f5v2yynuq3kr2vrxtiwvrnut6qteexitpyd7n4ef36usxji4v3uus47b4ekzba5of625r3js5vt66wggm2v6f/0802_finding_balance_report.pdf.

84. Moran, "Launching a Second Generation of Policy Research."

85. John Cantwell and Odile Janne, "O.E.M. Technological Globalization and Innovative Centers: The Role of Corporate Technological Leadership and Locational Hierarchy," *Research Policy* 28, nos. 2–3 (1999): 119–144. Cantwell and Janne find that foreign subsidiaries of even technologically advanced MNCs focus on the specific technologies where these MNCs lag behind.

86. Irene Brambilla, "Multinationals, Technology, and the Introduction of Varieties of Goods" (NBER Working Paper No. 12217, National Bureau of Economic Research, Cambridge, MA, May 2006).

87. See "Multinationals: Are They Good for America?" *Business Week*, February 28, 2008.

88. Andrew B. Bernard and Bradford Jensen, "Firm Structure, Multinationals, and Manufacturing Plant Deaths," *Review of Economics and Statistics* 89, no. 2 (May 2007): 193–204.

89. Matthew J. Slaughter, "How U.S. Multinational Companies Strengthen the U.S. Economy" (Paper prepared for the Business Roundtable and the United States Council Foundation, Spring 2009).

90. Mayer and Ottaviano, "The Happy Few."

Chapter 5: Southbound

1. Real GDP in chained dollars (2000), seasonally adjusted at annual rates. Bureau of Economic Analysis, available at http://www.bea.gov.

2. Standard & Poor's, "Standard & Poor's Global Stock Market Review" (Monthly Report, World by Numbers, December 2008), available at http://www2.standardandpoors.com/spf/pdf/index/123108_WorldbyNumbers-Report.pdf).

3. Standard & Poor's, "Standard & Poor's Global Stock Market Review."

4. U.S. Department of Treasury, "Daily Treasury Yield Curve Rates," available at http://www.ustreas.gov/offices/domestic-finance/debt-management/interest-rate/yield_historical_2008.shtml.

5. "China to Stick with U.S. Bonds," *Reuters*, February 12, 2009.

6. See David Levy, "Emerging Market Debt Spreads—How Things Have Changed," in *Notes on Credit Spreads* blog, November 18, 2008, available at http://www.spreadsoncredit.com/an-emerging-difference/.

7. "Caught in the Downward Current," *Economist*, March 19, 2009.

8. See United Nations Conference on Trade and Development (UNCTAD) Foreign Direct Investment database, available at http://www.unctad.org/Templates/Page.asp?intItemID=1923&lang=1.

9. UNCTAD, "Global and Regional FDI Trends in 2009," *Global Investment Trends Monitor*, no. 2, January 19, 2010, available at http://www.unctad.org/en/docs/webdiaeia20101_en.pdf.

10. United Nations Conference on Trade and Development, "Global Foreign Direct Investment."

11. Malcolm Beith, "Reverse Migration Rocks Mexico," *Foreign Policy*, Web Exclusive, February 2009.

Chapter 6: A Dangerous Time in Global Finance

1. This was the theme of the November 2008 G20 declaration, which read: "Policymakers, regulators and supervisors, in *some advanced countries*, did not adequately appreciate and address the risks building up in financial markets, keep pace with financial innovation, or take into account the systemic ramifications of domestic regulatory actions" (italics added).

2. See George Cooper, *The Origin of Financial Crises: Central Banks, Credit Bubbles, and the Efficient Market Fallacy* (New York: Random House, 2008); and Robert J. Shiller, *The Subprime Solution: How Today's Global Financial Crisis Happened, and What to Do about It* (Princeton, NJ: Princeton University Press, 2008).

3. Steven Gjerstad and Vernon L. Smith, "From Bubble to Depression," *Wall Street Journal*, April 6, 2009, A15.

4. See Martin Wolf, *Fixing Global Finance* (Baltimore, MD: Johns Hopkins University Press, 2008); and "Bernanke's Speech to Council on Foreign Relations," *Reuters*, March 10, 2009, available at http://www.reuters.com/article/businessNews/idUSTRE52939S20090310. China is the source of a third of the U.S. trade deficit. China's export boom owes in part to an undervalued Chinese currency and to a massive supply of cheap and capable labor for manufacturing consumer goods. Numerous concerns about the imbalances have been voiced especially since the U.S. trade deficit peaked in 2006. See, for example, Robert Rubin, Peter R. Orszag, and Allen Sinai, "Sustained Budget Deficits: Longer-Run U.S. Economic Performance and the Risk of Financial and Fiscal Disarray" (Paper presented at the AEA-NAEFA Joint Session, Allied Social Science Associations Annual Meetings, The Andrew Brimmer Policy Forum, "National Economic and Financial Policies for Growth and Stability," January 4, 2004, San Diego, CA; Maurice Obstfeld and Kenneth Rogoff, "The Unsustainable U.S. Current Account Position Revisited" (NBER Working Paper No.

10869, National Bureau of Economic Research, Cambridge, MA, November 2004); and Peter Peterson, *Running on Empty: How the Democratic and Republican Parties Are Bankrupting Our Future and What Americans Can Do about It* (New York: Farrar, Straus and Giroux, 2004). For the view that imbalances contributed significantly to the crisis, see, for example, Ben S. Bernanke, "Remarks on the Economic Outlook" Speech, International Monetary Conference, Barcelona, Spain, June 3, 2008; Martin Wolf, *Fixing Global Finance* (Washington, DC: Johns Hopkins University Press, 2008); and Brad Setser, "Bretton Woods 2 and the Current Crisis: Any Link?" Council on Foreign Relations Blog, 1 August 2008, available at http://www.blogs.cfr.org/setser/2008/12/01/bretton-woods-2-and-the-current-crisis-any-link/. For the opposing view, see, for instance, Michael P. Dooley, David Folkerts-Landau, and Peter M. Garber, "Bretton Woods II Still Defines the International Monetary System" (NBER Working Paper No. 14731, National Bureau of Economic Research, Cambridge, MA, February 2009).

5. Ron Nixon, "Study Predicts Foreclosure for 1 in 5 Subprime Loans," *New York Times*, December 20, 2006, available at http://www.nytimes.com/2006/12/20/business/20home.html.

6. Nixon, "Study Predicts Foreclosure."

7. See, for example, Jörg Bibow, "The International Monetary (Non-)Order and the 'Global Capital Flows Paradox'" (Working Paper No. 531, Levy Economics Institute and Skidmore College, April 2008).

8. Warren Buffett, "What Worries Me," *Fortune*, March 3, 2003.

9. Mark Landler, "World Leaders Vow Joint Push to Aid Economy," *New York Times*, November 16, 2008, A1.

10. See Elisa Gamberoni and Richard Newfarmer, "Trade Protection: Incipient but Worrisome Trends," International Trade Department, World Bank, *Trade Notes* 37 (March 2009), available at http://www.siteresources.worldbank.org/NEWS/Resources/Trade_Note_37.pdf .

11. Adam Nagourney and Megan Thee-Brenan, "Outlook on Economy Is Brightening, Poll Finds," *New York Times*, April 7, 2009, A1, available at http://www.nytimes.com/2009/04/07/us/politics/07poll.html?_r=1&scp=2&sq=poll&st=cse.

12. Two leading international relations theorists, Miles Kahler and David Lake of University of California, San Diego, argue that over past centuries, supranationalism has lost out to the other forms of global financial governance: hierarchies (one country plays a dominant role) and networks (cooperative rule setting between equal members and reciprocity as the mechanism of enforcement). For a few decades after 1950, the International Monetary Fund played the role of supranational nanny for emerging countries that hit the financial rocks, but even the IMF has had no such authority with respect to monetary affairs or financial governance in the major nations. See Miles Kahler and David A. Lake, "Economic Integration and Global Governance: Why So Little Supranationalism?" in *Explaining Regulatory Change in the Global Economy*, ed. Walter Mattli and Ngaire Woods (Princeton, NJ: Princeton University Press, 2009).

13. Alongside lofty objections rooted in sovereignty, a global super-regulator would face numerous practical difficulties. If oversight differentiates between countries, some will surely cry discrimination; if it does not, the regulations will be ill-suited to local circumstances and politics. If regulations are to be agreed by an assembly of national officials, it could take years to reach a consensus—witness the plodding pace of Basel II, the second generation of recommendations on banking practices issued by the Basel Committee on Banking Supervision. It would also be tough to ensure compliance in the absence of a dispute settlement body akin to the system in the World Trade Organization.

14. See Michael Gordy and Bradley Howells, "Procyclicality in Basel II: Can We Treat the Disease without Killing the Patient?" *Journal of Financial Intermediation* 15 (July 2006): 395–417.

15. A collateralized debt obligation (CDO) is an investment-grade security backed by a pool of bonds, loans, and other assets. A constant proportion debt obligation (CPDO) is a type of credit derivative sold to investors looking for long-term exposure to credit risk on a highly rated note.

16. See the Securities Class Action Clearinghouse, available at http://www.securities.stanford.edu.

17. The act also established a new quasi-public agency, the Public Company Accounting Oversight Board (PCAOB), to oversee accounting firms in their role as auditors, and entrusted the Securities and Exchange Commission (SEC) to issue regulations to carry out the new law.

18. Marshall Carter, "America's Capital Markets: Maintaining Our Lead in the 21st Century" (Testimony before the House Financial Services Subcommittee on Capital Markets, Insurance and Government Sponsored Enterprises, April 26, 2006).

19. Christian Leuz, Alexander Triantis, and Tracy Wan, "Why Do Firms Go Dark? Causes and Economic Consequences of Voluntary SEC Deregistrations" (Working Paper, Wharton School, University of Pennsylvania, November 2004).

20. Mercer and Russell Reynolds Associates, "How CFOs Are Managing Changes in Roles and Expectations," Research Report, February 2006, available at http://www.russellreynolds.com/sites/default/files/HowCFOsareManagingChanges_US.pdf.

21. See, for example, Peter J. Wallison, "Escape from New York," *The American*, February 20, 2008.

22. One reason that IPOs were launched abroad was the simple fact of well-capitalized financial centers outside the United States and the desire of Chinese companies to see their shares traded in Shanghai. Thompson Financial Study reported in the *Wall Street Journal Online* (February 20, 2007) that foreign IPOs accounted for 16 percent of the 208 IPOs launched in the United States in 2006—the highest proportion in twenty years—and raised $10.6 billion compared to $45.3 billion for U.S. IPOs in 2006, or 23 percent of the U.S. volume, the highest proportion since 1994. Some companies also preferred International Financial Reporting Standards compared to the Generally Accepted Accounting Principles recognized in the United States.

23. SEC chairman Christopher Cox noted in 2007 that the passage of SOX prompted other governments to follow the U.S. lead in establishing independent

auditor oversight bodies. See Christopher Cox, "Remarks to the U.S. Chamber of Commerce's First Annual Capital Markets Summit: Securing America's Competitiveness" (Washington, DC, March 14, 2007).

24. "A Taxonomy of Trouble," *Economist*, October 23, 2008.

25. Michael Pettis, "How Will China Deal with the U.S. Adjustment?" *Financial Times*, January 9, 2009, available at http://www.blogs.ft.com/wolfforum/2009/01/how-will-china-deal-with-the-us-adjustment/#more-303.

26. The Special Drawing Right (SDR is a virtual currency whose value is set by a currency "basket" made up of the U.S. dollar, the European euro, the British pound, and the Japanese yen, all of which qualify as reserve currencies, with the dollar being the leader).

27. This assumes that foreign private holders make no addition to their dollar accounts for ten years.

28. Openness to multinational investment in infrastructure is mixed. In a 2008 multicountry survey, all responding countries stated that multinational company (MNC) involvement was allowed in electricity generation, and at least 80 percent of the countries allowed MNCs to operate roads, seaports, airports, electricity distribution, mobile telecommunications, water supply, and sewage infrastructure. In most industries, developed countries are more open to both private and foreign company involvement. However, in airports and mobile telecommunications, the share of developing and transition economies that were open was higher than in developed countries (81 percent vs. 67 percent, and 88 percent vs. 86 percent, respectively). In so-called "network" industries, such as railways and electricity transmission, only 60 to 70 percent of those surveyed stated that MNCs were allowed to participate. Some three-quarters of developing economies allow MNC participation in water. See United Nations Conference on Trade and Development, *World Investment Report 2008* (Geneva: UNCTAD, 2008), 157.

29. See Philip Levy, "An 8.3% Deficit Is Plenty of Stimulus," *Wall Street Journal*, January 14, 2009, available at http://www.online.wsj.com/article/SB123189508831779607.html; and Paul Kennedy, "American Power Is on the Wane," *Wall Street Journal*, January 14, 2009, available at http://www.online.wsj.com/article/SB123189377673479433.html.

30. The bill authorized the secretary of the Treasury to "exercise any rights received in connection with troubled assets purchased," to "manage troubled assets purchased," and to "sell, or enter into securities loans, repurchase transactions, or other financial transactions in regard to any troubled asset purchased." Web sites were filled with criticism that the politicians had ignored constitutional checks and balances.

31. See, for example, Vincent R. Reinhart, "A Bill That Deserved to Pass," *The American*, October 6, 2008, available at http://www.american.com/archive/2008/october-10-08/a<->bill-that-deserved-to-pass.

32. Several banks tried to return money to Washington when they realized the strings were on too tight. But rules that are too loose will attract calls for help even when help is not vital. The heart of the matter is asymmetric information: private-sector players know their books and prospects better than government ever can.

33. See Allan Meltzer, "End Too-Big-to-Fail," *International Economy* (Winter 2009): 49.

34. Group of Thirty, "Financial Reform: A Framework for Financial Stability," Report, January 15, 2009, available at http://www.group30.org/pubs/recommendations.pdf.

35. Bank for International Settlements (BIS) economist William R. White draws an analogy to computer technology, noting that while seamless integration is more efficient than modular development, the modular is less likely to flop. This idea applies to international finance. See William R. White, "What Have We Learned from Recent Financial Crises and Policy Responses?" (BIS Working Paper No. 84, Bank for International Settlements, Basel, Switzerland, January 2000).

36. See, for example, Joseph Stiglitz, *Globalization and Its Discontents* (New York: W. W. Norton, 2002).

37. An IMF member's voting share can be expressed as $100^* [1/185^*\, S + \text{the member's quota share}^* (1 - S)]$, where S = the share of basic votes in total votes.

38. World Bank, *World Development Indicators 2007* (Washington, DC: World Bank, 2007).

39. See Paul Keating, "A Chance to Remake the Global Financial System," *Financial Times*, March 5, 2009.

40. See Richard N. Cooper and Edwin M. Truman, "The IMF Quota Formula: Linchpin of Fund Reform" (Peterson Institute for International Economics Policy Brief 07-1, February 2007), available at http://www.iie.com/publications/pb/pb07-1.pdf.

41. This objection could have been answered if all "rich industrial countries" would agree to limit their quota shares to 60 percent of their GDP shares (the current ratio for the United States and Japan), thereby leaving 14.4 percentage points of total quotas for transfer to other countries. See Cooper and Truman, "The IMF Quota Formula."

42. Vijay L. Kelkar, Praveen K. Chaudhry, and Marta Vanduzer-Snow, "Time for Change at the IMF," *IMF Finance & Development* (March 2005): 46–48, available at http://www.imf.org/external/pubs/ft/fandd/2005/03/pdf/kelkar.pdf.

43. This sum includes the funds provided by the Federal Deposit Insurance Corporation (FDIC) as well as the Treasury and the Federal Reserve. See Congressional Oversight Panel, "Assessing TARP Strategy" (Washington, DC, April 7, 2009), available at http://www.cop.senate.gov/documents/cop-040709-report.pdf.

44. A broad look at the vast literature on this subject offers considerable evidence that the insurance provided by the International Monetary Fund leads to moral hazard on the part of investors in bond markets. There is also evidence that debtor government policies are negatively influenced by the insurance—that is, they resort to more expansive policies leading to higher probabilities of IMF programs and shorter periods between programs when they are able to access the IMF window. See Axel Dreher, "Does the IMF Cause Moral Hazard? A Critical Review of the Evidence," Draft, University of Konstanz and Thurgau Institute of Economics (December 2004),

available at http://www.129.3.20.41/eps/if/papers/0402/0402003.pdf (May 13, 2009). Axel Dreher, "IMF and Economic Growth: The Effects of Programs, Loans, and Compliance with Conditionality," *World Development* 34, no. 5 (May 2006): 769–788.

Jong-Wha Lee and Kwanho Shin of Korea University analyzed the responses of sovereign bond spreads to the changes in the perceived probability of IMF bailouts of countries undergoing financial crisis. They found that the expectations of IMF lending attenuate the relationship between spreads and country fundamentals: a country comes out as looking less risky because of the potential access to the IMF window. This suggests the presence of IMF moral hazard. See Jong-Wha Lee and Kwanho Shin, "IMF Bailouts and Moral Hazard," *Journal of International Money and Finance* 27, no. 5 (September 2008): 816–830. Interestingly, there is quite a bit of repetition in the history of defaults: countries that have defaulted on their secured loans are quite likely to default again. Similarly, the nonbailout in Russia in 1997 created a natural experiment: it should have spooked risk-taking investors and profligate nations into believing that the IMF would no longer dash to their rescue. A team composed of IMF researchers, among others, found this to have happened. The nonevent in Russia had momentous implications, raising the level of spreads and the sensitivity with which spreads reflect country fundamentals. See Giovanni Dell'Ariccia, Isabel Schnabel, and Jeromin Zettelmeyer, "Moral Hazard and International Crisis Lending: A Test" (IMF Working Paper WP/02/181, International Monetary Fund, Washington, DC, October 2002).

45. William Rhodes, "The Fund Must Act to Protect Emerging Markets," *Financial Times* 23 (October 2008).

46. IMF Article IV requires that the IMF exercise "firm surveillance" over the exchange rate policies of members. The article also asks the IMF to initiate "special consultations" whenever one member's exchange rate policy has an important impact on other members. However, since the early 1980s, the IMF has initiated special consultations only twice, and firm surveillance is confined to smaller countries that get in serious trouble. The result is that the big countries have often addressed their currency misalignments, if at all, only bilaterally (as the United States and China did during the George W. Bush years or perhaps plurilaterally (the big examples being the Smithsonian agreement of 1971 and the Plaza accord of 1985).

47. See, for instance, Morris Goldstein, "Currency Manipulation and Enforcing the Rules of the International Monetary System," in *Reforming the IMF for the 21st Century*, ed. Edwin M. Truman (Washington, DC: Peterson Institute for International Economics, 2006).

48. For a thoughtful exposition of bottom-up forces in creating the fabric of global governance, see Horst Siebert, *Rules for the Global Economy* (Princeton, NJ: Princeton University Press, 2009).

49. See Charles P. Kindleberger, *The World in Depression: 1929–1939* (Berkeley: University of California Press, 1973).

50. See Jagdish Bhagwati and Arvind Panagariya, "Preferential Trading Areas and Multilateralism: Strangers, Friends or Foes?" in *The Economics of Preferential Trade*

Agreements, ed. Jagdish Bhagwati and Arvin Panagariya (Washington, DC: AEI Press, 1996), 1–78; Richard E. Baldwin, "A Domino Theory of Regionalism" (CEPR Discussion Paper No. 857, Center for Economic and Policy Research, Washington, DC, 1993); Jagdish Bhagwati, "Regionalism and Multilateralism: An Overview," in *New Dimensions in Regional Integration*, ed. Jaime de Melo and Arvind Panagariya (Cambridge: Cambridge University Press, 1993), 22–51; Paul Krugman, "Regionalism versus Multilateralism: Analytical Notes," in *New Dimensions in Regional Integration*, ed. Jaime De Melo and Arvind Panagariya (Cambridge: Cambridge University Press, 1993), 58–79; and Robert Gilpin, *The Political Economy of International Relations* (Princeton, NJ: Princeton University Press, 1987).

51. Ben Bernanke, "Nonmonetary Effects of the Financial Crisis in the Propagation of the Great Depression," *American Economic Review* 73 (June 1983): 257–276.

Chapter 7: Trade in Trouble

1. According to the World Trade Organization (WTO), in November 2008, India raised tariffs on some steel products, while Ecuador raised its tariffs reportedly between 5 and 20 percentage points on 940 products, including butter, turkey, crackers, caramels, blenders, cell phones, eyeglasses, sailboats, building materials, and transport equipment. Mercosur members—Argentina, Brazil, Paraguay, and Uruguay—meanwhile reached an agreement to raise their common external tariff by 5 percentage points, on average, on a number of specific items, including wine, peaches, dairy products, textiles, leather goods, and wood furniture. However, this agreement was not ratified at Mercosur's summit in mid-December 2008. Argentina has recently imposed nonautomatic licensing requirements on products considered sensitive, such as auto parts, textiles, TVs, toys, shoes, and leather goods. In December 2008, Indonesia limited the entry of certain imports—such as electronics, garments, toys, footwear, and food and beverages—to only five ports and certain international airports. South Korea announced a hike on crude oil tariffs from 1 to 3 percent, effective March 2009. Russia reportedly adopted measures in December 2008 to support domestic car manufacturers, including state subsidies, and in January 2009 raised import duties on cars and trucks. The size of the increases depends on the age of the vehicles and their engine size, but by way of example, import duties on cars less than five years of age are increased from 25 percent to 30 percent coupled with a specific duty denominated in rubles per cubic centimeter of engine capacity. In addition, legislated increases in export duties on wood have been temporarily delayed, although not repealed.

2. See "Nations Rush to Establish New Barriers to Trade," *Wall Street Journal*, February 6, 2009. Ukraine approved legislation in December 2008 to impose a temporary 13 percentage point import surcharge for balance of payments purposes, with the possibility of exempting selected imports. However, in January 2009, the president vetoed the legislation. If the legislation were to be returned to Parliament, it could override the veto with a two-thirds majority.

3. "Nations Rush to Establish New Barriers to Trade," *Wall Street Journal*, February 6, 2009.

4. See Gary Hufbauer, Luca Rubini, and Yee Wong, "Swamped by Subsidies: Averting a U.S.-EU Trade War after the Great Crisis" (Peterson Institute for International Economics Policy Note, Washington, DC, August 4, 2009).

5. For instance, the U.S. auto bailout likely meets three of the tests to qualify for a challenge under the WTO Agreement on Subsidies and Countervailing Measures (ASCM): that the bailout constitutes a "financial contribution" under Article 1 of the ASCM, that it is aimed at a specific industry or company, and that it confers a "benefit" to a company. The remaining question is whether the bailout causes "serious prejudice" toward auto producers in another country. See "Experts Say Auto Bailout Provides Illegal WTO Benefit, Risking Trade," *Inside U.S. Trade*, December 26, 2008.

6. For example, in March 2009, Ecuador raised a slew of tariffs from the applied rates to the rates bound in its WTO tariff schedules. This was perfectly legal, but certainly more protective than the *status quo ante*.

7. Paul Krugman, "The Conscience of a Liberal," *New York Times* blog, 2009, available at http://www.krugman.blogs.nytimes.com/.

8. Even a very minor degree of foreign emulation could, on balance, cost 6,500 U.S. jobs. See Gary Clyde Hufbauer and Jeffrey J. Schott, "Buy American: Bad for Jobs, Worse for Reputation" (Peterson Institute Policy Brief No. PB09-2, Peterson Institute for International Economics, Washington, DC, 2009). Some Canadian border towns that traditionally supply components to U.S. infrastructure projects have threatened "Buy Canadian" measures in response to the "Buy American" legislation. See "Fighting Back: Small Town Says Turn-Around Fair Trade in 'Buy America' Battle," *Associated Press*, May 12, 2009.

9. Elisa Gamberoni and Richard Newfarmer, "Trade Protection: Incipient but Worrisome Trends," *VOX*, March 4, 2009, available at http://www.voxeu.org/index .php?q=node/3183.

10. WTO Secretariat, "Report to the Trade Policy Review Body (TPRB) from the Director-General on the Financial and Economic Crisis and Trade-Related Developments" (World Trade Organization, Washington, DC, March 26, 2009).

11. See Simon J. Evenett, "Broken Promises: A G20 Summit Report by Global Trade Alert" (Global Trade Alert and the Center for Economic and Policy Research, September 2009).

12. World Trade Organization, *World Tariff Profiles 2008* (Switzerland: WTO Secretariat, 2008), available at http://www.wto.org/english/res_e/booksp_e/tariff_ profiles08_e.pdf.

13. At the time, S&D was endorsed by the renowned free trader and polymath Harry Johnson. Like most economists, Johnson could not foretell the insidious consequences of S&D.

14. Patrick Messerlin, "Walking a Tightrope: World Trade in Manufacturing and the Benefits of Binding" (Policy Brief, German Marshall Fund of the United States, 2008).

15. Under Article 19, escape clause relief requires that imports cause "serious injury" to the competing domestic industry. A Doha Round compromise might specify a lower threshold, such as "material injury."

16. In a last-minute move, China decided to align itself behind the immovable India in the "special safeguard mechanism" (SSM) debate. While China has a keen interest in export market access, the negotiators reportedly hold a grudge over the tough WTO accession conditions agreed in 2001. Moreover, political leaders in Beijing are sensitive to the interests of 193 million small farms in the Chinese hinterlands—half of the world's total. Finally, China was unwilling to cede leadership over developing country issues to India.

17. Matthew Adler, Claire Brunel, Gary Clyde Hufbauer, and Jeffrey J. Schott, "What's on the Table? The Doha Round as of August 2009," Peterson Institute Working Paper 09-6, Washington, DC (August 2009); and Anderson Kym and Will Martin, eds., *Agricultural Trade Reform and the Doha Development Agenda* (Washington, DC: World Bank, 2005).

18. The Doha Round led to yet another formulation, "aid for trade." According to the new twist, trade *could be* an engine of growth, but many developing countries cannot capture the gains without solid measures on the supply side of trade—infrastructure for producers to move their goods, export promotion programs to display the country's wares abroad, and real-time information about market conditions.

The Aid for Trade mantra (A4T) was also seen as a weapon to cajole the industrial nations into offering a better deal. Experts from development agencies and the WTO have met on numerous occasions to devise an A4T agenda and count the money that would be required. When the concept was vetted in 2005, Japan pledged $10 billion through 2008, the United States promised $2.7 billion a year, and the EU committed &euro$2 billion a year by 2010. As the Aid for Trade initiative does not fall under the Doha single undertaking, aid would flow regardless of Doha's fate. However, in the absence of meaningful trade opening, the initiative will soon be back to square one—aid, not trade.

19. Batshur Gootiiz and Aaditya Mattoo, "Services in Doha: What's on the Table?" (World Bank Paper, April 15, 2009).

20. Simon J. Evenett, "Doha's Near Death Experience at Potsdam: Why Is Reciprocal Tariff Cutting So Hard" (Policy Paper, University of St. Gallen and Center for Economic and Policy Research, June 23, 2007), available at http://www.evenett.com/publicpolicy/policypapers/DohaAfterPotsdam.pdf.

21. Simon J. Evenett, "Five Hypotheses concerning the Fate of the Singapore Issues in the Doha Round," *Oxford Review of Economic Policy* 23, no. 3 (2007): 392–414.

22. See, for example, Marion Dovis and Juliette Milgram-Baleix, "Trade, Tariffs and Total Factor Productivity: The Case of Spanish Firms," *World Economy* 32, no. 4 (2009): 575–605.

23. Antoine Bouët and David Laborde, "The Potential Cost of a Failed Doha Round" (Issue Brief 56, International Food Policy Research Institute, 2008).

24. Batshur Gootiiz and Aaditya Mattoo, "Services in Doha: What's on the Table?" (World Bank Paper, April 15, 2009).

25. Yvan Decreux and Lionel Fontagné, "A Quantitative Assessment of the Outcome of the Doha Development Agenda" (Centre d'Etudes Prospectives et d'Informations Internationales (CEPII) Working Paper No. 2006-10, May 1, 2006).

26. Simeon Djankov, Caroline Freund, and Cong S. Pham, "Trading on Time" (Working Paper, World Bank, November 2008).

27. See, for example, Antoni Estevadeordal and Kati Suominen, with Jeremy Harris and Matthew Shearer, *Bridging Trade Agreements in the Americas* (Washington, DC: Inter-American Development Bank, 2009).

28. See, for example, Antoni Estevadeordal and Kati Suominen, *Gatekeepers of Global Commerce: Rules of Origin and International Economic Integration* (Washington, DC: Inter-American Development Bank, 2008).

29. For a review, see Bart Driessen and Folkert Graafsma, "The EC's Wonderland: An Overview of Pan-European Harmonized Origin Protocols," *Journal of World Trade* 33, no. 4 (1999).

30. See Patricia Augier, Michael Gasiorek, and Charles Lai-Tong, "The Impact of Rules of Origin on Trade Flows," *Economic Policy* 20, no. 43 (July 2005), 567–624; and Patricia Augier, Michael Gasiorek, and Charles Lai-Tong, "Multilateralising Regionalism: Relaxing the Rules of Origin or Can Those Pecs Be Flexed?" (Centre for the Analysis of Regional Integration at Sussex (CARIS) Working Paper No. 03, 2007). Jeremy Harris and Kati Suominen take the idea further to examine the effects of cumulation zones over the past fifty years, finding that adding partners representing 10 percent of world output to a "cumulation zone" was associated with a 3 percent increase in the bilateral trade of small countries. Importantly, this is a net effect, including any reduction in trade due to trade diversion. See Jeremy Harris and Kati Suominen, "Connecting Regional Trade Agreements: What Are the Trade Effects?" (Unpublished Paper, Inter-American Development Bank, Washington, DC, 2008).

31. See, for instance, Richard Baldwin, Simon Evenett, and Patrick Low, "Beyond Tariffs: Multilateralising Deeper RTA Commitments" (Paper presented at WTO-HEI Conference on "Multilateralising Regionalism," World Trade Organization, Geneva, Switzerland, September 10–12, 2007).

32. In his treatment of PTAs as "termites" in the world trading system, committed multilateralist Jagdish Bhagwati has a delightful argument about the difficulties in crafting multilateral "pizza" from regional "lasagna plates." Jagdish Bhagwati, *Termites in the Trading System: How Preferential Agreements Undermine Free Trade* (Oxford: Oxford University Press, 2008).

33. See Baldwin, Evenett, and Low, "Beyond Tariffs."

34. See Carsten Fink and Mario Jansen, "Services Provisions in Regional Trade Agreements: Stumbling or Building Blocks for Multilateral Liberalizations" (Paper presented at WTO-HEI Conference on "Multilateralising Regionalism," World Trade Organization, Geneva, Switzerland, September 10–12, 2007). See also Baldwin, Evenett, and Low, "Beyond Tariffs." The authors cite the NAFTA-style telecommunications

provision as an agent of multilateralization due to the sheer number of countries adhering to it, and because harmonization to a single regulatory regime for telecommunications frees trade in the same way that adoption of an international standard liberalizes technical barriers to trade: a common set of rules that governments apply to private firms in many nations tends to foster competition and trade.

35. In the area of tariff liberalization, an easy-to-monitor definition of substantially all trade, such that at least 90 percent of industrial tariff lines *and* 90 percent of industrial trade liberalized by year ten could be considered. But such quantitative tests have never been adopted by the WTO.

36. The General Agreement on Tariffs and Trade (GATT), signed in 1948 by twenty-three countries, was the companion to those other Bretton Woods institutions, the World Bank and the International Monetary Fund. Formed to reduce tariffs and nontariff barriers, GATT's first round yielded some 45,000 tariff concessions affecting about 20 percent of global trade. At the heart of the GATT system was nondiscrimination. The agreement marked the formation of 123 bilateral agreements that were subsequently generalized via the most favored nation (MFN) clause. However, the problem with the system was free-riding—countries would use the MFN clause to benefit from concessions made by other countries, while doing little themselves. The Torquay Round mandated that the GATT negotiations be multilateral, and the Kennedy Round put multilateralism into practice. However, the concept of "special and differential treatment" reopened the door to free riding for developing countries and allowed them to retain high-tariff and nontariff barriers.

37. Among other recommendations, the report declares: "Clearly, the WTO needs an efficient-size sub-group of members for the purpose of discussing, debating and negotiating draft decisions that can be put to the entire membership for adoption. What needs changing is the basis for putting together such a sub-group, for deciding which delegations will be in the room and which delegations are excluded. The new basis needs to be one that is fully transparent, predictable, equitable and legitimate in the eyes of all WTO members."

38. Robert Z. Lawrence, "Rulemaking amidst Growing Diversity: A Club-of-Clubs Approach to WTO Reform and New Issue Selection," *Journal of International Economic Law* 9, no. 4 (December 2006): 823–835.

39. Patrick Low, "Regionalism: Challenges for the WTO," Conference Presentation, ADBI/HEID Conference, Tokyo, September 18–19, 2008.

Chapter 8: Anxious Workers

1. Robert Z. Lawrence, *Blue-Collar Blues: Is Trade to Blame for Rising U.S. Income Inequality?* (Washington, DC: Institute for International Economics, 2008).

2. Kati Suominen, "New Age of Protectionism? The Economic Crisis and Trans-Atlantic Trade Policy" (Brussels Forum Paper Series, German Marshall Fund of the United States, Washington, DC, March 2009).

3. *New York Times*-CBS News Poll, March–April 2008, available at http://www.graphics8.nytimes.com/packages/pdf/politics/20080403_POLL.pdf. The 24 percent figure is the lowest in twenty years.

4. See the Pew Global Attitudes Project, "World Publics Welcome Global Trade, but Not Immigration: 47-Nation Pew Global Attitudes Survey" (Pew Foundation, Washington, DC, October 4, 2007), available at http://www.pewglobal.org/reports/pdf/258.pdf. While Europeans embrace trade more enthusiastically than Americans, they seem less keen on capitalism. In a 2008 BBC World Service poll, 62 percent of Germans and Italians, 59 percent of British, and only 41 percent of French agreed with the statement that "the free enterprise system and free market economy is the best system on which to base the future of the world." By contrast, the figure was 70 percent for the United States, 64 percent for Canada, 66 percent for China, and 68 percent for India. Disconcertingly, in all eighteen surveyed countries, the support had plunged by some 5 to 10 percentage points from 2002. In seventeen of the eighteen countries surveyed, a majority or a plurality agreed that "the free enterprise system and the free market system work best in society's interest when accompanied by strong government regulation." Even the free market–loving Chinese endorsed regulation by 87 percent. See BBC World Service Poll, "Widespread Unease about Economy and Globalization—Global Poll," February 7, 2008, available at http://www.worldpublicopinion.org/pipa/articles/btglobalizationtradera/446.php?lb=btgl&pnt=446&nid=&id=.

5. Since the North American Free Trade Agreement (NAFTA), Republican support for trade measures has generally increased, while Democratic support has varied depending on the pact. Democratic support reached a recent low level with the Oman and CAFTA-DR free trade agreements, but a high level with the Morocco FTA. The evolution of a less-favorable political backdrop for trade over time provides context for the highly critical tone in the 2008 presidential race.

6. See "People Fear Losing Job the Most: Poll," CNBC, February 19, 2009, available at http://www.cnbc.com/id/29275784.

7. The American Federation of Labor and Congress of Industrial Organizations (AFL-CIO) has called for "new administration priorities and benchmarks" for the three pending free trade agreements and a new template for future trade agreements. The union strongly backs the TRADE Act, which would restore congressional primacy in setting mandates for U.S. trade negotiators and order U.S. officials to write enforceable labor rights into the text of new trade agreements. The AFL-CIO was a major force behind the legislation that repudiated U.S. obligations with respect to Mexican trucks. "Buy American" was also the fruit of union lobbying, and regulations that spell out the new provisions enable state and local governments to discriminate against suppliers based in Canada, Mexico, and other countries that thought they had access to the U.S. government procurement market.

8. The Smoot-Hawley Tariff began with an effort to protect American farmers against rising agricultural imports, but industrial interests soon grabbed the legislation. When the dust settled, the United States had raised tariffs on more than twenty

thousand imported goods to record heights—and the pleas of hundreds of economists were ignored.

9. Before the 2009 expansion, Trade Adjustment Assistance (TAA) provided: seventy-eight weeks of income maintenance payments and free training; a Health Coverage Tax Credit (HCTC), which provided a 65 percent refundable tax credit to offset the cost of maintaining health insurance for up to two years; wage insurance, under which workers over fifty years old and earning less than $50,000 a year were eligible to receive half the difference between their old and new wages, subject to a cap of $10,000, for up to two years; 90 percent of the costs associated with job search, up to a limit of $1,250; and 90 percent of the costs associated with job relocation, up to a limit of $1,500. Some of these provisions were made more generous in the 2009 legislation.

10. Howard F. Rosen, "Designing a National Strategy for Responding to Economic Dislocation" (Testimony before the Subcommittee on Investigation and Oversight House Science and Technology Committee, June 24, 2008), available at http://www.iie.com/publications/papers/paper.cfm?ResearchID=967.

11. "Business Lobbies for Program to Help Workers Hurt by Trade," *Workforce Management*, June 11, 2008, available at http://www.workforce.com/section/oo/article/25/58/88.html.

12. U.S. Government Accountability Office, "Trade Adjustment Assistance: Most Workers in Five Layoffs Received Services, but Better Outreach Needed on New Benefits," GAO, Washington, DC, January 2006, available at http://www.gao.gov/new.items/d0643.pdf. Those who did not receive assistance—mostly younger male employees—often said they needed to find a job right away and thus had no time to visit a center, or they did not think they needed help finding a new job.

13. U.S. Government Accountability Office, "Trade Adjustment Assistance: Reforms Have Accelerated Training Enrollment, but Implementation Challenges Remain," GAO, Washington, DC, September 2004, available at http://www.gao.gov/new.items/d041012.pdf.

14. U.S. Government Accountability Office, "Trade Adjustment Assistance: Program Provides an Array of Benefits and Services to Trade-Affected Workers," GAO, Washington, DC, June 14, 2007, available at http://www.gao.gov/new.items/d07994t.pdf.

15. Organization for Economic Cooperation and Development, *OECD Employment Outlook 2006: Boosting Jobs and Incomes* (Paris: OECD, 2006).

16. Organization for Economic Cooperation and Development, *OECD Employment Outlook 2006*.

17. Peter Katzenstein, *Small States in World Markets* (Ithaca, NY: Cornell University Press, 1985).

18. In 1995, Paul Krugman observed that European policies designed to prevent a decrease in the relative wage of unskilled labor—mainly as a result of information technology—had the unintended consequence of raising unemployment. In America and Britain, where flexible wages are the norm, information technology increased inequality—by driving down wages for low-skilled workers and driving up wages for

high-skilled workers—but had little effect on employment. See Paul R. Krugman "Growing World Trade: Causes and Consequences," *Brookings Paper on Economic Activity* 1 (1995): 327–377. The same arguments can be extended to trade, but Bill Gates did far more to reduce demand for unskilled labor than all the trade with China.

19. Efforts to coordinate national decisions at the EU level, through the so-called Lisbon Agenda, have had little practical effect.

20. Robert Kuttner, "The Copenhagen Consensus: Reading Adam Smith in Denmark," *Foreign Affairs* (March/April 2008).

21. The EGF is not altogether new. The 1957 Treaty of Rome, the founding document of the European Union, created the European Social Fund (ESF) that was designed to enhance geographical and occupational mobility in the Common Market. During its first ten years, the ESF provided grants for vocational training and resettlement to workers hurt by restructuring operations of their companies; later, the ESF focused on vocational training for young people. In the mid-1980s, the ESF was geared to "social harmonization," bringing newly admitted Spain and Portugal, with their lower wages, closer to par with the rest of Europe in order to avoid "social dumping" to the wealthier members. While the ESF was a very modest program in its early years, today it accounts for 10 percent of the EU budget (around 0.12 percent of GDP). See Andre Sapir, "An Agenda for a Growing Europe: Making the EU System Deliver," Report of an independent high-level group established at the initiative of the president of the European Commission, July 2003 (other members of the group: Philippe Aghion, Giuseppe Bertola, Martin Hellwig, Jean Pisani-Ferry, Dariusz Rosati, José Viñals, and Helen Wallace), available at http://www.europa.eu.int/comm/dgs/policy/advisers/experts_groups/ps2/docs/agenda_en.pdf.

22. As a welcome nod to the idea of not picking winners, only workers are covered, not industries and companies. However, the EGF aid is not limited to workers of the company or sector experiencing hardship, but also extends to workers at supplier firms, if they also face difficulty.

23. Except for vague pronouncements that plants have closed due to "subsequent concentration of manufacturing in the most efficient sites," there are few explanations of where jobs have migrated. In the Finnish case, the petitioners argue that "redundancies can be linked . . . to major structural changes in world trade patterns, in particular the delocalization of production of mobile phones to countries in Asia, specifically China and India." Redundant workers in the filed cases have most often been the ones at the lower rungs of the skill and salary scales. See European Commission, Employment, Social Affairs and Equal Opportunities, "EGF—European Globalisation Adjustment Fund," available at http://www.ec.europa.eu/social/main.jsp?catId=582&langId=en.

24. Stuart M. Butler, "Evolving beyond Traditional Employer-Sponsored Health Insurance" (Hamilton Project Discussion Paper No. 2006-07, Brookings Institution, Washington, DC, May 2007). See also Sherry A. Glied and Phyllis C. Borzi, "The Current State of Employment-Based Health Coverage," *Journal of Law, Medicine and Ethics* (Fall 2004): 404–409.

25. See Michael Lind, "Next Social Contract: A Citizen-Based Social Contract" (Principles Paper, New America Foundation, Washington, DC, July 2007).

26. Butler, "Evolving."

27. Fernando Ferreira, Joseph Gyourko, and Joseph Tracy, "Housing Busts and Household Mobility" (Working Paper, Wharton School, University of Pennsylvania, August 28, 2008), available at http://www.real.wharton.upenn.edu/~gyourko/Working%20Papers/housingcycles-mobility-August%2028%202008.pdf.

28. See Rosen, "Designing a National Strategy."

29. States with the highest maximum weekly benefits include Massachusetts ($551 to $826), Minnesota ($350 to $515), New Jersey ($521), and Rhode Island ($492 to $615). The replacement rates of the employees' average weekly earnings are also varied, from less than a quarter in the District of Columbia to almost a half in Hawaii. Benefits normally last for twenty-six weeks. A third of unemployment insurance recipients exhaust their benefits before finding new jobs.

Kletzer and Rosen estimate that with a recipiency rate of 50 percent and a million eligible each year, the total cost would be an additional $7.4 billion annually. This is a significant sum, but small if it paves the path to continued globalization. See Lori G. Kletzer and Howard F. Rosen, "Reforming Unemployment Insurance for the Twenty-First Century" (Hamilton Project Discussion Paper No. 2005-06, Brookings Institution, Washington, DC, September 2006).

30. See, for example, Robert J. LaLonde, "The Case for Wage Insurance" (Council on Foreign Relations, New York, September 2007), available at http://www.cfr.org/content/publications/attachments/WageInsuranceCSR.pdf.

31. Robert W. Fairlie, "Kauffman Index of Entrepreneurial Activity 1996–2007" (Kauffman Foundation, April 2008), available at http://www.kauffman.org/uploadedFiles/KIEA_041408.pdf.

32. Douglas Holz-Eakin, "Public Policy toward Entrepreneurship," *Small Business Economics* 15 (2000): 283–291.

33. See Organization for Economic Cooperation and Development, "Income Inequality and Poverty Rising in Most OECD Countries" (Press Release, OECD, Paris, October 21, 2008).

Chapter 9: New Frictions

1. The main emitting sectors are energy generation and transportation. Manufacturing activity and industrial processes are less-important greenhouse gas (GHG) sources, although certain industries like cement manufacturing spew out much more CO_2 than, say, computer production. The United States has been a leading source of GHG emissions, both in total tonnage and on a per capita basis, but China is racing ahead on total emissions.

2. Gary Clyde Hufbauer, Steve Charnovitz, and Jisun Kim, *Global Warming and the World Trading System* (Washington, DC: Peterson Institute for International Economics, 2009).

3. There was speculation after the North American Free Trade Agreement (NAFTA) was passed that U.S. companies would migrate to Mexico to escape U.S. environmental laws. Mexico has reasonable laws, but lax enforcement. However, subsequent evidence did not show that U.S. companies flocked to Mexico to smoke in peace. In sectors where plant vintage determines the level of pollution, countries can benefit from their ability to employ new technologies after trade liberalization—as was the case with the Mexican steel sector. In sectors where pollution is a function of "end of pipe" technology, such as the paper industry, pollution levels are determined by regulation and enforcement, somewhat weaker in Mexico. Thus, some industries that are the dirtiest in the world economy are actually cleaner in Mexico than in the United States, while other industries are dirtier in Mexico.

4. The evidence for "leakage" is far less robust than the political argument—the World Bank has found some confirming evidence, but the International Energy Agency has not. Whatever the evidence, the Clinton administration was compelled to negotiate an environmental side agreement to NAFTA, owing to a marriage of convenience between labor unions and environmental opponents of the pact. This approach has come to be the standard for U.S. free trade agreements.

5. The EU's "20-20-20" plan in Phase III envisages a 20 percent reduction in greenhouse gas emissions, a 20 percent share for renewable energy, and a 20 percent boost to energy efficiency, starting in 2013, all to be achieved by 2020.

6. For an analysis, see Sallie James, "A Harsh Climate for Trade: How Climate Change Proposals Threaten Global Commerce" (Cato Institute Trade Policy Analysis 41, Cato Institute, Washington, DC, September 9, 2009).

7. Supposedly, this oil entails higher GHG emissions than conventional petroleum sources, but on a "well to wheels" basis, gasoline derived from the Alberta oil sands has about the same CO_2 footprint as oil from traditional sources in Saudi Arabia or Venezuela.

8. However, similar fees may be imposed by the United States, since California, Connecticut, New Mexico, and Pennsylvania, together with certain cities and environmental organizations, jointly filed a petition in 2007 asking the federal government to apply fuel efficiency regulations to all airplanes, including those of foreign airlines, that land or take off from U.S. airports. Decisions made in such cases will be central both to global trade and climate change regimes, as both air and maritime travel has so far remained outside the United Nations Framework Convention on Climate Change (UNFCCC) system.

9. World Bank, *International Trade and Climate Change: Economic, Legal, and Institutional Perspectives* (Washington, DC: World Bank, 2007).

10. One major difference in approaches is whether pollution permits are assigned to private companies, thereby conferring valuable quota rents on the recipients, or whether limits are imposed by way of auction or tax systems so that the government collects substantial revenues. Another major difference is the choice of activity where

limits are designed to "bite": for example, on power generation and refineries or also on transportation and manufacturing.

11. "Climate Change: WTO Director-General Warns against 'Spaghetti Bowl' of Unilateral Policies" (Press Release, European Parliament, May 30, 2008).

12. Hufbauer, Charnovitz, and Kim, *Global Warming*.

13. The quoted language comes almost word for word from the chapeaus of GATT Article 20, the General Exceptions article that can be invoked, in appropriate circumstances, to override other GATT provisions.

14. See National Foreign Trade Council, *WTO Compatibility of Four Categories of U.S. Climate Change Policy* (Washington, DC: NFTC, December 2007).

15. See Hufbauer, Charnovitz, and Kim, *Global Warming*.

16. See Hufbauer, Charnovitz and Kim, *Global Warming*.

17. The Multi-Fiber Arrangement (MFA) did not have social or environmental provisions, but other trade provisions have contained social provisions regarding labor conditions (notably the Generalized System of Preferences, GSP).

18. WTO Secretariat, "Trade and Environment at the WTO" (Background Paper, April 23, 2004).

19. Committee on Trade and Environment Special Session, "Continued Work under Paragraph 31 (III) of the Doha Ministerial Declaration: Non-Paper by Canada, the European Communities, Japan, Korea, New Zealand, Norway, the Separate Customs Territory of Taiwan, Penghu, Kinmen and Matsu, Switzerland, and the United States of America," April 2007, available at http://www.mfat.govt.nz/downloads/NZ-WTO/wto-doha-ministerialdeclaration27apr07.pdf.

20. The new liberalization would cover environmental, energy, construction, architectural, engineering, and integrated engineering services. See U.S. Trade Representative, "Summary of U.S. and EC Proposal for Liberalizing Trade in Environmental Goods and Services in the WTO DDA Negotiations," 2007, available at http://www.ustr.gov/assets/Document_Library/Reports_Publications/2007/asset_upload_file479_13638.pdf.

21. One concept invoked to measure this relationship is environmental return on investment (EROI). For example, the EROI of conventional oil is estimated to be between 11:1 and 18:1—meaning that for every barrel of oil expended to lift oil from the ground, some eleven to eighteen barrels are sent to the market. This is well below the figure of about 100:1 when oil was first discovered and oil reserves were close to the surface. The EROI of cane-based ethanol is estimated at 8:1; the EROI for corn-based ethanol is a mere 1.5:1, and negative under some estimates—meaning that corn ethanol production consumes more energy than it creates.

22. Preferential trade agreements (PTAs) would be particularly useful if used as vehicles for new and WTO rule making on environmental goods and services (EGS). PTAs, liberalizing as they are, tend to open trade in EGS. PTAs, particularly those of the United States and Canada, have long occupied a parallel universe in trade-climate battles. Their deals tend to include such provisions as the obligation for the parties to

enforce their own environmental laws and procedural guarantees in environmental matters, as well as different types of enforcement and dispute settlement mechanisms. Some agreements, such as Mercosur, strive for harmonization of member states' environmental laws. The risk of relying on PTAs alone, of course, is that they may also result in trade diversion from countries that are most effective at producing environmental goods and services when such countries are not members of the PTA. Moreover, developing countries—particularly China and India—would be needed to play ball both because of their growing shares of global trade and because of the rising share of coal-fired power in their emissions profiles.

23. See Gary Clyde Hufbauer and Kimberly Elliott, *Economic Sanctions Reconsidered*, 3rd edition (Washington, DC: Peterson Institute for International Economics, 2007), table 1.

24. Diana Farrell, Susan Lund, Oscar Skau, Charles Atkins, Jan Philipp Mengeringhaus, and Moira S. Pierce, *Mapping Global Financial Flows*, 5th edition (San Francisco: McKinsey Global Institute, 2008), available at http://www.mckinsey.com/mgi/reports/pdfs/fifth_annual_report/fifth_annual_report.pdf.

25. Finfacts Team, "Global Economic Confidence Has Halved in the Two Years since April 2007: OECD Says One in Ten Workers in Its Thirty Member Countries Will Be Without a Job in 2010," March 31, 2009, available at http://www.finfacts.ie/irishfinancenews/article_1016328.shtml.

26. The body politic wavered on the benefits of foreign acquisition of U.S. assets. While a narrow majority of 53 percent had a negative view of foreign investors owning U.S. companies, the figure is considerably below the 70 percent of 1989, at the height of the Japan scare. Younger and wealthier Americans are more disposed to inward foreign investment. Further, as many as 24 percent of Americans were very concerned, and 34 percent somewhat concerned, that the Dubai Ports World scandal may have angered important allies in the Middle East. People under age thirty saw foreign investment in the United States as positive by a 71 percent to 26 percent margin. By comparison, majorities of those ages sixty-five and older tend to see both foreign ownership (57 percent) and foreign investment (53 percent) in a negative light. Americans in households earning $75,000 or more annually are the most supportive of foreign ownership and investment, with nearly three-quarters saying that investment is good for the country. Americans in low-earning households tend to say both are bad for the country.

27. The top five SWFs include Abu Dhabi Investment Authority, Norway's Government Pension Fund, Kuwait Investment Authority, Singapore's Government Investment Corporation, and China Investment Corporation. In 2007–2008, SWFs invested more than $60 billion in some of the largest financial sector companies in the world. While the United States was the largest recipient, European countries were also a major target.

28. See, for instance, Brad Setser's analyses, available at http://www.blogs.cfr.org/setser/category/sovereign-wealth-funds/. Also, Red Truman notes that Chinese CIC makes investments with political interests in mind. See Edwin M. Truman,

"Sovereign Wealth Funds: New Challenges from a Changing Landscape" (Testimony before the Subcommittee on Domestic and International Monetary Policy, Trade and Technology, Financial Services Committee, U.S. House of Representatives, September 10, 2008), available at http://www.petersoninstitute.org/publications/papers/truman0908.pdf.

29. For an exhaustive review, see Edward Graham and David Marchick, *U.S. National Security and Foreign Direct Investment* (Washington, DC: Peterson Institute for International Economics, 2005), available at http://www.petersoninstitute.org/publications/chapters_preview/3918/01iie3918.pdf. The CFIUS process fundamentally serves two functions. The first is to vet the buyer—assess its behavior and the policies of its home government to determine whether the buyer would be an appropriate steward of U.S. business assets. The second is to screen the acquired asset—evaluate whether the proposed investment would risk the transfer of sensitive technology or have other security implications. In the wake of 9/11, the CFIUS mandate was expanded to cover the potentially adverse impact of an acquisition on homeland security.

The U.S. president delegated his authority to investigate individual transactions to CFIUS. The Exon-Florio statute applies only when a transaction affects national security, the case for a small percentage of the overall number of foreign direct investments in the United States. According to the Treasury Department, historically less than 10 percent of foreign direct investments in U.S. companies were reviewed by CFIUS. While application for a CFIUS review is voluntary, firms that are subject to an Exon-Florio review that do not notify CFIUS remain indefinitely subject to the Exon-Florio review and appropriate action by the president. The president can suspend or prohibit a foreign acquisition of a U.S. company when he finds credible evidence that the foreign entity exercising control might take action that threatens national security.

30. Edwin M. Truman, "A Blueprint for Sovereign Wealth Fund Best Practices" (Policy Brief 08-3, Peterson Institute for International Economics, Washington, DC, 2008), available at http://www.petersoninstitute.org/publications/pb/pb08-3.pdf.

31. U.S. Government Accountability Office, "Foreign Investment Laws and Policies Regulating Foreign Investment in 10 Countries" (GAO Report 08-320), available at http://www.gao.gov/new.items/d08320.pdf.

32. See Jacques de Jong, "The Third EU Energy Market Package: Are We Singing the Right Song?" (CIEP Briefing Paper No. 8, The Hague, Clingendael Institute, February 2008), available at http://www.clingendael.nl/publications/2008/20080200_ciep_briefingpaper_jong.pdf.

33. Julie Ray and Neli Esipova, "Most Russians Oppose Foreign Purchases of Companies, but 42% See Foreign Investments as Beneficial," *Gallup*, May 12, 2008, available at http://www.gallup.com/poll/107200/Most-Russians-Oppose-Foreign-Purchases-Companies.aspx.

34. Openness to multinational investment in infrastructure is mixed. In a 2008 multicountry survey, all responding countries stated that MNC involvement was

allowed in electricity generation, and at least 80 percent of the countries allowed MNCs to operate roads, seaports, airports, electricity distribution, mobile telecommunications, water supply, and sewage infrastructure. In most industries, developed countries are more open to both private and foreign company involvement. However, in airports and mobile telecommunications, the share of developing and transition economies that were open was higher than in developed countries (81 percent vs. 67 percent, and 88 percent vs. 86 percent, respectively). In so-called "network" industries, such as railways and electricity transmission, only 60 to 70 percent of the countries surveyed stated that MNCs were allowed to participate. Some three-quarters of developing economies allow MNC participation in water. See United Nations Conference on Trade and Development, *World Investment Report 2008* (Geneva: UNCTAD, 2008), 157.

35. U.S. Trade Representative, *National Trade Estimate Report on Foreign Trade Barriers 2009* (Washington, DC: USTR, 2009).

36. These include such bills as the 2006 Foreign Investment Security Improvement Act, the Port Security Act, and the Smart and Effective Foreign Investment Act.

37. See Edward Graham and David Marchick, *U.S. National Security and Foreign Direct Investment* (Washington, DC: Peterson Institute for International Economics, 2005).

38. Committee on Foreign Investment in the United States, "Annual Report to Congress, Public Version," December 2008, available at http://www.treas.gov/offices/international-affairs/cfius/docs/CFIUS-Annual-Rpt-2008.pdf.

39. It also expands the number of agencies that are members of CFIUS, while curtailing the delegation of major decisions in any agency below the level of under secretary. A 2008 executive order tasks the director of national intelligence (DNI) to provide CFIUS with threat assessments posed by a foreign purchase and adds a requirement for the DNI to assess the "potential consequences" of a foreign deal involving a U.S. company.

40. Control is defined as the "power, direct or indirect, whether or not exercised . . . to determine, direct, or decide important matters affecting an entity." The rules state that private equity and other structures that create ownership interests do not necessarily create control, but joint ventures will be considered reviewable transactions to the same extent as direct acquisitions. Rather than automatic reviews of specific categories of transactions, CFIUS can review proposed investments based on the individual characteristics of the transaction. The threshold for considering acquisitions is a 10 percent or greater ownership position.

41. Most countries also have established time frames for the review and can place conditions on transactions prior to approval. For example, a country may place national citizenship requirements on company board members. However, sector-based lists of national security assets are rare. The context of a national security determination is not clear-cut, and the ever-increasing complexity of global business makes it very hard to announce *ex ante* lists.

42. See also Council on Foreign Relations, "Global FDI Policy: Correcting a Protectionist Drift" (Transcript, June 26, 2008), available at http://www.cfr.org/publication/16695/global_fdi_policy.html.

43. See Truman, "Sovereign Wealth Funds." Ted Truman pioneered a scorecard of SWF governance, behavior, and accountability. At the top of his list are pension funds from the United States and other developed countries, plus Thailand, Timor-Leste, Azerbaijan, China's pension fund, Chile, and Kazakhstan; at the middle, funds from Russia, Mexico, Kuwait, and Singapore; at the bottom two funds from Abu Dhabi—each of which has an excellent reputation in financial markets. Among non-pension funds, Hong Kong and Russia are in the middle, while China's investment corporation, Abu Dhabi, and Qatar tend toward the bottom, as do Venezuelan, Iranian, Nigerian, and Algerian funds.

44. See Graham and Marchick, *U.S. National Security and Foreign Direct Investment*.

45. "Treasury Gets New CFIUS Authority," *Washington Times*, January 24, 2008, available at http://www.washingtontimes.com/news/2008/jan/24/treasury-gets-new-cfius-authority.

46. See, for example, Tom Ashby and Caryle Murphy, "UK Calls for New Deals with GCC," *The National*, June 22, 2008, available at http://www.thenational.ae/article/20080622/BUSINESS/923588024/1001&profile=1001.

47. David M. Marchick and Matthew J. Slaughter, *Global FDI Policy: Correcting a Protectionist Drift* (New York: Council of Foreign Relations, June 2008), available at http://www.cfr.org/content/publications/attachments/FDl_CSR34.pdf.

48. Truman, "A Blueprint."

49. The OECD has also revised its declarations pertaining to SWFs. However, the preliminary drafts provide relatively meek protection for SWF investments. Moreover, OECD rules do not cover China and the Middle Eastern countries. Any OECD member's decision to invoke the national security "exemption" from a policy of open investment is not subject to appeal or even discussion.

Chapter 10: Afterword

1. Claude Barfield and Philip I. Levy, "In Search of an Obama Trade Policy" (AEI Outlook Series, American Enterprise Institute for Public Policy Research, Washington, DC, August 2009).

2. Mark Horton, Manmohan Kumar, and Paolo Mauro, "The State of Public Finances: A Cross-Country Fiscal Monitor" IMF Staff Position Note SPN/09/21 (International Monetary Fund, Washington, DC, July 30, 2009).

3. Catherine L. Mann, "International Capital Flows and the Sustainability of the U.S. Current Account Deficit," in *The Long-Term International Economic Position of the United States*, ed. C. Fred Bergsten (Washington, DC: Peterson Institute for International Economics). Mann explains the drop in the dollar exchange rate during 2002–2008 (about 25 percent on a trade-weighted basis) by noting that foreigners would

have had to allocate more than 100 percent of the total increase in their international portfolios to U.S. assets to fund the U.S. deficits during that period without changes in exchange rates and interest rates.

4. See David Barboza, "China Faces Delicate Task of Reining in Bank Lending," *New York Times,* August 7, 2009.

5. Assuming foreign private holders make no addition to their dollar accounts for ten years.

INDEX

Abu Dhabi Investment Authority,
  30–31, 228, 237
acquisitions. *See* mergers and acquisitions
adjustment assistance, 196–200
Adler, Matthew, 54, 92
adverse selection, 110
Africa, 46
Agreement on Subsidies and Counter-
  vailing Measures (ASCM), 96
Agreement on Technical Barriers to
  Trade, 219
agricultural subsidies, 175–76
agricultural tariffs, 69–70, 172, 175–78
agriculture, 62–63, 98, 172
Aid for Trade (A4T), 283n18
airplanes, 7, 54, 56
Aldonas, Grant, 69
Alliant Techsystems, 229
America Movil, 228
American consumers, 126–27
American Federation of Labor and
  Congress of Industrial Organiza-
  tions (AFL-CIO), 197–98, 286n7
Anti-Bribery Convention, 107
Antidumping Agreement, 186, 259n28
antidumping filings, 66, 168–69, 195
Apple, 113
applied tariffs, 173–75

Arcelor, 90, 228
Argentina, 46, 60, 281n1
Argentine financial crisis, 157, 162
Asia, 241–42. *See also specific countries*
Asian financial crisis, 2, 29, 41, 45–46,
  134, 146–47, 157
Asian Monetary Fund, 157, 242
Asian savings glut, 134, 147
Asian tigers, 50
Asia-Pacific Economic Cooperation
  (APEC), 21, 182–83, 224
asset bubbles, 133, 142
asset losses, 119–20
Association of Southeast Asian Nations
  (ASEAN), 62
AT&T, 228
Augier, Patricia, 183
Australia, 229, 231
auto industry bailouts, 153, 169, 282n5

bailouts, 152–56, 169, 282n5
balance of payments, 123, 146–51, 161,
  281n2
Baldwin, Richard, 63, 103, 183
Bangladesh, 68
bank failures, 12, 139, 156
Bank for International Settlements
  (BIS), 279n35

297